Living in Christ

The Church

Christ in the World Today

Martin C. Albl

with Christine Schmertz Navarro and Joanna Dailey

saint mary's press

The Subcommittee on the Catechism, United States Conference of Catholic Bishops, has found that this catechetical high school text, copyright 2011, is in conformity with the *Catechism of the Catholic Church* and that it fulfills the requirements of Course IV: "Jesus Christ's Mission Continues in the Church" of the *Doctrinal Elements of a Curriculum Framework for the Development of Catechetical Materials for Young People of High School Age.*

Nihil Obstat: Rev. William M. Becker, STD
                    Censor Librorum
                    October 1, 2010

Imprimatur: †Most Rev. John M. Quinn, DD
                    Bishop of Winona
                    October 1, 2010

The nihil obstat and imprimatur are official declarations that a book or pamphlet is free of doctrinal or moral error. No implication is contained therein that those who have granted the nihil obstat or imprimatur agree with the contents, opinions, or statements expressed, nor do they assume any legal responsibility associated with publication.

The publishing team included Maura Thompson Hagarty, PhD, theological reviewer; Christine Schmertz Navarro, development editor with Steven McGlaun and Brian Singer-Towns; Joanna Dailey, section 4 sidebar and section 5 author; prepress and manufacturing coordinated by the production departments of Saint Mary's Press.

Cover Image: © The Crosiers / Gene Plaisted, OSC

1149 (PO3893)

ISBN 978-1-59982-060-6, Print
ISBN 978-1-59982-106-1, Digital

Contents

Introduction 7

Section 1: The Church: Christ's Continued Presence and Work in the World

Part 1: The Origin of the Church 9

Article 1: The Meaning of Church 10

Article 2: God's Call to Israel Foreshadows the Church 13

Article 3: Christ Instituted the Church 15

Part 2: The Holy Spirit and the Church 20

Article 4: Introducing the Holy Spirit 21

Article 5: Pentecost: The Church Revealed to the World . . . 23

Article 6: The Meaning of Pentecost 25

Article 7: The Holy Spirit Animates, Sanctifies, and Builds the Church 27

Article 8: Life according to the Holy Spirit 30

Article 9: The Holy Spirit Gifts the Church 32

Part 3: The Work of the Early Church 38

Article 10: The Mission of the Apostles 39

Article 11: Spreading the Gospel 42

Article 12: Persecution and Martyrdom 45

Part 4: Images of the Church 49

Article 13: The Church Is the People of God 50

Article 14: The Church Is the Body of Christ 53

Article 15: The Church Is the Temple of the Holy Spirit 57

Section 2: The Church Is One, Holy, Catholic, and Apostolic

Part 1: The Church Is One................62

Article 16: The First Mark of the Church 63

Article 17: Bonds of Unity 66

Article 18: Wounds to Unity 70

Article 19: Ecumenism...............................74

Part 2: The Church Is Holy.................79

Article 20: Why Is the Church Holy? 80

Article 21: The Church Makes Us Holy through God's Grace84

Article 22: The Communion of Saints 87

Article 23: The Saints: Models and Intercessors..........89

Article 24: Mary: Perfect Model of Holiness 92

Part 3: The Church Is Catholic.....................97

Article 25: The Meaning of the Word *Catholic*...........98

Article 26: Catholicity: The Fullness of Christ in the Church............................100

Article 27: The Church's Relationship with All People.....102

Article 28: Universality and Diversity 106

Part 4: The Church Is Apostolic..................111

Article 29: The Apostles Continue Jesus' Mission 112

Article 30: Apostolic Tradition 114

Article 31: The Successors to Peter and the Apostles 117

Article 32: The Apostolate of the Laity................120

Section 3: The Church's Salvation and Mission

Part 1: The Church and Salvation 125

Article 33: The Fullness of Truth and Salvation 126

Article 34: Salvation for Those Outside the Church 129

Article 35: Who Needs Organized Religion? 132

Part 2: The Church and the World 137

Article 36: Engaging the World 138

Article 37: Engaging Modern Culture. 140

Article 38: The Church and Evangelization 141

Section 4: The Lived Mission of the Church

Part 1: The Leadership Structure of the Church. . . . 149

Article 39: The Church and Hierarchy 150

Article 40: The Pope: Visible Head of the Church 153

Article 41: The Role of the Bishops in the Church
Hierarchy. 156

Article 42: The Priesthood 160

Article 43: The Diaconate. 163

Part 2: Many Vocations to Holiness. 168

Article 44: The Evangelical Counsels. 169

Article 45: The Mission of the Laity 172

Article 46: The Work and Vocation of the Laity 176

Article 47: The Consecrated Life: Religious Orders 179

Article 48: Other Types of Consecrated Life 182

Part 3: The Magisterium: The Teaching Office of the Church   186

Article 49: The Magisterium. 187

Article 50: Indefectibility and Infallibility. 190

Article 51: The Magisterium and Truth. 193

Section 5: The Church and Young People

Part 1: You Have Been Called. 198

Article 52: Called by God to Belong to the Church 199

Article 53: Christ Enriches Us through Participation in
the Life of the Church. 202

Article 54: Called to Community 206

Part 2: Sent with the Holy Spirit................211

Article 55: Sent as a Disciple........................212
Article 56: Discipleship in Daily Life...................215
Article 57: Empowered by the Holy Spirit..............219

Glossary...224

Index...234

Acknowledgments................................244

Introduction

Dear Reader,

You are about to begin your study of the Church. In many ways studying this subject will be similar to studying any other subject: you will learn new vocabulary, become familiar with some famous people in the Church, and be introduced to some new concepts and ways of thinking.

But in other ways, this study will be unique, because the subject matter is unique. The Church is unlike any other reality on earth, because she is both within history and beyond it. She is both human and divine. In the Church we meet God.

This study will engage not only your brain but also your heart and your spirit—in other words, your whole self. You will be challenged mentally to understand teachings about the nature of the Church and gain a sense of how she has been present in the world throughout history. You also will be challenged in other ways—challenged to pray more deeply with the Church and challenged to become a more committed and active member of the Church. After all, you are a holistic person, made up of body, mind, and spirit. This study will challenge you to broaden and deepen all aspects of yourself.

In writing this book, the editors and I have expanded our knowledge about the Church, have thought in new ways about the Church, and have grown in our own commitment to and love for her. I invite you to share in that experience.

Sincerely,

Martin C. Albl

The Church

Christ's Continued Presence and Work in the World

Part 1

The Origin of the Church

As you begin your study of the Church, it makes sense to address questions about where the Church came from and who founded it. The Church was always part of the Father's plan. It was instituted by his Son, Jesus Christ, and is given life by the Holy Spirit.

The word *Church* refers to the assembly of people whom God calls together to be in a special relationship with him. The Church was part of God's saving plan from all eternity. It is both the means of salvation and the goal of his plan. All people who are saved will be gathered into the perfected Church at the end of time.

God formed a special relationship with Israel as his Chosen People, which foreshadowed his subsequent relationship with the Church. God's covenants with Israel prepared for the New Covenant established through Jesus' death and Resurrection.

Jesus' gift of the Eucharist and his saving death on the cross gave birth to the Church. Jesus inaugurated the Church by preaching about the Kingdom of God, healing people in mind and body, and calling people to be part of his family. Jesus also established a structure for the Church, based on the Twelve Apostles' and Peter's leadership. This structure will last until the fulfillment of the Kingdom.

The topics covered in this part are:

- Article 1: "The Meaning of Church" (page 10)

- Article 2: "God's Call to Israel Foreshadows the Church" (page 13)

- Article 3: "Christ Instituted the Church" (page 15)

Article 1 The Meaning of Church

Let's begin by clarifying the meaning of the word *church*. In the everyday English language, the word *church* can refer to different realities, such as a building ("the big church downtown"), a parish ("I'm a member of Saint Mary's Church"), a Christian eccesial community ("the Lutheran Church"), and the Catholic Church. To understand how these are related, it is helpful to see how the earliest Christians understood and used this word.

Defining *Church*

The hierarchy of bishops and cardinals come from a wide range of nationalities, ethnicities, and backgrounds, reflecting the diversity of the Church.

© Franco Origlia/Sygma/Corbis

The New Testament Greek word translated as *church* is *ekklesia*. It is related to the Greek verb *ek-ka-lein*, "to call out," and thus refers to the convocation or assembly of people whom God calls together to be in a special relationship with him. In the Greek Old Testament, *ekklesia* is used to refer to the people of Israel, an assembly chosen by God. The first Christians applied the term *ekklesia* to themselves to show that they were heirs of the assembly of Israel. In the Church, God calls people together from all over the earth.

The word *Church* has three meanings in Christian usage, all of which involve God's call:

* the entire community of God's People around the world

- the local community, which is a **diocese** or archdiocese, such as the Archdiocese of Chicago
- the community assembled for **liturgy**, especially the Mass (for example, the people gathered at Saint Charles Borromeo Parish to celebrate the Eucharist at 10:00 a.m. on Sunday)

It is impossible to separate these meanings from one another. The Church is all the people God gathers in the world, but she exists concretely in local communities and is made real in the assembly that gathers for liturgy, especially to celebrate the Eucharist. "She draws her life from the word and the Body of Christ and so herself becomes Christ's Body" (*Catechism of the Catholic Church, [CCC]*, 752).

The Father Planned the Church from the Beginning

Calling together human beings is central to the Father's plan of salvation, as he wishes to gather us as his own people, the People of God, in order to save us. Jesus Christ, the only Son of God, who is himself fully God, established the Church when he proclaimed and ushered in the Kingdom of God.

Even before the Church was instituted, the Father's eternal plan of calling together a holy people had already been taking shape in history. The Father's call to the people

diocese
Also known as a "particular" or "local" Church, the regional community of believers, who commonly gather in parishes, under the leadership of a bishop. At times, a diocese is determined not on the basis of geography but on the basis of language or rite.

liturgy
The Church's official, public, communal prayer. It is God's work, in which the People of God participate. The Church's most important liturgy is the Eucharist, or the Mass.

Live It!

Living the Three Meanings of Church

You have many opportunities to live out each of the three meanings of the word *Church* in different ways:

1. Develop a better sense of the universal nature of the Church by learning about Catholic customs in other countries or praying for Catholics in other nations, especially those suffering persecution. You might also have an opportunity to attend World Youth Day.
2. Get involved with your local diocese. Attend diocesan events for teens. If your diocese has a youth board, consider serving as a member.
3. Participate fully in the liturgy at your parish. You may have opportunities to serve in special roles, such as singing in the choir or lectoring.

How does celebrating the Eucharist in our local parish reflect the three meanings of the word *Church*?

of Israel to enter into a covenant relationship with him was the clearest preparation for the Church. God desires that the whole human race, rather than simply one people, may come together as one People of God. Thus from all eternity, God planned to form a Church as a means of fulfilling that plan. ☩

God Created the Earth for the Church

The Shepherd of *Hermas* is an ancient Christian writing dating from the second century. The first part records a series of visions given to Hermas, a Christian slave. In one, he sees an old woman carrying a book that reveals future events and the secrets of people's hearts. Later, in a dream, a young man tells Hermas that the old woman is the Church. Hermas wonders why she is old, and is told: "Because she was created first of all, for this reason she is old. And for her sake the world was made" (*Visions* 2.4).

Article 2 God's Call to Israel Foreshadows the Church

Have you ever wondered why more than half of the Bible is composed of books that were written before the time of Christ? The reason is that the Old Testament still has enormous value. Together with the New Testament, it hands on God's Revelation and makes known to us his plan of salvation. The Old Testament records the history of salvation from Creation through God's Covenant with the Israelites, which foreshadows and prepares for the Church.

foreshadow

To represent or prefigure a person before his or her life or an event before it occurs.

God's Covenants with Israel

The community of Israel **foreshadows** the Church. Just as God chooses us to be saved as part of the Church, so too did God call Israel as a nation to be his Chosen People as part of his larger plan of salvation.

God called Abraham to leave his own country, promising him that he would father a great nation, Israel (see Genesis 12:2). Later God made a covenant with him, promising him land for himself and his descendants (see 12:15). Still later God entered into the Sinai Covenant. As the people's part of the Covenant, God gave them his Law through Moses at Mount Sinai. The Law is summarized in the Ten

© Scala / Art Resource, NY

When the Israelites turned away from God, Moses interceded with God on their behalf. How does this foreshadow Jesus' role as our Savior?

Commandments. Through the covenants, God established a special relationship with Israel as his Holy People.

Universal Implications of God's Call to Israel

God's special relationship with Israel was not just about Israel: it had a deeper meaning for the rest of the world as well. The prophets proclaimed a future when all nations would gather together with Israel in true worship (see Isaiah 2:2–5, Micah 4:1–4). The gathering of the people of Israel foreshadows the future gathering of all nations into one People of God.

The Israelites, however, could not fulfill and were not always faithful to their Covenant with God, straying away to worship other gods, for example. The prophet Jeremiah spoke of God's plan for a New Covenant between God and his People (see Jeremiah 33:31–34).

The perfect fulfillment of the Sinai Covenant, of the Law, is the Son of God, Jesus Christ. As a Jew he was born under the Law, but by taking the people's sins upon himself, he transformed the Law engraved on stone and engraved it upon his own heart. He is then the "covenant of the people" (Isaiah 42:6), God's Servant who brings justice. In fulfilling the Law of Sinai, however, Jesus did not abolish it. Instead he revealed its true meaning. Jesus thus initiated the New Covenant at the Last Supper: "This cup is the new covenant in my blood, which will be shed for you" (Luke 22:20). ✝

Old Testament Images of the Church

In describing herself, the Church often draws on Old Testament images. Israel is pictured as God's flock of sheep (see Psalm 77:20). Jesus refers to his followers as his "little flock" (Luke 12:32). Isaiah compares Israel to a vineyard (see chapter 5). Jesus calls his disciples the branches of the vine (see John 15:5).

Christians often compare the Church to Israel's Temple. They call themselves "living stones" who form a "spiritual house" (1 Peter 2:5). Their community is "the temple of God" (1 Corinthians 3:16, 2 Corinthians 6:16) with Christ as the cornerstone (see 1 Peter 2:7, Matthew 21:42).

Another image, dear to the Church Fathers, is the prefiguring of the Church in Noah's ark. The ark saves from flood waters, while the Church saves from sin.

Article 3 Christ Instituted the Church

When you think of people instituting an organization or corporation, you may think of a ceremony or of men and women dressed in business suits and hard hats using shovels to dig up the first dirt. Jesus did not institute the Church in this way. This article explores how Jesus instituted the Church.

Jesus Preached the Kingdom of God

At the time appointed by God, Jesus Christ, the eternal Word of the Father, became man and lived among us on earth. He took on a human nature without losing his divine nature. The mystery of the union of the divine and human natures in one Divine Person is called the Incarnation.

During his earthly ministry, Jesus inaugurated the Church through his preaching: "This is the time of fulfillment. The Kingdom of God is at hand" (Mark 1:15; see also *CCC*, 763). Jesus was drawing on the hope announced by the Old Testament prophets, who looked forward to a coming age when God's will would be done on earth: "Then will the eyes of the blind be opened, / the ears of the deaf be cleared" (Isaiah 35:5).

Catholic Wisdom

Vatican II Teaching on the Church's Relation to the Jewish People

The Vatican II document *Declaration on the Relation of the Church to Non-Christian Religions* (*Nostra Aetate*, 1965), affirms that God loves the Jewish people and decries all oppression of Jews. Many Jews have suffered unjust treatment because the sins of the Jews involved in Jesus' death were wrongly extended to include all Jewish people, even those in different times and places.

> Nevertheless, God holds the Jews most dear for the sake of their Fathers; He does not repent of the gifts He makes or of the calls He issues—such is the witness of the Apostle. . . . Although the Church is the new people of God, the Jews should not be presented as rejected or accursed by God, as if this followed from the Holy Scriptures.

> (*Relation of the Church to Non-Christian Religions*, 4)

Jesus' message was intended for all people. Yet in a special way, Jesus directed his message to the poor and proclaimed that the nations would be judged on how well they took care of people who were hungry and thirsty (see Matthew 25:31–46). Jesus also directed his message toward sinners, calling them to repentance and assuring them of the Father's great mercy. Jesus' message often took the form of parables, which challenged listeners to make the radical choice whether to truly follow him.

Jesus' listeners learned about the Kingdom not only from his words but also from his actions. Jesus' miracles and his healing of the sick were signs that the Kingdom had already begun on earth.

Jesus Sent Disciples

To help him establish the Kingdom of God, the Father gathered people to become Jesus' first followers. Jesus sent out these disciples to preach the Kingdom and to make disciples

During his earthly ministry, Jesus preached the Kingdom of God. How does the Gospel message continue to be taught today?

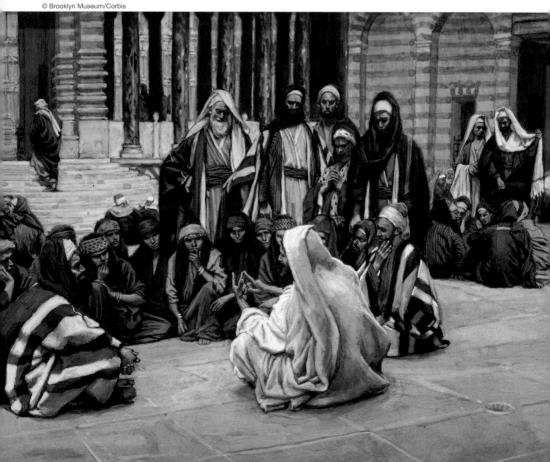

of the nations, calling all people to join Christ's Church. This group of followers, his disciples, became the Church, Jesus' true family, and the seed and beginning of the Kingdom on earth. The Church is thus a sign, as well as the actual beginning, of that perfect peace and happiness that all of us desire: the Reign of God mysteriously present in the world.

Jesus Gave Himself Fully for the Church

Jesus established the Church primarily by the saving gift of himself. This gift, which was fulfilled on the cross, was anticipated when Jesus instituted the Eucharist. Jesus' words, "This is my body . . ." (Luke 22:19), expressed his complete self-giving in handing over his life for the sake of humanity. By participating in the Eucharist today, we share, in a mystical way, in Christ's sacrifice, and also in the grace that his sacrifice gives the Church. This Sacrament also increases the unity of the People of God and enables us to share in the divine life.

Pray It!

Praying the Psalms

Jews and Christians continue to share the custom of praying the Psalms. Pray with the following excerpt, especially at times when you may struggle with your self-worth:

You formed my inmost being;

you knit me in my mother's womb.

I praise you, so wonderfully you made me;

wonderful are your works!

My very self you knew;

my bones were not hidden from you,

When I was being made in secret,

fashioned as in the depths of the earth.

Your eyes foresaw my actions;

in your book all are written down;

my days were shaped, before one came to be.

(Psalm 139:13–16)

Jesus Created the Structure of the Church

hierarchy

In general, the line of authority in the Church; more narrowly the Pope and the bishops, as successors of the Apostles, in their authoritative roles as leaders of the Church.

Have you ever wondered why the Church is governed by a pope and bishops? Jesus set up this structure himself. He appointed the Twelve Apostles as the leaders of the community gathered around him (see Mark 3:14–19), and he gave Peter a special role as the head (see Matthew 16:18–19, Luke 22:31).

In order to build the Church and to proclaim the faith, Christ sent out his Apostles, giving them a share in his own mission. He gave them, and those who have succeeded them, the power to act in his place. The bishops are the Apostles' successors, and the Pope, the Bishop of Rome, is the successor of Peter. The structure and **hierarchy** of the Church established by Christ continues to this day and will remain until the Kingdom is fully established at the end of time.

Whom Does Jesus Call?

When Jesus gathered followers to help him proclaim and establish the Kingdom, he did not call the most talented and powerful; rather, he chose ordinary fishermen (see Mark 1:16–20) and even a tax collector (see 2:13–17)—a person despised by most Israelites. Jesus' choices are consistent with Paul's reminder that "God chose the weak of the world to shame the strong" (1 Corinthians 1:27). God's call comes to everyone, even (or perhaps especially) to those who think they may not be worthy.

Jesus' choice of Twelve Apostles reflects the Twelve Tribes of Israel, God's Chosen People. This aspect of Jesus' inauguration of the Church recalls the Jewish hope that someday the Twelve Tribes, scattered in exile, would be gathered together again. ✝

Part Review

1. What are three meanings of the word *Church* in Christian usage?

2. What is the Church's role in the Father's plan to save us?

3. Why was God's Covenant with Israel significant for the rest of the world?

4. How is Jesus the perfect fulfillment of the Sinai Covenant?

5. How did Jesus establish the Church through his preaching?

6. How is Jesus' self-giving on the cross related to his establishment of the Church?

Part 2

The Holy Spirit and the Church

In this section we study the Holy Spirit's action in the Church. The first article introduces the Holy Spirit, the Third Divine Person of the Holy Trinity. We see that although the Holy Spirit is revealed throughout the Scriptures, he was not fully revealed until Pentecost, after Jesus had died, risen from the dead, and ascended into Heaven. The Holy Spirit and Christ are inseparable in their mission.

We then look at the actual account of Pentecost in the Acts of the Apostles and see how Christ poured out the Holy Spirit upon the Church that day. Subsequently, we look at the significance of Pentecost as the Revelation of the Church, the Holy Spirit, and the Trinity.

We consider the ways the Holy Spirit animates, sanctifies, and builds the Church. We learn what Saint Paul means when he describes a new kind of life according to the Holy Spirit. A life according to the Holy Spirit is full of love and joy instead of selfishness, conflict, and a blind focus on short-term pleasure. The Holy Spirit's role in this new life includes teaching us to pray.

We conclude this part by learning about special gifts from the Holy Spirit, known as charisms. These include extraordinary gifts, such as speaking in tongues and miraculous healing, but also more ordinary gifts, such as leadership and teaching.

The topics covered in this part are:

- Article 4: "Introducing the Holy Spirit" (page 21)

- Article 5: "Pentecost: The Church Revealed to the World" (page 23)

- Article 6: "The Meaning of Pentecost" (page 25)

- Article 7: "The Holy Spirit Animates, Sanctifies, and Builds the Church" (page 27)

- Article 8: "Life according to the Holy Spirit" (page 30)

- Article 9: "The Holy Spirit Gifts the Church" (page 32)

^{Article} 4 Introducing the Holy Spirit

Because you are familiar with the Old Testament and the Gospels, you have had the opportunity to get to know the Father, the Son, and the Holy Spirit, the Third Divine Person in the Trinity. The Holy Spirit first appears in the Scriptures in the Book of Genesis, in the first account of Creation. Here, the Holy Spirit is present in the form of a mighty wind that sweeps over the waters (see Genesis 1:2). Throughout the Old Testament, the Holy Spirit is present and participates with the Father and the Son in the work of salvation. However, the Holy Spirit's greatest participation in the work of salvation can be witnessed in the New Testament, beginning with the Incarnation (see Luke 1:27–35). The Holy Spirit is fully revealed at Pentecost, when he descended upon the Apostles, with Mary present among them (see Acts 2:1–4).

The Holy Spirit and Christ

Although the Holy Spirit and Jesus Christ have possessed a common mission since the beginning of time, the Holy Spirit was fully revealed to us when he was poured out on the Church by Jesus at Pentecost. Jesus did refer to the Holy Spirit in his conversations with his Apostles and in some more public settings but did not fully reveal the Holy Spirit until after his death, Resurrection, and Ascension.

© Zvonimir Atletic/Shutterstock.com

The mission of Jesus and the Holy Spirit are conjoined and inseparable. Whenever God sends his Son, he also sends his Spirit, so when we recite the Nicene Creed, we should see all of Jesus' actions in the second section as a joint mission with the Holy Spirit.

Two symbols of the Holy Spirit are a dove and fire. What might these symbolize about the Holy Spirit?

The Holy Spirit's Mission

Although Revelation and salvation are the common work of the three Divine Persons, the Holy Spirit is the principal agent of the Church's mission. Over time the Holy Spirit reveals the mission of Christ. The Church continues Christ's path, and because he shared the Good News with the poor, the Church must also do so. Following Christ means sharing in his poverty, obedience, service, and self-sacrifice, and even in his willingness to sacrifice his life.

Sisters of the Holy Spirit and Mary Immaculate

In 1893 the order of the Sisters of the Holy Spirit and Mary Immaculate was established in Texas. This was the first community of religious women established in that state. One Sunday Margaret Mary Healy-Murphy heard a letter from the bishops of the United States asking people to reach out to African American people who did not have many opportunities for an education.

With the help of the Holy Spirit, she discerned that she was called to serve and educate African American children who were poor. She built a church and a small schoolhouse, named Saint Peter Claver Academy. When she had trouble recruiting volunteers, she, with the help of the local bishop, established a religious community. She gathered a group of young women who dedicated their lives to serving those living in poverty.

After Saint Peter Claver Academy closed in 1971, the sisters established the Healy-Murphy Center, an alternative school for young people at risk, such as teenage mothers and those who have not been successful in traditional high school settings. The sisters also opened day care centers for the teens' children. In addition to their work at the Healy-Murphy Center, the Sisters of the Holy Spirit and Mary Immaculate now minister in seven dioceses in Texas, five in Louisiana, two in Mississippi, and one in Mexico.

(This material is taken from the Web site for the Healy-Murphy Center.)

Where does the Holy Spirit lead the Church? Through the power of the Holy Spirit, the Church carries out its mission to bring all people into union with the Trinity. Because people live in harmony with one another only when they are in union with God, the Church is also a means of creating unity among human beings. This unity has begun, but it will not be complete until sometime in the future. The Church is a sign and instrument of the full realization of this unity, that final and eternal perfection in which people will truly be one in union with the Trinity.

An important step in this mission occurred when the Holy Spirit revealed the Church to the world. The Holy Spirit inspired the Apostles and other disciples to share the Good News with Jews and Gentiles.✝

Article 5 Pentecost: The Church Revealed to the World

It seems that whenever we pick up a newspaper, watch the news on television, or surf the Internet, we hear reports of violent conflicts. However, God made human beings to live in harmony with him and with one another. The Church, revealed on **Pentecost,** is a means to this **communion.**

The Day of Pentecost

After Jesus' Ascension his followers gathered together in Jerusalem (see Acts of the Apostles 1:15) at the time of the Feast of Weeks, the Jewish festival also known as Pentecost, which is Greek for "fiftieth," as it was celebrated fifty days after Passover.

The account in the Acts of the Apostles tells us that suddenly a noise like a strong, driving wind filled the house where Jesus' Apostles were. Tongues as of fire rested on each one of them, and they were filled with the Holy Spirit. They began to preach in different languages. A crowd gathered, formed of Jews from Egypt, Rome, modern-day Turkey and Iraq, Palestine, and other places, who were all in Jerusalem for the Pentecost festival. Miraculously, each heard the message of the Apostles in his own language. This multilingual chorus caused some bystanders to think that the Apostles were drunk (see Acts of the Apostles 2:13). Peter, the

Communion
Refers to receiving the Body and Blood of Christ. In general, your companionship and union with Jesus and other baptized Christians in the Church. This union has its origin and high point in the celebration of the Eucharist. In this sense the deepest vocation of the Church is Communion.

Pentecost
The fiftieth day following Easter, which commemorates the descent of the Holy Spirit on the early Apostles and disciples.

In the account of the Tower of Babel, God confused the speech of humanity. Why does he reverse this in the preaching of the Apostles at Pentecost?

Apostles' leader, clarified that these events were fulfilling Old Testament prophecies (see 2:14–32), especially the Prophet Joel's words:

> It will come to pass in the last days, God says,
>   "that I will pour out a portion of my spirit
>   upon all flesh.
> Your sons and your daughters shall prophesy,
>   your young men shall see visions,
>   your old men shall dream dreams."
>
> (Acts of the Apostles 2:17; see also Joel 3:1)

Peter explained that the glorified Jesus himself was pouring the Holy Spirit upon the Apostles and enabling them to miraculously speak in such a way that they could be understood by all members of the audience (see Acts of the Apostles 2:33).

Peter instructed his listeners to repent and be baptized so that their sins would be forgiven, so they too would receive the Holy Spirit. Three thousand people were baptized that day (see 2:37–41).

Pentecost and the Tower of Babel

Pentecost contrasts greatly with the Tower of Babel event described in Genesis. At that time, when the whole world spoke one language (see Genesis 11:1), some people wished to build a tower up to the sky, in order to "make a name for [them]selves" (11:4). Instead God scattered them throughout the earth, confusing their languages so they could no longer communicate.

At Pentecost, however, the Holy Spirit enabled people speaking various languages to hear the same message. At the Tower of Babel, God put up barriers to understanding; at Pentecost he broke them down.

Article 6 The Meaning of Pentecost

You may sometimes hear Pentecost referred to as the birthday of the Church. This can be misleading if we mean that the Church began on Pentecost. Recall that the Father and his Son were involved with the Church before the descent of the Holy Spirit on the Apostles. The Church was born primarily of Christ's total self-giving for our salvation, anticipated when he instituted the Eucharist, and fulfilled in his death on the cross. A helpful analogy for the revelation of the Church at Pentecost may be a child's day of birth.

At a child's birth, we see her or him with our eyes for the first time, but the child has been prepared for several months within her or his mother. In a similar yet greater way, the outpouring of the Holy Spirit at Pentecost revealed the Church to the world for the first time. The Church itself was not a new entity, however, as she had been in God's plan from before the world was created.

On Pentecost, God as the Trinity was fully revealed for the first time. Jews who followed Jesus at the time of Pentecost worshipped the God of Abraham, Isaac, and Jacob and also believed that Jesus was the Divine Son of

© Francis G. Mayer/CORBIS

At Pentecost the Holy Spirit broke through into our world in a new way. How did the action of the Holy Spirit make the Blessed Trinity known to us?

God the Father. The action of the Holy Spirit at Pentecost enabled these Jewish followers to become aware of their encounter with God the Holy Spirit, the Third Divine Person of the Trinity. For the first time in salvation history, God fully revealed himself as the Blessed Trinity. This mystery of the Trinity—one God in three Divine Persons, Father, Son, and Holy Spirit—is the central mystery of our faith. God alone can make this mystery known to us.

The Age of the Church

In God's plan of salvation, Pentecost marked the beginning of the Church's mission on earth, when the Apostles were able to begin their work of evangelization and to baptize in Jesus' name. No longer present on earth in the same way as before his death and Resurrection, Christ now lived and acted in the world through his Church. In this way, and through his sending of the Holy Spirit, Jesus fulfilled his promise to his disciples: "I am with you always, until the end of the age" (Matthew 28:20). ♰

Celebrating Pentecost

We celebrate Pentecost fifty days after Easter. Pentecost marks the ending of the Easter season in the liturgical year, a season in which we celebrate the life, death, Resurrection, and Ascension of Jesus and the redemption he won for us. You may have noticed that the priest celebrating the Mass on Pentecost wears red, but do you know why? Red symbolizes the transforming power of the Holy Spirit.

A second special component of the Pentecost liturgy is the singing or recitation of "Veni, Sancte Spiritus," or "Come, Holy Spirit," a Latin sequence that dates from the twelfth century. (See the sidebar "Come, Holy Spirit" for the text of this sequence.)

© Robert Young/Shutterstock.com

Article 7 The Holy Spirit Animates, Sanctifies, and Builds the Church

We hear phrases such as "school spirit" or the "spirit of teamwork." These phrases refer to a kind of energy or atmosphere in a group or organization that we can't see but that we know is real and active. When this energy brings people together and strengthens their relationships and ability to share in a common mission for the sake of others, it gives us a glimpse of the Holy Spirit's way of working in the world.

The Holy Spirit, given to the Church's members by Christ, builds, animates, and sanctifies the Church. These three elements of the Holy Spirit's mission are evidence of the Holy Spirit's energy!

Pray It!

Come, Holy Spirit

"Come, Holy Spirit" (in the original Latin, "*Veni Sancte Spiritus*") is a chant, dating from the Middle Ages, that is still sung or recited in the Mass for Pentecost. It has been recorded in many beautiful arrangements, including Gregorian chant.

Come, Holy Spirit, and send down from heaven the ray of your light.

Come, father of the poor, come, giver of gifts, come, light of the hearts.

Best consoler, sweet host of the soul, sweet refresher.

Rest in work, cooling in heat, comfort in crying.

O most blessed light, fill the innermost hearts of your faithful.

Without your power nothing is in man, nothing innocent.

Clean what is dirty, water what is dry, heal what is wounded.

Bend what is rigid, heat what is cold, lead what has gone astray.

Grant to your faithful who trust in you, your sevenfold holy gift.

Grant us the reward of virtue, grant us final salvation, grant us eternal joy.

(The Choral Public Domain Library)

The Holy Spirit Animates the Church

animate
To give life to.

sanctify, sanctification
To make holy; sanctification is the process of becoming closer to God and growing in holiness, taking on the righteousness of Jesus Christ with the gift of sanctifying grace.

The Holy Spirit **animates** or gives life to the Church. Saint Augustine said that what the soul is to the human body, so the Holy Spirit is to the Body of Christ, the Church. Prior to his Ascension, Jesus told his disciples, "You will receive power when the Holy Spirit comes upon you" (Acts of the Apostles 1:8). At Pentecost, tongues as of fire, symbolizing the transforming energy of the Holy Spirit, came upon the disciples. This power converted a group of disciples who had been huddling behind closed doors out of fear (see John 20:19) into bold missionaries, proclaiming their faith in the Risen Christ.

The Holy Spirit Sanctifies the Church

The Church is **sanctified** or made holy by the Holy Spirit. The Holy Spirit works to "build up" the holiness of the Church's members in various ways: through the Sacraments, through the virtues by which we live a moral life, and by the many gifts the Holy Spirit gives to each person. Church members first receive the Holy Spirit through Baptism, the first Sacrament of Christian Initiation. Baptism brings each person into the Body of Christ. Paul says, "For in one Spirit we were all baptized into one body" (1 Corinthians 12:13).

The Holy Spirit Builds the Church
At Pentecost the Holy Spirit's power to build the Church was made known. Once the Apostles had received the Holy Spirit, more than three thousand people were baptized!

Catholic Wisdom

A Challenge from Pope Benedict XVI to Youth

The Pope delivered this challenge at World Youth Day 2008 in Sydney, Australia:

Dear young people, let me now ask you a question. Are you living your lives in a way that opens up space for the Spirit in the midst of a world that wants to forget God, or even rejects him in the name of a falsely conceived freedom? How are you using the gifts you have been given, the "power" which the Holy Spirit is even now prepared to release within you? What legacy will you leave to young people yet to come? What difference will you make?

How is Baptism by total immersion symbolic of dying to our old life and rising to new life in Christ?

After Jesus told his followers they would receive the Holy Spirit, he also told them what to do next: "You will be my witnesses in Jerusalem, throughout Judea and Samaria, and to the ends of the earth" (Acts of the Apostles 1:8). The mission of the Church is to bring people into communion with the Trinity. The Holy Spirit builds individuals' faith lives, builds community, and attracts new members to join the Church, which builds the Church's actual numbers. ✝

The Holy Spirit, Breath, and Wind

In Greek, the language of the New Testament, the word for Spirit is *pneuma*, but this word can also mean "wind" or "breath." In Hebrew, the primary language of the Old Testament, the word *ruach* has these same meanings.

The Scripture writers take full advantage of this range of meaning. Jesus breathes on his disciples and says, "Receive the holy Spirit" (John 20:22). This recalls God's action in Genesis 2:7, where the Lord God blew into the nostrils of man the breath of life, and man became a living being. When the Holy Spirit came upon the disciples at Pentecost, there was "a noise like a strong driving wind" (Acts of the Apostles 2:2).

Jesus says, "The wind (or Spirit) blows where it wills, and you can hear the sound it makes, but you do not know where it comes from or where it goes; so it is with everyone who is born of the Spirit" (John 3:8).

Article 8 Life According to the Holy Spirit

Sometimes people go through dramatic changes in their lives. Let's say Lauren, who has always been somewhat rude and inconsiderate, suddenly becomes much nicer and thoughtful. You might say something like, "It's like Lauren is a different or new person!" The Gift of the Holy Spirit brings this kind of startling change of life.

Life Ignoring the Holy Spirit

We may know about the transforming power of the Holy Spirit, but we have the free will to ignore him, or, as Paul would say, to live "according to the flesh" (Romans 8:4). The Apostle Paul contrasted a holy life lived according to the power of the Holy Spirit with a life lived according to the flesh. The person who lives according to the flesh focuses on immediate gratification of his or her own needs. As a result, this person's life will be filled, as Paul said, with hatred, jealousy, lack of self-control, and selfishness. According to Paul, this person may well abuse alcohol and be sexually promiscuous in relationships (see Galatians 5:19–21). The person who ignores the Holy Spirit is so focused on meeting his or her own immediate desires that he or she has no time to consider other people.

The Holy Spirit, the Dove, and the Scriptures

The Scriptures and Christian art often portray the Holy Spirit as a dove. Luke tells us that the Holy Spirit descended upon Jesus at his Baptism in the form of a dove. In his poem "God's Grandeur," the Jesuit poet Gerard Manley Hopkins (1844–1889) used the image of the dove:

And though the last lights off the black West went

Oh, morning, at the brown brink eastward, springs —

Because the Holy Ghost over the bent

World broods with warm breast and with ah! bright wings.

Life in the Holy Spirit

Paul contrasted this selfish life with a life "according to the Spirit" (Romans 8:4). Paul spoke of the fruits of the Spirit: "love, joy, peace, patience, kindness, generosity, faithfulness, gentleness, self-control" (Galatians 5:22–23). The person living according to the Spirit is not focused on himself or herself but rather on the needs and well-being of others. Paul said, "The love of God has been poured out into our hearts through the holy Spirit that has been given to us" (Romans 5:5). This life in the Holy Spirit is the beginning, the first-fruits, a kind of sneak preview of our life in Heaven, where we will share in the perfect love and happiness of the Trinity. Think of people you know who are filled with the Spirit—they radiate calm and joy even during tough times.

The Holy Spirit allows us to deepen our relationship with himself, the Father, and the Son, showing us that we are "children of God" (Romans 8:16), and thus we can cry out, "Abba, Father" (Romans 8:15, Galatians 4:6).

The Holy Spirit helps teach us how to pray. The next time you pray, begin by asking the Holy Spirit to guide you.

© Bill Wittman / www.wpwittman.com

petition
A prayer form in which one asks God for help and forgiveness.

intercession
A prayer on behalf of another person or group.

charism
A special gift or grace of the Holy Spirit given to an individual Christian or community, commonly for the benefit and building up of the entire Church.

The Teaching of the Holy Spirit

The Holy Spirit has a teaching role in the Church. Jesus told his disciples, "He will teach you everything and remind you of all that I told you" (John 14:26). "When he comes, the Spirit of truth, he will guide you to all truth" (16:13). The Holy Spirit also helps us understand the truths of faith.

The Holy Spirit also teaches us to pray. Have you ever had the experience of feeling that you would like to pray, or that you should pray, but you don't know what to say? Ask the Holy Spirit for help! The Apostle Paul tells us, "The Spirit too comes to the aid of our weakness; for we do not know how to pray as we ought, but the Spirit itself intercedes with inexpressible groanings" (Romans 8:26). When we do not know how to pray, it's good to know that we can call on the Holy Spirit, the "master of prayer," to help us.

The Holy Spirit, as the master of prayer, not only intercedes for us but also instructs us in our prayer life, inspiring us to express new forms of the basic types of prayer: blessing, **petition, intercessions,** thanksgiving, and praise. The Holy Spirit has been teaching people to pray for thousands of years. The Holy Spirit operates through Tradition, the living transmission of God's truth to us. The Holy Spirit is like a well of living water within the heart of a person who prays, but the Holy Spirit also points the praying person to the source of the living water, Jesus Christ. From the medieval Gregorian chants to the latest praise and worship songs, from the Eucharistic Prayers of the Mass to our own spontaneous prayers before we fall asleep at night, the Holy Spirit is endlessly creative in our prayer lives. ✝

Article 9 The Holy Spirit Gifts the Church

The Holy Spirit gives various gifts, or **charisms,** to the members of the Church for the benefit of the whole Church and, through the Church, the whole world. As Saint Paul wrote, "To each individual the manifestation of the Spirit is given for some benefit" (1 Corinthians 12:7).

Paul's Description of the Charisms

Saint Paul listed the following charisms in his First Letter to the Corinthians: the expression of knowledge or wisdom, faith, gifts of healing, mighty deeds, prophecy, discernment of spirits, the "variety" or gift of tongues and interpretation of tongues (see 12:8–10).

These charisms should not be confused, however, with the Gifts of the Holy Spirit, the seven gifts that describe dispositions or prevailing tendencies rather than specific skills. The seven Gifts of the Holy Spirit, based on Isaiah 11:2, are wisdom, understanding, right judgment (counsel), courage (fortitude), knowledge, reverence (piety), and wonder and awe (fear of the Lord).

Ordinary Charisms

There are extraordinary charisms and more ordinary ones, both of which are important. On any given day, you can see these ordinary charisms at work all around you. Teachers share their talents of knowledge and wisdom with their students. A nurse or doctor demonstrates the capacity to heal a patient. A friend may have the ability to learn languages and use it to help recent immigrants to the country.

Live It!

Being Open to the Spirit

How can you be more open to the activity of the Holy Spirit in your own life? Following are a few suggestions:

- Make time for quiet reflection and prayer. If we are constantly busy, it is difficult to hear the voice of the Holy Spirit within us. Many people find it helpful to set aside a specific prayer time in the mornings. Spending an hour in Eucharistic Adoration on a weekly basis is another great opportunity to hear the Holy Spirit.
- Join or form a prayer or Bible study group. Many groups read and discuss the readings for the upcoming Sunday Mass. The Holy Spirit often guides participants into a deeper understanding of the Scriptures.
- Discover or develop the particular gifts that the Holy Spirit has shared with you. Volunteer opportunities often give us a chance to discover or develop talents and abilities; a trusted adult can often help you to discern your own particular gifts.

The Holy Spirit, the Dove, and the Scriptures

The term **charismatic** refers to Christians who place special emphasis on the Gifts of the Spirit, in particular the extraordinary gifts. The modern charismatic renewal movement in the Catholic Church began in 1964 among university students and faculty and has since spread into all areas of the Church. Although not an official "organization," it is a recognizable movement of the Spirit.

The following are some characteristics of those involved in the Catholic Charismatic Renewal:

- desire for personal holiness and a personal relationship with Jesus Christ
- openness to the movement of the Holy Spirit in their lives, including (but not limited to) the extraordinary gifts, such as speaking in tongues and healing
- preference for lively and enthusiastic worship of God
- acceptance of the authority of the Church **Magisterium** to discern what is truly beneficial in the Charismatic Movement

The Charismatic Renewal has been affirmed as a legitimate movement of the Holy Spirit and a gift to the Church since Pope Paul VI in 1975.

© Corbis

Extraordinary Charisms

Some of the Holy Spirit's Gifts are extraordinary, involving spiritual powers beyond normal human abilities. A person's extraordinary charism of healing, for example, might be visible to others through a miraculous cure that has no scientific explanation. Some people have the gift of prophecy, or the gift of speaking in tongues and the interpretation of tongues. Speaking in tongues is the gift of praying in a spiritual language; no one else can understand it unless it is interpreted by someone with the charism of interpreting tongues (see 1 Corinthians 14:2,14).

Charisms of Leadership

Sometimes we describe political or other leaders as charismatic, meaning they possess a certain power of personality or speaking ability that draws people to them. The Church too has charisms of leadership, but these are Gifts of the Holy Spirit that enable a leader to provide benefit to the whole Church. In his discussion on gifts, Paul says that God has designated believers to be Apostles, prophets, teachers, administrators, and assistants (see 1 Corinthians 12:28).

Founders of religious orders or congregations often have specific charisms that their followers also pursue. Saint Benedict's charism of combining work and prayer has inspired the spiritual life of vowed Benedictines and their associates for centuries. Saint Francis's charism of embracing a life of poverty and simplicity inspired thousands to follow in his footsteps.

As leaders and teachers of the Church, the Pope and the bishops in union with him, have the charism of **infallibility** so that the Church may always avoid error in her teaching on faith and morals. Infallibility extends to the whole of divine Revelation. One way the gift of infallibility is exercised is when the Pope, as supreme pastor and teacher, defines a doctrine as infallible. The most recent infallible teaching was Pope Pius XII's proclamation of the Assumption of the Blessed Virgin Mary in 1950. Another way infallibility is exercised is when the bishops, together with the Pope, agree, especially in an Ecumenical Council, on a teaching that all must hold because it is divinely revealed.

charismatic
The word refers to a person gifted with the charism or graces of the Holy Spirit such as healing, prophecy, and speaking in tongues. Because self-deception is always possible, the charisms claimed by such a person must be verified by the Church.

Magisterium
The Church's living teaching office, which consists of all bishops, in communion with the Pope, the Bishop of Rome.

infallibility
The gift given by the Holy Spirit to the Pope and the bishops in union with him to teach on matters of faith and morals without error.

The Church Needs All Charisms

The Holy Spirit gives gifts to every member of the Church, no matter how humble, because each person can contribute to building up the Church. Some have a musical gift, others have the charism of leadership or coaching, and yet others have the gift of patient listening and the ability to give wise advice. As a young person, you may already know some of your gifts. You will discover more as you mature. ✝

Each one of us has gifts we can contribute to the building up of the Church. These gifts may be obvious, such as musical abilities, or subtle, like being a good listener. What gifts do you possess that you can share with the Church?

© Diane White Rosier/iStockphoto.com

Part Review

1. What does it mean to say that the works of Jesus and the Holy Spirit are inseparable?

2. Where does the Holy Spirit lead the Church?

3. Describe the events of Pentecost.

4. What did Peter say would happen to those people who repented and were baptized on the day of Pentecost?

5. Why is it appropriate to say that the Church is revealed rather than born on Pentecost?

6. Why was Pentecost the Revelation of the Holy Trinity as well as the Church?

7. What are three important elements of the Church's mission?

8. How did the Holy Spirit transform Jesus' disciples?

9. Contrast a life lived ignoring the Holy Spirit and one lived in the Holy Spirit.

10. How does the Holy Spirit help us to pray?

11. What is the subtle difference between a charism and a Gift of the Holy Spirit?

12. Describe how founders of religious orders often had specific charisms that their followers also pursued.

Part 3

The Work of the Early Church

In this part we see how the Apostles, sent by Jesus and empowered by the Holy Spirit, participated in the universal mission of the Church by spreading the Gospel throughout the Mediterranean world. Although Jesus had offered his Apostles a share in his mission of preaching the Good News and healing before he died, after his Ascension he sent the Holy Spirit to be with them and guide them. Christ's love and the presence of the Holy Spirit gave these Apostles and other disciples the motivation and energy to share the truth of Christ with those they encountered.

Saint Paul, sometimes referred to as the Apostle to the Gentiles, preached to both Jews and Gentiles. Paul preached to Jews in terms of the Old Testament, while he spoke to Gentiles in terms they would be accustomed to. He also used imagery familiar to people who live in cities to illustrate the meaning of the Gospel message he was sharing.

The Jews in Jerusalem and the Romans did not always welcome the Gospel message, however, which led to persecution and, at times, martyrdom. Martyrs inspired others to be strong in their faith. But persecution and suffering is not isolated to this time period. The Scriptures and Tradition reveal that there will be a final trial or tribulation at the end of the world.

The topics covered in this part are:

- Article 10: "The Mission of the Apostles" (page 39)

- Article 11: "Spreading the Gospel" (page 42)

- Article 12: "Persecution and Martyrdom" (page 45)

Article 10 The Mission of the Apostles

When we first receive good news—we pass a difficult test, we hear that a sick friend is getting better—our first inclination is to share that news. In a similar but even greater way, the early Apostles were motivated to share the Good News about Jesus with everyone.

The Church Continues Christ's Mission

The mission of the Apostles in the early Church began during their time with Jesus, prior to his death, Resurrection, and Ascension. Jesus proclaimed the Good News and healed people and sent the Apostles out to do the same (see Matthew 10:5–15). The Risen Jesus made it clear that the Apostles' mission was universal, or for everyone:

> Go, therefore, and make disciples of all nations, baptizing them in the name of the Father, and of the Son, and of the holy Spirit, teaching them to observe all that I have commanded you.
>
> (Matthew 28:19–20)

Jesus provided the Apostles with a significant charge when he said to make disciples of all nations. It is no wonder, then, that the Church spread rapidly in communities throughout the Mediterranean area.

The Spread of Christianity

Acts of the Apostles records that within a few years of Jesus' death and Resurrection, the Apostles and disciples had proclaimed the faith from Jerusalem to Samaria, Damascus, Phoenicia, and Antioch (see chapters 8–11). Saint Paul traveled to various cities in Asia Minor and Greece and had plans to travel as far as Spain before he was executed in Rome. Scholars tell us that the Church also spread south into Egypt and further into eastern Syria within a few short years of Jesus' death and Resurrection.

Why did these Apostles and early disciples travel so far and work so hard to spread the Good News? The universal love of God, who desires that all be saved, provided the motivation and energy for the Apostles and early disciples to

Trinitarian
Of or relating to the Trinity or the doctrine of the Trinity.

evangelization
The proclamation of the Good News of Jesus Christ through words and witness.

By modern standards Paul did not travel very far, but through these journeys Paul established and supported numerous churches that led to the spread of Christianity throughout the known world.

© Thomas Nelson, Inc./maps.com

travel throughout the known world sharing the truth of the Gospel with those who would listen. Saint Paul said, "For the love of Christ impels us" (2 Corinthians 5:14). The Church needed to be missionary so as to share the truth that many people already longed for.

The Holy Spirit and the Apostles' Mission

Acts of the Apostles records the events of Pentecost and how the Holy Spirit was involved in every aspect of the missionary spread of Christianity. The Holy Spirit came to repentant sinners who were baptized and aided them in making decisions, assigning Paul and Barnabas to a certain task (see 13:2), ruling on what laws Gentile converts to Jesus must follow (see 15:28), and guiding Paul and Timothy to preach only in certain areas (see 16:6–7).

Yet the Holy Spirit was not working alone, because the Church's mission is essentially **Trinitarian**. This means that the work of the Church is the work of the three Divine Persons in the Trinity—the Father, the Son, and the Holy Spirit. According to the Father's eternal plan, the Church continues

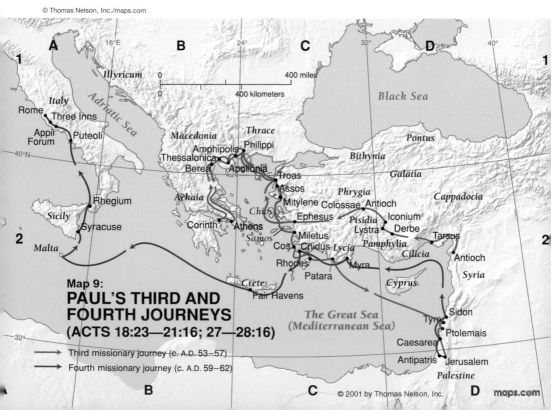

Map 9:
PAUL'S THIRD AND FOURTH JOURNEYS
(ACTS 18:23—21:16; 27—28:16)

→ Third missionary journey (c. A.D. 53–57)
→ Fourth missionary journey (c. A.D. 59–62)

© 2001 by Thomas Nelson, Inc.   maps.com

How Did Christianity Spread So Quickly?

What were other factors that helped the Apostles and disciples to spread the Christian message in the regions surrounding the Mediterranean as far east as Armenia, northern Africa and modern-day Ethiopia, and what we know as Europe? Certainly the expansion of the Church's mission to include outreach to Gentiles increased the potential audience for **evangelization.** Paul's ability to phrase important Christian truths in the Greek language, which enabled people from Greco-Roman culture to understand the faith, also attracted more intellectual members in addition to believers who were less educated.

The Roman Empire itself greatly helped the Church in its mission. The empire was large and unified and had a good road system for travel. It also provided a certain level of protection from bandits and other threats. By the fourth century, scholars estimate that approximately 10 percent of the people in the Roman Empire were Christian. Later in the same century, the Emperor Constantine's tolerant support of Christianity freed the Church from persecution. Missionaries took the Good News to additional places such as southern Europe, parts of the Balkans, the eastern Mediterranean, and northern Africa. Later centuries brought Christianity to northern Europe and the British Isles.

Catholic Wisdom

Pope John Paul II on Mission

The Pope challenges the Church about her own mission:

Today, as never before, the Church has the opportunity of bringing the Gospel, by witness and word, to all people and nations. I see the dawning of a new missionary age, which will become a radiant day bearing an abundant harvest, if all Christians, and missionaries and young churches in particular, respond with generosity and holiness to the calls and challenges of our time.

(John Paul II, *Redemptoris Missio,* 92)

the mission of the Son and the Holy Spirit. The ultimate purpose of the Apostles' mission was to cooperate with the Holy Trinity's plan and invite people to share in the communion between the Father and the Son in the Holy Spirit. ✝

Gentile

A non-Jewish person. In the Scriptures the Gentiles were the uncircumcised, those who did not honor the God of the Torah. In the New Testament, Saint Paul and other evangelists reached out to the Gentiles, baptizing them into the family of God.

Hellenistic

Of or relating to Greek history, culture, or art after Alexander the Great.

Article 11 Spreading the Gospel

A good teacher knows that all students do not learn in the same way. Some students learn best by reading silently, others by listening to a lecture, yet others by discussing the content. In a similar way, the Church recognizes that she must adapt her manner of spreading the Gospel to diverse audiences and the great variety of learners, or disciples, on earth. (The Greek word for *disciple* in the New Testament, *mathetes*, literally means "learner.")

Saint Paul Preached to Both Jews and Gentiles

Although he was called to be the Apostle to the Gentiles at his conversion, Saint Paul preached both to Jews and to **Gentiles.** In his missionary work, Paul always tried to communicate the Gospel to his audience in a way they would best understand. Paul himself was comfortable in the cultural worlds of both Jews and Gentiles. Though he was a devout Jew who belonged to the party of the Pharisees, Paul was born and raised in the **Hellenistic** city of Tarsus in modern-day Turkey and wrote in an excellent Greek style.

Live It!

How Do You Preach the Gospel?

There is no one single way to spread the Gospel today. The Holy Spirit has gifted some people with the skills and personality to speak boldly and publicly about their faith, while other people witness to the truth and power of their faith by a simple, humble life of serving others.

Many types of witnesses have allowed Christ to transform their lives. Once that true inward transformation has begun, the outward effects cannot be hidden, whether those effects are proclaimed from the rooftops or quietly lived out among friends and family.

© Victoria & Albert Museum, London / Art Resource, NY

When preaching to a Jewish audience, Paul focused primarily on the Old Testament, explaining to his fellow Jews that the Scriptures prophesied the life, death, and Resurrection of Jesus (see Acts of the Apostles 13:16–43). When he spoke to a Gentile audience, however, Paul changed his approach. When he preached to Greeks in Athens, for example, Paul began by relating the Good News in a familiar context. Paul said that among the many altars set up to worship various gods, such as Zeus and Apollo, he had noticed one altar dedicated to an "unknown God." This unknown God, Paul proclaimed, was the one true God who had created all things! Paul then quoted from Greek poets to further support his points, as the Athenians would have been unfamiliar with the Old Testament (see Acts of the Apostles 17:16–34).

Paul summed up his own methods in this way, referring to the Gentiles when he spoke of those outside the law: "To the Jews I became like a Jew to win over Jews. . . . To those outside the law I became like one under the law . . . to win over those outside the law" (1 Corinthians 9:20–21).

Today the Good News of Jesus Christ continues to be shared through preaching, much like Paul did on his journeys. Think about preachers you have heard. What makes someone an effective preacher?

Paul Used Familiar Imagery

Just as Jesus, who preached in rural Galilee, used images familiar to his audience, such as a farmer sowing seed and fishermen using nets, so Paul used examples suitable to his largely urban audience. Some of these images included athletes competing in a stadium (see 1 Corinthians 9:24), military armor and weapons (see Ephesians 6:10–17), musical instruments such as gongs and cymbals (see 1 Corinthians 13:1), and temples (see 1 Corinthians 6:19).

Paul's ways of presenting the faith changed with his audience, but he never changed the truths of the faith. Effective evangelization includes a presentation that is appropriate for those who are learning or listening, but it does not distort the message. ✝

Francis Xavier: Patron Saint of Foreign Missions

Saint Francis Xavier (1506–1552) was born to a noble family of the Kingdom of Navarre in what is modern-day Spain. Giving up a promising career as a professor of philosophy, he joined Saint Ignatius of Loyola to become one of the original members of the Society of Jesus, or the Jesuits.

Leaving Europe in 1541, Francis spent the rest of his life as a missionary, working in Mozambique, India, southeastern Asia, and Japan. He baptized and taught the basics of the faith to thousands of people and planned to evangelize China, but died on an island just off the mainland.

Francis preferred to live and work among the poor, often ministering to the sick in addition to his preaching. Like Saint Paul, he changed his methods of presenting the faith to suit his audience. He taught people at their level of understanding by teaching catechism, for example, to children using rhyming verses set to popular tunes. He also engaged in theological and philosophical discussions with the more educated. His ministry was accompanied at times by miraculous signs, including the gift of healing.

© Murillo, Bartolome Esteban (1618-1682) Saint Francis Xavier. c. 1670. Oil on canvas. 85 5/16 x 63 7/8 in. The Ella Gallup Sumner and Mary Catlin Sumner Collection Fund. 1937.3 Location: Wadsworth Atheneum Museum of Art, Hartford, Connecticut, U.S.A. Photo Credit: Wadsworth Atheneum Museum of Art / Art Resource, NY

^{Article} 12 Persecution and Martyrdom

Let's face it. Being a serious disciple of Christ is not always easy and often not popular. Refusing to attend parties where underage drinking is going on, for example, can alienate some of your peers. Resisting the temptation to have sexual relations before Marriage can potentially clash with other friends' values. Living out your faith as a teen might at times lead to suffering, mockery, and loss of popularity. Yet the Church calls all of us to be witnesses to the truth of Christ, both in our words and our deeds, whether this is popular or not.

Persecution of the Church by Jewish and Roman Authorities

Early Christians witnessed to the truth of Christ and some suffered persecution from both Jewish leaders and Roman authorities. Jewish leaders did not accept Jesus as the Messiah, and they regarded claims that Jesus was divine as blasphemous, because they believed that God alone could be fully divine. Because of this charge of **blasphemy,** Paul, a devout Pharisee, sought to destroy the Church (see Galatians 1:13) before his conversion to Christianity.

Roman authorities persecuted the Church because early Christians often refused to offer sacrifices to the Roman Emperor. They regarded this as idolatry. Roman authorities, however, interpreted this refusal as disloyalty to the emperor, a crime punishable by death. Despite the threats of execution, many Christians still refused to compromise their faith in Christ, at times suffering the ultimate consequence.

Martyrs of the Early Church

The highest form of Christian witness is giving up one's life for the sake of Christ. The Greek word *martys* reveals this connection as it literally means "witness," and is also the basis for our English word *martyr.*

Stephen was the first martyr of the Christian faith. After Jesus' Ascension the Jewish leaders in Jerusalem put him on trial for blasphemy (see Acts of the Apostles 6:8—7:60). At the trial an enraged crowd dragged him out of the city and

blasphemy
Speaking, acting, or thinking about God, Jesus Christ, the Virgin Mary, or the saints in a way that is irreverent, mocking, or offensive.

martyr
A person who suffers death because of his or her beliefs. The Church has canonized many martyrs as saints.

© Scala / Art Resource, NY

Early Christians often faced persecution and death for practicing and sharing their faith. What obstacles do you face in practicing your faith and sharing it with others?

stoned him to death. Stephen witnessed to his faith to the end, saying as he died, "Lord Jesus, receive my spirit" and "Lord, do not hold this sin against them" (7:59–60).

After Stephen's death a general persecution of the Jerusalem Church broke out, causing many Christians to flee (see Acts of the Apostles 8:1). Later King Herod had James, one of the Twelve, killed, and had Peter arrested (see 12:1–3). Eventually both Peter and Paul were martyred in Rome for their faith.

As hard as it may be to believe, followers of Jesus often accepted their suffering with joy. Saint Ignatius of Antioch, awaiting his execution at Rome around the year 100, wrote: "It is better for me to die [in order to unite myself] to Christ Jesus than to reign over the ends of the earth. . . . My birth is approaching. . . ." [1] (*CCC*, 2474). The martyrs were honored to die for Christ, convinced that by sharing in the suffering and the death of Christ, they would also share in his glorious Resurrection.

Far from destroying the Church, persecution produced brave martyrs whose examples encouraged other Christians to remain steadfast in their faith. As the Church Father Tertullian wrote, "The blood of martyrs is the seed of Christians" [2] (*CCC*, 852). ✝

Pray It!

A Martyr's Prayer

Around the year 150, when he was eighty-six years old, Bishop Polycarp of Smyrna was burned at a stake for refusing to deny his Christian beliefs and worship the Roman Emperor. His prayer follows:

I bless you for having judged me worthy from this day and this hour to be counted among your martyrs. . . . You have kept your promise, God of faithfulness and truth. For this reason and for everything, I praise you, I bless you, I glorify you through the eternal and heavenly High Priest, Jesus Christ, your beloved Son. Through him, who is with you and the Holy Spirit, may glory be given to you, now and in the ages to come. Amen. [3]

(CCC, 2474)

This stained-glass image depicts the martyrdom of Saint Polycarp of Smyrna. Take a moment and read his prayer in the Pray It! sidebar on page 46. Why do you think he is giving thanks to God for being martyred?

© The Crosiers / Gene Plaisted, OSC

The Church's Final Trial

Both the Scriptures and Tradition teach us that in the last days of the Church, before Christ's second coming, the Church will undergo a final persecution (see Matthew 24:3–28). No one, however, knows the precise events and timing of the end times except the Father; even the Son himself does not know the exact date and hour (see Mark 13:32). One scriptural prediction is that the antichrist, a false messiah who will set himself up in the place of God, will deceive many at that time (see 2 Thessalonians 2:3–12).

What might an antichrist really be like? We see previews of the antichrist's deception when any *earthly* power tries to claim the *ultimate* power and authority of God. Examples include the Nazi party claim in Germany that their master race was the key to history's meaning, and the Marxist claim that the proper economic system would eventually lead to a Heaven on earth.

We must resist these human claims to have ultimate answers. We know that God alone has those answers, and we also know that God's love is more than enough to support us, even during times of suffering and persecution.

Part Review

1. Why did the Apostles and early disciples travel so far and work so hard to spread the Good News?

2. What are three ways the Holy Spirit was involved in the missionary spread of Christianity?

3. Explain how Paul's preaching to the Jews differed from his preaching to the Gentiles.

4. Explain how Paul made his message more understandable to an urban audience.

5. Explain why the early Christians were often persecuted.

6. Identify some early martyrs of the Church. Describe the attitude of these Christians toward martyrdom.

Part 4

Images of the Church

In this section we explore the mystery of the Church through several important images from the Sacred Scriptures: the People of God, the Body of Christ, and the Temple of the Holy Spirit. These images help us not only to grasp more fully the Mystery that is the Church because the metaphors are frequently used in the Church but also to understand the Sacred Scriptures and the liturgy, especially the Mass.

The Church is the People of God. The People of God could potentially include every person on the planet. Under the first Covenant, membership was a birthright. Under the New Covenant, Christ invites all people to have faith in him and to be baptized so as to belong to the People of God, to form one family.

The Body of Christ is a second important image for the Church. This name reveals the extremely close relationship between Christ and believers as well as the intimate relationship among the believers themselves.

The Church as the Temple of the Holy Spirit emphasizes that she is a dwelling place for the Holy Spirit. For the Jewish people, God dwelt in the Temple. Paul said that the Holy Spirit now lives in the Church and in each one of us.

The topics covered in this part are:

- Article 13: "The Church Is the People of God" (page 50)

- Article 14: "The Church Is the Body of Christ" (page 53)

- Article 15: "The Church Is the Temple of the Holy Spirit" (page 57)

community
A body of individuals that is unified.

Article 13 The Church Is the People of God

Where do you feel that you belong? Groups to which you belong can tell others something about you. "I belong to the drama club," suggests that besides your love of drama, you likely also feel at home with the other members of that club who share your interest. "I belong to the Asian-American student association," suggests that you appreciate the company of others who want to know more about your cultural heritage. To say, "I belong to the People of God," conveys the message that it is important to you to spend time with others who share your relationship with Christ, that you see yourself as part of the Catholic Church.

Amazingly, the People of God is a **community** to which every person is welcome and truly belongs—no particular skills or talents needed! God invites all people to belong to the People of God, to form one family.

God Wants All People to Be His

What diversity exists within your parish community?

God creates every human being with a desire for him and continuously calls each person to himself. By nature we are religious beings. God made people to live in communion

© Bill Wittman / www.wpwittman.com

with him and to find happiness through this communion. There is a place for every person in the People of God.

The New People of God

God chose the people of Israel to be his People and made a Covenant with them. Jews became part of the People of God by birth. When Christ offered the New Covenant at the Last Supper, he created the new People of God, the Church, based on this New Covenant. Followers of Christ became members of this People not through physical birth but through the spiritual birth of Baptism and their faith in Christ, who invites all human beings to be part of this People. God offers membership in the Church to all, so that they can become one family, one People of God.

The People of God Are United

If you have ever been on a sports team or involved in another activity where everyone can participate, you know you will find participants at all levels of ability and interest. It can be hard for the coach or leader to meet everyone's needs.

Because the Church draws people from all parts of the world, she includes people with different customs and languages and of various levels of understanding and interest. How then has she become a global community of over one billion people? It is no surprise that this unity comes from God. The universal Church is united as a people from the unity of the Father, the Son, and the Holy Spirit. ✝

Catholic Wisdom

We Are Part of a Greater Whole

None of us is alone in this world; each of us is a vital piece of the great mosaic of humanity as a whole.

(Pope John Paul II, "Message of the Holy Father to the Young People of Israel and Palestine")

Who Are the People of God?

Imagine that at Baptism you received an official welcome booklet. It began: "Welcome to the People of God! Here is what you need to know about us!" What would it say? Read on!

We are called the People of God, not because we "own" God (no one owns God!) but because God "owns" us and claims us.

- We become members of this People by Baptism.
- Our Head is Jesus Christ, the Messiah.
- As members we enjoy the dignity and freedom of the children of the Father.
- The Holy Spirit dwells in our hearts.
- Our law is given by Jesus: "I give you a new commandment: love one another. As I have loved you, so you also should love one another" (John 13:34).
- Our mission is to infiltrate the world, bringing it salt (a loving and joyful flavor) and light (the light of Christ).
- Our destiny is nothing less than the Kingdom of God.

Welcome to the People of God!

Article 14 The Church Is the Body of Christ

If the phrase the "Body of Christ" brings up more than one image in your mind, then you may be on your way to understanding this central yet complex image of the Church. This article examines three aspects of this image: the unity of the members of the Church with one another through their unity with Christ, Christ's role as Head of the Body, and the Church as the Bride of Christ.

The Church is the Body of Christ. When you learned about the Body of Christ in preparation for First Communion, your study may have been limited to the important truth that we receive the Body and Blood of Christ in the Eucharist. The intimate union we have with Christ in the Eucharist is a good foundation for learning about the close relationship we can have with him through his Body, the Church. Christ told us, "Whoever eats my flesh and drinks my blood remains in me and I in him" (John 6:56).

We know that during the Consecration in the Mass, the bread and wine become the Body and Blood of Christ. This change is called **Transubstantiation.** Christ himself is present in a true, real, and substantial manner. Reception of the Eucharist intensifies the union we always have with Christ, as he dwells in us and we dwell in him. Because we actually consume the Eucharist, it might be easy to comprehend that Christ abides in us. In a way we cannot begin to understand, we also dwell supernaturally as communicants in Christ.

Transubstantiation

In the Sacrament of the Eucharist, this is the name given to the action of changing the bread and wine into the Body and Blood of Jesus Christ.

chalice

The cup used during the Mass that holds the wine before the Consecration and the Blood of Christ after the Consecration. It represents the cup used at the Last Supper and is a symbol of Jesus' sacrifice and eternal life.

The Unity of the Cup and the Unity of the People

Many theologians have pointed out the essential connection between the Eucharist, the unity of the Church, and the unity of the world. Bishop Malarias of Metz wrote that when the priest makes the Sign of the Cross over the **chalice** with the consecrated host, the Body of Christ, during the Mass, he touches the four sides of the chalice to show how the Body of Christ reunites the whole human race, gathered from the four corners of the earth, into one Body.

Communion in Christ with Others

Because we, as members of the Body of Christ, are in intimate communion with Christ as individuals, we are also all closely related to one another. People of diverse backgrounds, languages, countries, and experiences belong to the Body of Christ. We are united in Christ. The comparison between the Church and the human body illustrates how intimate our relationship is with Christ and with other Church members.

We not only come from many different places but we possess different gifts and, therefore, assume different roles in the Church. We contribute to the Church in different ways, much like the leg and foot contribute to the good of the human body differently than an ear or an eye.

Because we belong to Christ and are in communion with him, we grow in love and other virtues. This growth makes us more sensitive to fellow members of the Body as well as all people. Because we are a community (people in communion), we share joys and sorrows, and we try to show special concern for members most in need, especially people who are poor and persecuted. "If [one] part suffers, all the parts suffer with it; if one part is honored, all the parts share its joy" (1 Corinthians 12:26). Things that sometimes divide us, such as gender, race, or socioeconomic status, do not matter in the Body of Christ. As Paul says, "You are all one in Christ Jesus" (Galatians 3:28).

© Bill Wittman/www.wpwittman.com

Through the Eucharist we share in the Body of Christ in a special way. How does physically receiving the Body and Blood of Christ unite us with him and one another?

Christ Is the Head of the Body

Christ is the Head of the Body, which is the Church. Christ lives in and with her. The Church receives her life from Christ. She lives in him and for him. Christ unites the members of the Church with his life so that all may come to resemble him more and more. He unites us with his suffering, death, and Resurrection. Amazingly, when we bring our suffering to Christ, he transforms it. He has the power to bring new life out of it.

Why is this all important? In addition to gaining eternal life for us, Christ also conquered evil in a significant way. Evil never wins in the end. Good always does. This truth does not mean we do not suffer in life. It means we suffer with Christ in hope of new life, trusting that Christ can bring good from painful experiences. No matter how bad a situation seems, Christ can transform it and bring new life.

Exploring the nature of the Church as the Body of Christ with Christ as the Head helps us to understand ourselves as members of this Body. The head helps the body to grow toward the head; Christ helps us to grow toward him. Just as a Head and the members make up one Body, Christ and the Church are one Body and together make up the "whole Christ."

Loving Participation in the Body of Christ

Just because members of the Church belong to the Body of Christ does not mean they always act in a way that reflects this union. Saint Paul had to scold early Christian Churches because he saw unloving behavior that did not promote unity. He found factions and divisions in the Christian community. He knew this because some were not sharing their food with the poor.

Paul made his point: "Now you are Christ's body, and individually parts of it" (1 Corinthians 12:27). It was no accident that Saint Paul concluded his instruction on *being* the Body of Christ with his great instruction on love (see 1 Corinthians, chapter 13). Love is the way to fully become what we receive—the Body of Christ.

© Russell McBride/iStockphoto.com

The Church Is the Bride of Christ

Although Christ and the Church are one, it is possible to talk about the Church and Christ using the language of personal relationship to both distinguish the two and reveal their unity. Christ is the bridegroom who loves the Church, his bride. What is incredible about this union is that Christ gave himself up for his bride, the Church, in order to make her holy and to join her with himself in an everlasting covenant!

Saint Paul compares the intimate relationship between a husband and wife with the intimate relationship between Christ and the Church, saying, "Husbands, love your wives, even as Christ loved the church and handed

When a man and woman are married in the Sacrament of Holy Matrimony, they make an everlasting covenant to love and care for each other. In the same way, Christ has made a covenant with the Church to love and care for her for all eternity.

Pray It!

Prayers of Petition

Do you begin your religion class and other classes with a prayer? If so, perhaps the person who leads prayer invites you and your classmates to mention someone or something you would like the whole class to pray for. You might pray in petition for an academic or athletic challenge that you or others will soon encounter. You might ask others to pray with you for a loved one who is hurting in some way. Sometimes you may pray for people you hear about in the media who are in trouble.

By these prayers of petition, you participate in the Church as the Body of Christ. You are praying not only for others but also for the class. You are calling others to communion with the Father, the Son, and the Holy Spirit and you are also affirming the truth that we are in prayerful communion with people near and far through Christ's Body.

himself over for her to sanctify her" (Ephesians 5:25–26). This image may be hard to understand at first; even Saint Paul teaches, "This is a great mystery, but I speak in reference to Christ and the church" (5:32).

The unity of Christ, the bridegroom, and the Church, his bride, reveals to us something of the intimate relationship God intends for a husband and wife. The relationship between Christ and the Church can be described as two becoming one flesh (see *CCC,* 796). This is the case for a husband and wife too. In his **Theology of the Body,** Pope John Paul II teaches us not to shy away from a deeper understanding of the sexual imagery involved in this comparison. For a married couple, sexual intercourse is a profound "sign" of unifying love: a sign of the total self-giving of each spouse, and of the profound mystery of the two becoming one flesh. Thus, Christian Marriage becomes an effective sign or sacrament of the covenant of Christ and the Church, and the faithfulness of the spouses to one another gives witness to God's faithful love (see *CCC,* 1617, 1648). ✝

Theology of the Body

The name given to Pope John Paul II's teachings on the human body and sexuality delivered via 129 short lectures between September 1979 and November 1984.

mystical

Having a spiritual meaning or reality that is neither apparent to the senses nor obvious to the intelligence; the visible sign of the hidden reality of salvation.

Article 15 The Church Is the Temple of the Holy Spirit

In trying to explain to early Christians the mystery of the Church, Saint Paul offered this image: "Do you not know that you are the temple of God and that the Spirit of God dwells in you? . . . the temple of God, which you are, is holy" (1 Corinthians 3:16–17). In the Old Testament and in Jewish history, the Temple was the building in which God was present to the people of Israel in a special or unique way. Thus this passage from Saint Paul is saying that the Holy Spirit is present in a unique way now in the Church.

The Holy Spirit Is the Soul of the Church

The Holy Spirit is the center of the Church's life. Another way to say that is to say the Spirit is the soul of the **Mystical** Body of Christ. The Holy Spirit is the source of the Church's life, unity, gifts, and charisms. The Holy Spirit is present in the Body of Christ, the Church. Jesus Christ has poured the Holy Spirit onto all the members of the Church, making the Holy Spirit part of everything the Church is and does.

© Erich Lessing/Art Resource, NY

Ancient Israelites believed that God dwelt in the innermost part of the Temple, foreshadowing the Church as the dwelling place of the Holy Spirit.

The Holy Spirit is the source of the Church's life and is active in the liturgy. He reveals Christ's presence in the community gathered, in the proclamation of the Scriptures, in the presider, and in the physical signs of the liturgical celebration. But the Holy Spirit is at work even before that, preparing us to receive Christ in the liturgy. And the Holy Spirit does more than just reveal Christ in the liturgy. Through the Holy Spirit, the saving work of Christ is actually made real and present in the liturgy. Also through the Spirit, we are brought into communion with Christ. This gift of communion builds up and animates the Church, and increases her holiness.

The Holy Spirit also empowers the members of the Church to acquire and develop human **virtues.** These are "stable dispositions of the intellect and the will that govern our acts, order our passions, and guide our conduct in accordance with reason and faith" (*CCC,* 1834). The four pivotal human virtues, called the cardinal virtues, are prudence, justice, fortitude, and temperance. All other human virtues can

Live It!

Our Bodies Are Not Our Own

You may remember that Saint Francis of Assisi considered all of creation to be his brothers and sisters. He called the sun Brother Sun and the moon Sister Moon. He called his body Brother Donkey because, in his view, it carried him around from place to place. On his deathbed Saint Francis apologized to Brother Donkey for not taking very good care of him. He realized, too late, that his body was a great gift from God. His body deserved respect and proper consideration.

Think of your body as a Temple of the Holy Spirit, and consider some implications. Do you give it the right food, enough rest, and proper exercise? Do you get regular physical and dental check-ups? Do you take unnecessary risks that might result in bodily harm to you or others? Spend a few moments asking yourself these questions. Choose one way to live a healthier lifestyle. Then start soon!

© Kirk Strickland/iStockphoto.com

be grouped around these four. The Holy Spirit also gives us talents and skills that enable us to contribute to the Church's mission.

When Jesus told his Apostles about the Holy Spirit, he used the word *advocate*. A human advocate speaks or writes in your favor, supports you, and recommends you. Imagine how much more the Holy Spirit does for us! The next time you are in a difficult situation, call on the Holy Spirit. ✝

When we care for our bodies through exercise, rest, and proper diet, we are caring for the Temple of the Holy Spirit that God has given us.

virtue
A habitual and firm disposition to do good.

Dwelling Places of the Holy Spirit

Long ago, as a young king of Israel, David had a profound thought: "Here I am living in a house of cedar, while the ark of God dwells in a tent!" (2 Samuel 7:2). It was to be King David's son, the wealthy Solomon, who built the great Temple of Jerusalem.

Jesus told us that the Temple would not stand—and it was finally destroyed by the Romans in AD 70—but that we ourselves would become the dwelling places of the Holy Spirit:

Whoever believes in me, as scripture says,

"Rivers of living water will flow from within him."

He said this in reference to the Spirit that those who came to believe in him were to receive.

(John 7:38–39)

Being a dwelling place for the Holy Spirit means respecting ourselves and others in body, mind, and heart. Being a dwelling place for the Spirit means being a place not of anger or envy or bitterness but of hope and love, helpfulness and prayer. It means being a place where the Holy Spirit can say, deep in our hearts, "Here, I am at home."

Part Review

1. How can someone become a member of the People of God?

2. How is the Church, numbering over one billion people globally, unified?

3. How does belonging to the Body of Christ make us grow in holiness?

4. Explain why the Church is the Bride of Christ.

5. What connection is there between the Temple of the Old Testament and the Church as the Temple of the Holy Spirit?

6. How is the Holy Spirit the source of the Church's life?

The Church

Is One, Holy, Catholic, and Apostolic

Part 1

The Church
Is One

In this section we look at the four marks (essential features or characteristics) of the Church: the Church is One, Holy, Catholic, and Apostolic. This part explores the first mark: The Church is one.

The Church is one because the Church's example for unity and source of unity is the three Divine Persons in the Trinity: the Father, the Son, and the Holy Spirit. Unity does not mean uniformity, however, as the Church is diverse in many ways. The unity of the Church is sustained by God's love and can be seen through several bonds, including the profession of one faith, common worship, and Apostolic Succession.

Unity among Christians has been threatened over time by heresies, schism, and other breaks. The results of these breaks can be seen today in the different Churches and ecclesial communities that exist. Ecumenism, the movement to restore unity among Christians and, ultimately, of all humans through the "whole wide world," is an effort to bind the wounds caused by these breaks.

The topics covered in this part are:

- Article 16: "The First Mark of the Church" (page 63)

- Article 17: "Bonds of Unity" (page 66)

- Article 18: "Wounds to Unity" (page 70)

- Article 19: "Ecumenism" (page 74)

16 The First Mark of the Church

The first of the **marks of the Church** is that the Church is one. The New Testament is perfectly clear: there is only one Church, one Body of Christ, and it is characterized by oneness or unity. Paul writes, "For in one Spirit we were all baptized into one body, whether Jews or Greeks, slaves or free persons, and we were all given to drink of one Spirit" (1 Corinthians 12:13). Paul also speaks of "one body and one Spirit . . . one Lord, one faith, one baptism; one God and Father of all" (Ephesians 4:4–6). This teaching has been affirmed many times over the Church's history as well.

marks of the Church
The four essential features or characteristics of the Church: One, Holy, Catholic (universal), and Apostolic.

Christ gave the Church the gift of unity, and it is a gift she cannot lose. In order for the unity to increase, however, members of the Church need to pray and to work to keep the unity and make it increasingly perfect. Jesus prayed prior to his death that his community of followers would be one as he is with the Father (see John 17:21). The Holy Spirit also calls us to this work, animates us in doing it, and lives within each member of the Church.

The Source of the Church's Unity

The ultimate example for and source of the Church's unity is the eternal unity of the three Divine Persons of the Trinity,

The Pope as a Symbol of Unity

As the successor to Peter, the Pope is the visible principle and foundation of the unity of the whole Church. As the shepherd of the whole Church, he is the "visible sign and guarantor of unity" (*Ut Unum Sint: On Commitment to Ecumenism,* 88). As the Vicar of Christ, the Pope is the visible representative of Christ on earth.

The Pope does not lead the Church by domination and power; rather, he leads as the *servus servorum Dei*—the "servant of the servants of God." Although this term has been used for centuries, the newly elected Pope Benedict XVI used this term in his first message, "Striving to Be the *Servus Servorum Dei*," on April 20, 2005.

Pope John Paul II called on non-Catholic Christians to work with Catholics to develop ways of expressing this universal role of the Pope in a way that would be acceptable to all Christians.

© Bildarchiv Preussischer Kulturbesitz / Art Resource, NY

How is the Holy Trinity the source of the Church's unity?

the Father, the Son, and the Holy Spirit. The Trinity actually brings the people of the universal Church into unity with the Trinity and with one another.

The Church is one because of her founder, Jesus Christ. Through his Passion, death, Resurrection, and Ascension, Jesus reconciled all people with God, thus restoring unity and allowing them to be reconciled to one another and to form one People, one Body.

The Church is also one because of the Holy Spirit, the "soul" of the Church, who lives within each member of the Church and draws them together in communion with one another and in Christ.

Diversity

Unity should not be confused with uniformity. The belief that the Church of Christ is "one" does not mean that all the Church members are striving to be the same. On the contrary, there is great diversity within the one Church.

In his first letter to the Corinthian Church, Paul noted this diversity within unity:

> There are different kinds of spiritual gifts but the same Spirit; there are different forms of service but the same Lord; there are different workings but the same God who produces all of them in everyone. (12:4–6)

People are diverse and so are the gifts they are given. The Holy Spirit gives each person his or her own gifts, and they are all necessary for increasing the unity of the Body of Christ (see 1 Corinthians 12:14–31).

The Church gathers people from various cultures and nations. Pope Paul VI captures this reality in the *Dogmatic Constitution on the Church* (*Lumen Gentium,* 1964):

Though there are many nations there is but one people of God, which takes its citizens from every race, making them citizens of a kingdom which is of a heavenly rather than of an earthly nature. (13)

The Church draws its members from all over the world. If we think of members from different cultures, each with varied gifts and callings, we can begin to imagine the great diversity in the Church.

Diversity and Unity of Worship

People of every race, nationality, culture, and age belong to the Church. The Diocese of Oakland, California, for example, offers Masses in at least twelve languages, including Portuguese, Korean, Latin, and American Sign Language.

The diversity of the Church is visible in the variety of languages in which the Mass is celebrated. In what languages is the Mass celebrated in your parish?

Although the essentials of the Mass are the same everywhere, there are aspects of liturgical celebrations that can be adapted to the culture of the people in the assembly. The liturgical music, the artwork, or the liturgical dance within a church, for example, can reflect a particular culture. Yet the integrity of the Church's worship is guaranteed because the ritual has been passed down from the Apostles through the bishops.

Sin and Unity

Sin and its aftermath threaten Christ's gift of Church unity. The Apostles could see this challenge in the early Church and warned Christians to do their part to maintain and perfect the gift of unity. Today we also see this challenge, and we are called to do our part in praying and working for the unity of all Christians and all humanity. ☩

WEEKEND MASS SCHEDULE

Saturday: 12:30 p.m. (Korean), 5:30 p.m. (English)
Sunday: 9:00 a.m., 11:00 a.m., 7:00 p.m.

DAILY MASSES

Monday - Friday: 5:30 p.m.

Sacrament of Reconciliation: (Confessions)
Monday - Friday: 4:30 - 5:00 p.m.
Wednesday: 8:30 - 9:30 p.m.
Saturday: 4:00 - 5:15 p.m. and by appt.

Sacrament of Baptism of Infants:
Held on the fourth Sunday of every month, in English at 1:00 p.m. and in Spanish at 2:00 p.m. Scheduling is done at the Baptism Class.

Baptismal Classes: (a prerequisite to have your child baptized)
Classes in English and Spanish meet on the second Monday of each month at 7:30 p.m. in the Catholic Center. Attendance at a Baptism preparation class is required for parents and godparents.

Article 17 Bonds of Unity

creed

Based on the Latin credo, meaning, "I believe," a creed is an official presentation of the faith, usually prepared and presented by a council of the Church and used in the Church's liturgy. Two creeds occupy a special place in the Church's life: the Apostles' Creed and the Nicene Creed.

How does the Church retain its unity? Church members are connected by both visible and invisible bonds of unity. The greatest bond of unity is God's love, which binds us together in an invisible way. Several visible characteristics of the Church also bind her in unity: the profession of one faith, the common celebration of divine worship, and the recognition of the ordained leaders of the Church who are successors of the Apostles.

Unity of Faith

People all over the world profess the one faith by praying the Nicene Creed. The Nicene Creed is one of two **creeds** that have special places in the Church's life. The second is the Apostles' Creed. The Apostles' Creed is a statement of Christian faith developed from the baptismal creed of the ancient Church of Rome; the Nicene Creed was developed at the Church's first two Ecumenical Councils—the Council of Nicaea (AD 325) and the Council of Constantinople (AD 381).

Next Sunday when you recite the Creed, imagine scores of people around the world joining with you and all those assembled with you in the profession of the one faith. This is a visible (and audible) sign of unity and an affirmation of the basic beliefs we share. When we profess what we believe, we also commit ourselves to what we believe.

The Creed summarizes truths about the Father ("I believe in one God, the Father almighty . . . "), the Son ("I believe in one Lord Jesus Christ . . . "), the Holy Spirit ("I believe in the Holy Spirit, the Lord, the giver of life . . ."), as well as belief in the Church ("I believe in one, holy, catholic and apostolic Church") and other essential beliefs.

Although the Creed summarizes the key points of the faith, the profession of faith goes far beyond the Nicene and Apostles' Creeds. Think of the size of the *Catechism of the Catholic Church* and the Bible as closer to the amount of knowledge Catholics should have about their faith. Learning about the faith through Catholic schools, parish religious education programs, or personal study enables us to understand, articulate, and share the faith.

Apostles' Creed

I believe in God, the Father Almighty, Creator of heaven and earth, and in Jesus Christ, his only son, our Lord, who was conceived by the power of the Holy Spirit, and born of the Virgin Mary. He suffered under Pontius Pilate, was crucified, died, and was buried; he descended into hell; on the third day he rose again from the dead; he ascended into heaven, and is seated at the right hand of God the Father almighty; from there he will come to judge the living and the dead.

I believe in the Holy Spirit, the holy catholic Church, the communion of saints, the forgiveness of sins, the resurrection of the body, and the life everlasting. Amen.

Nicene Creed

I believe in one God, the Father almighty, maker of heaven and earth, of all things visible and invisible.

I believe in one Lord, Jesus Christ, the Only Begotten Son of God, born of the Father before all ages. God from God, Light from Light, true God from true God, begotten, not made, consubstantial with the Father; through him all things were made. For us men and for our salvation he came down from heaven, and by the Holy Spirit was incarnate of the Virgin Mary, and became man.

For our sake he was crucified under Pontius Pilate, he suffered death and was buried, and rose again on the third day in accordance with the Scriptures.

He ascended into heaven and is seated at the right hand of the Father. He will come again in glory to judge the living and the dead and his kingdom will have no end.

I believe in the Holy Spirit, the Lord, the giver of life, who proceeds from the Father and the Son, who with the Father and the Son is adored and glorified, who has spoken through the Prophets. I believe in one, holy, catholic and apostolic Church. I confess one baptism for the forgiveness of sins and I look forward to the resurrection of the dead, and the life of the world to come. Amen.

Apostolic Succession

The uninterrupted passing on of apostolic preaching and authority from the Apostles directly to all bishops. It is accomplished through the laying on of hands when a bishop is ordained in the Sacrament of Holy Orders as instituted by Christ. The office of bishop is permanent, because at Ordination a bishop is marked with an indelible, sacred character.

Unity of Worship

We are also united in our participation in divine worship and the Sacraments. The Seven Sacraments create bonds of unity within the Church, especially the Eucharist. The Eucharist is both a sign of the unity of the Church and a means for bringing about that unity; this Sacrament is the totality and summary of our faith. Paul taught, "Because the loaf of bread is one, we, though many, are one body, for we all partake of the one loaf" (1 Corinthians 10:17). Our Eucharistic celebrations always include the same essential elements: the proclamation of the Word of God, thanksgiving to God for all his benefits, the consecration of bread and wine, and our receiving the Body and Blood of Christ.

Unity of the Apostolic Succession

We are united by recognizing the authority of the same Church leaders: the bishops in union with the Pope. The bishops and the Pope have received their authority by means of **Apostolic Succession** through the Sacrament of Holy Orders. The bishops, as successors of the Apostles, and the Pope, as the successor of Peter, provide us a concrete guarantee that we are still following the same faith and sacramental worship that was passed down from Jesus and the Apostles. ✝

Catholic Wisdom

Young People in Prayer

The Taizé community in France welcomes thousands of young people each year to pray and sing with them. Here, a brother from the community reflects on these young people:

> We brothers are often impressed by the ability of the young people to remain in our church, sometimes for hours on end, in silence or supported by meditative singing.
>
> What enables the young people to become truly open to an inner dialogue in prayer? How do we manage to let them discover that, even without knowing how to pray, even without knowing what to ask for or what to expect, God has already placed in us the longing for a communion?

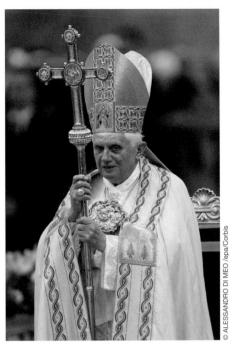

"The Roman Pontiff, as the successor of Peter, is the perpetual and visible principle and foundation of unity of both the bishops and of the faithful" (*Lumen Gentium*, 23). Pope Benedict XVI is the 265th Roman Pontiff.

Sharing the Eucharist

To Christians who are not Catholic, it may seem as if the Catholic Church is arrogant and intolerant in not sharing the Eucharist with them. Let's look closer at the Church's reasoning in order to understand why that is not the case.

The Eucharist is a sign of the oneness of the faith, liturgy, and leadership of the Church. Unfortunately, however, Christians currently are not fully united. Many Christians belong to congregations that are outside the Apostolic Succession. Though those congregations share many beliefs and practices with us, they do not share them fully. It would be dishonest to celebrate a sign of unity together before the Church is actually united or before the friend comes into full communion with the Catholic Church.

If you have friends who would like to become Catholic, suggest that they talk with your school's campus minister or a priest or staff member at a nearby Catholic parish.

Article 18 Wounds to Unity

The Church is united by bonds of professed faith, worship, and Apostolic Succession. Although the Apostles urged the early Christians to preserve the gift of unity they had received, we know that they later Christians found it challenging to be one. Heresy and schism were principal causes of divisions within the Church.

Heresy

In our society today, we value a diversity of opinions and become nervous when one group insists that it possesses the truth. Though considering different opinions can be beneficial in certain circumstances, differences in key areas of theology or practice have led to confusion and division among Christians.

A heresy occurs when a person consciously and deliberately rejects a dogma of the Church. The word comes from *haeresis*, a Greek word meaning "party or faction," revealing the fact that heresies have often led to the establishment of opposing groups within the Church, especially in its first several centuries. Early Church heresies include Gnosticism, Arianism, Nestorianism, Monophysitism, and Appolinarianism.

Schisms

A Church in **schism** with the Catholic Church is one that does not recognize the supreme authority of the Pope or refuses to be in communion with the Church. Schisms sometimes occurred when a community did not accept the teachings of a Council. The Assyrian Church of the East did not accept the outcome of the Council of Ephesus, for example, while the Oriental Orthodox Churches rejected the definitions from the Council of Chalcedon.

The ancient Roman Empire was divided in half, into East and West. Constantine's successors ruled the Greek-speaking Eastern half, the Byzantine Empire, from its capitol, Constantinople, while emperors ruled the Latin-speaking West from Rome. The current schism between Eastern Orthodox Christianity and the Catholic Church is often dated to 1054, although the East and the West were distanced by communication difficulties and disagreements in the prior years.

In 1054 Pope Leo IX sent a delegation from Rome to the Orthodox Patriarch Michael of Constantinople. After a series of disagreements, the Roman delegation **excommunicated** the patriarch, and the patriarch in turn excommunicated the delegation. Other events, including the destruction of Constantinople in 1204 by Western crusaders, eventually led to a complete break in relations between the Eastern Orthodox Churches and the Roman Church.

You may be familiar with the Russian Orthodox Church, the Greek Orthodox Church, or others. The Center for the Study of Global Christianity estimates that there were approximately 216,574,000 Orthodox Christians worldwide in 2004.

Despite differences, the Catholic Church considers itself to be almost in full communion with the Orthodox Churches. (See the next article, "Ecumenism," for some reasons why these two Churches are close but not in full communion.)

schism
A major break that causes division. A schism in the Church is caused by the refusal to submit to the Pope or to be in communion with the Church's members.

excommunication
A severe penalty that results from grave sin against Church law. The penalty is either imposed by a Church official or happens automatically as a result of the offense. An excommunicated person is not permitted to celebrate or receive the Sacraments.

The Church of Christ

Jesus Christ established the Church, sometimes referred to as the Church of Christ, and appointed Saint Peter and the Apostles to lead her. The Church of Christ, which in the Nicene Creed we profess to be one, holy, catholic, and apostolic, subsists (exists) in the Catholic Church.

Toward the Healing of Ancient Schisms

In 1984 Pope John Paul II and Moran Mar Ignatius Zakka II, who was Patriarch of Antioch and All the East and Supreme Head of the Universal Syrian Orthodox Church, declared that the past schism between their Churches was due to differences in terminology and culture, rather than to any true differences in belief. The Churches pledged to continue to work toward full communion.

Only the Catholic Church has kept the structure of leadership that Christ established. The Kingdom of God is already in her and will be perfected at the end of time. When the Kingdom of God is perfected, the just will reign with God in Heaven for eternity, their souls united with their glorified, resurrected bodies. God will be all in all because the whole of the creation will be in perfect and direct relationship with its Creator.

The Protestant Reformation

The Protestant Reformation in the early sixteenth century also divided Christians. At that time the conflicts arose that led some Christians to break away from the Catholic Church and form new ecclesial communities. These communities became known as Protestants, from the verb *to protest.* The term *Protestant* now describes the Christians that descended from this movement. A key figure in the Protestant Reformation was Martin Luther, a German monk, priest, and Scripture scholar. Among Church practices criticized by Luther was that of selling **indulgences.** Luther could not resolve his conflict with the Church, and was excommunicated. People who then followed Luther in forming a new ecclesial community became known as Lutherans.

The Catholic Church shares a special relationship with the Eastern Orthodox churches in part because they have maintained Apostolic Succession and celebrate true Sacraments.

© Atlantide Phototravel/Corbis

Theological principles that were central to the Protestant Reformation were *sola scriptura* and *sola gratia,* ideas that contradict the truth of Catholic teaching. The first phrase means that "Scripture alone," rather than the Scriptures and Tradition, should be the basis for Church teaching. *Sola gratia* means that salvation comes through God's grace alone rather than through any human effort. This sole focus on grace contradicts the truth that while God's grace is ultimately the source of salvation, human beings can cooperate with it through their good works, or deny it. (See the sidebar "Dialogue with Non-Catholics" on page 77 for information about this ecumenical dialogue.)

Not long after the start of the Protestant Reformation and Luther's break with the Church, other Christian ecclesial communities were established in Northern Europe. Among these were the Calvinists, led by John Calvin. In 1530, King Henry VIII broke with the Catholic Church following a dispute with the Pope over his right to divorce and remarry. Henry VIII established the Church of England and declared himself the head of that Church. In later centuries, ecclesial communities such as Presbyterians, Baptists, Methodists, and Episcopalians evolved from congregations that had split with the Catholic Church in the early sixteenth century.

indulgence
The means by which the Church takes away the punishment that a person would receive in Purgatory.

Pray It!

Praying for Christian Unity

The following prayer is taken from *Resources for the Week of Prayer for Christian Unity and throughout the year 2009,* prepared jointly by the Pontifical Council for Christian Unity and the Commission on Faith and Order of the World Council of Churches. This week is observed every January 18–25, including the feasts of Saints Peter and Paul.

> Lord our God, we thank you for the wisdom we gain from your scriptures. Grant us the courage to open our hearts and our minds to neighbors of other Christian confessions and of other faiths; the grace to overcome barriers of indifference, prejudice or hate; and a vision of the last days, when Christians might walk together towards that final feast, when tears and dissension will be overcome through love. Amen.

(Prayer for Day 7)

© Hulton-Deutsch Collection/CORBIS

Martin Luther is known for his posting of the *95 Theses on the Power and Efficacy of Indulgences.* Martin Luther did not intend to cause a split in the Church; instead he hoped the Church would discuss and resolve the points he was raising.

The Church made efforts to address the issues at the heart of the division created by the Protestant Reformation through the Counter-Reformation, most notably, at the Council of Trent (1545–1563). Although the council brought positive change, it did not restore unity to the Church. ✝

19 Ecumenism

Article

Do you have a friend or family member who is a member of a Christian community but is not a Catholic? Although all Christians are not unified, all those baptized in Christ and brought up in the faith of Christ are Christians and are brothers and sisters with one another and with the Church.

Catholics and Other Christians

All Catholics are Christians but not all Christians are Catholic. We share many elements of holiness and truth with other Christians: the Bible; the life of grace; faith, hope, and love; Gifts of the Holy Spirit; and many visible elements as well. Christ uses other Churches and ecclesial communities as a means of salvation. Yet the possibility of these Christian communities being used as a means of salvation is based ultimately on the fullness of the heritage of faith that Jesus entrusted to the Catholic Church.

Non-Catholic Churches and Ecclesial Communities

The Eastern Orthodox Church, though not in full communion with the Catholic Church, is especially close to the Catholic Church, as it has maintained Apostolic Succession. The Orthodox Church has true Sacraments, especially Holy Orders and the Eucharist. One major cause of continuing

© OSSERVATORE ROMANO/X01934/Reuters/Corbis

division, however, is that the Orthodox Church does not recognize the primacy of the Pope, or the Pope's authority over the whole Church.

The Catholic Church recognizes that all those "who believe in Christ and have been properly baptized are put in some, though imperfect, communion with the Catholic Church" (*Decree on Ecumenism* [*Unitatis Redintegratio*, 1964], 3). All who are baptized are made part of the "crucified and glorified Christ" (22), and are rightly called brothers and sisters in Christ. However, ecclesial communities, such as those that originated in the Protestant Reformation, who do not receive apostolic authority from the Apostles and their successors, the bishops, through the Apostolic Succession, do not have the fullness of the Sacraments or of salvation.

While visiting Turkey in 2006, Pope Benedict XVI met with leaders of the Orthodox Church to deepen the relationship between the two Churches.

ecumenism
The movement to restore unity among all Christians.

The Ecumenical Movement

The ecumenical movement, or **ecumenism,** is an effort by Christians from different churches and ecclesial communities to be more open to one another and to work to restore unity among all Christians. The movement has focused on two immediate goals: (1) to achieve better mutual understanding and (2) to cooperate in various fields (for example,

assisting people who are poor, or making Bible transla-
tions). Pope John Paul II was clear that the ultimate goal of
the ecumenical movement was to return all Christians to a
visible unity and full communion. The Catholic Church is

The Unity of the Martyrs

Pope John Paul II spoke about Catholic and other Christians who have
been willing to give their lives as martyrs and went further. He said, "I
now add that this communion is already perfect in what we all consider
the highest point of the life of grace, *martyria* unto death, the truest
communion possible with Christ who shed his Blood" (*Ut Unum Sint: On
Commitment to Ecumenism*, 84).

The Church of England makes its own ecumenical tribute to martyrs.
In London, above Westminster Abbey's West door, built into the stone,
are the figures of ten twentieth-century martyrs. The statues include
the Dietrich Bonhoeffer (a Lutheran pastor), Dr. Martin Luther King Jr.
(a Baptist minister), Oscar Romero (a Catholic Archbishop), the Grand
Duchess Elizabeth of Russia (a member of the Orthodox Church), and
the Lucian Tapiedi (a member of the Anglican Church).

Though Pope John Paul II speaks of Christian martyrs being in communion with Christ, the Church does not necessarily recognize all those who
die for their faith as saints, even those who are Catholic. For example,
Bishop Oscar Romero, who in 1980 was assassinated in El Salvador
while celebrating Mass because of his outspoken stance on human rights
abuses in that country, has not been canonized. A cause for his beatifi-
cation and canonization was opened in 1997 and the process of studying his life and his martyrdom continues.

fully committed to the ecumenical movement; many Vatican II documents addressed this issue, including the important *Decree on Ecumenism.*

Although you and I can deepen our understanding of non-Catholic communities in conversation with Christian friends, an essential part of the movement is dialogue between official representatives of the Catholic Church and of other communities. The Catholic Church has participated in a number of these exchanges, yielding concrete results. In 1965 Pope Paul VI and the Athenagoras I, the Patriarch of Constantinople, created a joint Catholic-Orthodox declaration in which they apologized to one another for the offensive actions surrounding the 1054 schism, nullified the excommunications, and stated that they deplore the events before and after the schism that led to their break in communion.

Essential Elements of the Movement Toward Unity

The commitment to the ecumenical movement involves several essential elements for all Church members (see *CCC,* 821):

- growing in holiness through a constant renewal of the Church
- conversion of heart

Live It!

Dialogue with Non-Catholics

Because our world is diverse, it is likely that you have daily interactions with non-Catholic Christians as well as with members of non-Christian faiths. Following are two practical guidelines to follow whenever you find yourself discussing religious topics with those who are not Catholic:

- Develop a solid understanding of your own faith. If others challenge your beliefs, be ready to explain them in a clear and calm way (see 1 Peter 3:15–16).
- Be open to learning about other faiths. The Church affirms that the Holy Spirit works through Christians who are not Catholic, and she rejects nothing of what is true and holy in non-Christian religions.

We can thus be open to learning from these other traditions, while at the same time being ready to share the truth of our Catholic faith.

theologian

A person who studies theology. Theology is "the study of God"; the academic discipline and effort to understand, interpret, and order our experience of God and Christian faith; classically defined as "faith seeking understanding."

- prayer for unity, including joining together in prayer with other Christians

- deeper knowledge of each other and our traditions

- formation for ecumenical dialogue for all the faithful, especially priests

- ecumenical dialogue and meetings among **theologians** and other Christians

- collaboration between Catholics and other Christians in various areas of service to all of humanity

Achieving Christian unity is a work of the whole Church but cannot come from human effort alone. Through prayer and other actions, we participate in the Trinity's work of reconciling all Christians. ☦

Part Review

1. What is the example for and source of the Church's unity?

2. What is the difference between unity and uniformity?

3. What are the visible bonds of unity in the Church?

4. Why does the Catholic Church not allow all Christians to receive the Eucharist?

5. What were the final events that led to the schism between the Roman Catholic and Eastern Orthodox Churches?

6. Explain the two theological principles that were at the heart of the Protestant Reformation.

7. What are the elements of holiness and truth that are shared between Catholics and other Christians?

8. What is the ecumenical movement, and what is the Catholic Church's approach toward it?

Part 2

The Church Is Holy

Why is the Church holy? Why is she different than other organizations that do good things? This part answers those questions.

Unlike any other organization, the Church is made up of a human and a divine element. The divine element can be seen with the eyes of faith. The eyes of faith tell us that the Church is holy because she was created by the most holy God, who has given her the gifts to be an instrument of salvation, and because the Holy Spirit dwells in her. The holiness of the Church on earth is real yet imperfect because her members cannot be perfectly holy in this life even though they take steps toward holiness.

The Church depends completely on the free gift of God's grace to be holy. Through this grace we are prepared to respond to God's invitation of love and able to grow in holiness.

The Church recognizes the power of the Holy Spirit as she identifies certain people as saints to serve as models of holiness for us. We also pray to the saints to intercede for us or others with God. Mary, who by God's grace is perfectly holy, is the model toward which all other Church members strive. She responded perfectly to the Father by agreeing to be the Mother of the Father's only Son, Jesus.

The topics covered in this part are:

- Article 20: "Why Is the Church Holy?" (page 80)

- Article 21: "The Church Makes Us Holy through God's Grace" (page 84)

- Article 22: "The Communion of Saints" (page 87)

- Article 23: "The Saints: Models and Intercessors" (page 89)

- Article 24: "Mary: Perfect Model of Holiness" (page 92)

Article 20 Why Is the Church Holy?

We know we live in a world of both good and evil. Why is the Church holy if she is obviously part of this sinful world?

The Church Is Both Human and Divine

Let's explore a truth about the Church that helps us to understand her holiness. She is one but is made up of two elements, one human and one divine. We see the human, visible reality of the Church in such things as people gathered for the Eucharist; the church buildings; the Pope, bishops, and priests; young people praying on retreats and serving others; the Bible; and so on.

But the Church is more than what we can see. The Church also has an invisible dimension as a bearer of divine life. This is a mystery that we see only with the eyes of faith. It builds on the visible reality. Through the action of the Holy Spirit, the aspects of the Church that we can see communicate and put us in touch with the divine dimension of the Church.

The Holy Spirit assures us that the Church is carrying out Christ's mission, despite the sins and failures of the members. Through us God is doing what we could never do on our own. Our work is participation in the real, but unseen, divine life of the Trinity. The earthly structure of the Church exists for the sole purpose of sanctifying the members or making them holy.

When we understand the true nature of the Church as human and divine, we see that she is not limited to her visible aspects, and we recognize the source of her holiness. The Church is holy because the most holy God created her. Christ, her Bridegroom, loves her and gave up his life for her to make her holy (see Ephesians 5:25–26). He also joins himself to her as his Body and gave the Holy Spirit to the Church. The Spirit of holiness gives the Church her life.

The Church Is Holy Because She Has God's Holy Gifts

The Church is holy because she is united with Christ and he has given her the means of salvation. In other words, God has given her the gifts that enable her to sanctify. She is his instrument of salvation. Christ has gifted the Church, for example, with the Holy Scriptures, the Sacraments, models of holiness, the leadership of the Apostles and their successors, and everything else that is required for salvation.

The Call to Holiness

The holiness of the Church on earth is real but imperfect. Christ calls all members of the Church to perfect holiness, but this perfection always lies in the future and cannot be fully achieved in the present. Perfect holiness will be achieved in Heaven, the state of supreme and definitive happiness with the most Holy Trinity and the Communion of Saints that is the ultimate fulfillment of all human longing.

Love is at the heart of holiness, and encounters with human and divine love can give us glimpses into what eternal communion with God might be like. Love is the means

Live It!

The Desire to Be Holy

We have all felt the pressure to go along with the crowd and accept the standards of the culture. But once a person gets a true taste of the life of holiness, he or she will want to live it more and more. Many worldly promises are ultimately false and hollow; only holiness brings true and lasting happiness.

Here are a few practical steps for building up an increasingly holy life:

- **Take time for prayer, reflection, and worship.** It is difficult to grow in holiness when we are caught up in the "busyness" of the world, causing us to lose the big picture of life's true meaning.
- **Choose your friends wisely.** If you choose friends who are serious about living a holy life, their example will rub off. A true friend will challenge you to become even more holy.
- **Fill your heart and mind with holy things.** We live what is in our hearts and imagination. So if we deliberately choose to read holy literature, watch inspiring movies, or listen to spiritual songs, our hearts will become holier, and our actions will reflect that inner change.

by which the Church sanctifies her members. We encounter the love of God in the Scriptures, in the Sacraments, in personal prayer, in relationships with loved ones, and in learning about the faith. Saint Thérèse of Lisieux describes love as the principle vocation or calling of each person. The more specific vocations, such as priesthood, consecrated life, or Marriage are different ways to live out the calling to love.

Holiness and Sinners

Despite the holiness of the Church, her members include sinners. In fact all of the members of the Body, including her leaders, are sinners. Because the Church sanctifies, it is natural that she embrace sinners. Her holiness lies in the truth that with Christ and in Christ, she is fully focused on saving people from sin. The presence of sinners in the Church does not detract from her holiness.

Recall Jesus' parable of the weeds among the wheat (see Matthew 13:24–30) in which an enemy plants weeds in the same place where the farmer sowed his wheat. Although his slaves ask if the farmer wants them to pull the weeds up, the farmer says to wait until harvest to separate them. His concern is that if the slaves pull out the weeds, they might

One way we can grow in holiness is through reading and praying with the Scriptures. What opportunities for growing in holiness are available to you in your school or parish?

pull out some of the wheat as well. Each of us is a mix of wheat and weeds within. "In everyone, the weeds of sin will still be mixed with the good wheat of the Gospel until the end of time. Hence the Church gathers sinners already caught up in Christ's salvation but still on the way to holiness"[1] (*CCC*, 827).

Affirming the Church's holiness and her role in sanctifying people is not to say that members of the Church do not need to constantly do penance and seek purification and renewal. Repentance and **conversion** are important means of growing in holiness. They involve sorrow for and abhorrence of the sins we have committed and the intent to avoid sin in the future. The Church calls all her members to a "second conversion." The first occurs with the forgiveness of sins and the gift of new life at Baptism. This second one is a lifelong effort to hear Christ's call to conversion and become increasingly holy. ✝

conversion
A change of heart, turning us away from sin and toward God.

The Church's Role within History

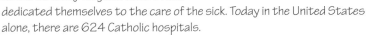

The mysterious aspects of the Church can be seen only with the eyes of faith and cannot be fully comprehended by humans. However, the accomplishments of the Church throughout history are visible signs of this divine reality of salvation. Consider just a few examples. Following the example of Jesus the healer, the Church has always been active in health care. Early on, the Church played a central role in the development of hospitals. Through the centuries many religious orders have dedicated themselves to the care of the sick. Today in the United States alone, there are 624 Catholic hospitals.

The Church's monasteries played a major role in preserving knowledge throughout the late ancient and medieval periods, studying and copying not only the Scriptures and Church writers, but also classical philosophy and literature. In the Middle Ages, the Church was a great patron of the arts. Pope Julius II, for example, commissioned Michelangelo's great paintings in the Sistine Chapel. These are only a few of the outward manifestations of the hidden sources of healing, knowledge, and creativity that lie within the mystery of the Church.

Article 21 The Church Makes Us Holy through God's Grace

grace
The free and undeserved gift of God's loving and active presence in the universe and in our lives, empowering us to respond to his call and to live as his adopted sons and daughters. Grace restores our loving communion with the Holy Trinity, lost through sin.

supernatural grace
Transcending the power of human intellect and will.

You are likely familiar with the spiritual song "Amazing Grace." In this article we explore how truly amazing grace is.

As we have discussed already, each member of the Church is called to be holy. Jesus said, "Be perfect, just as your heavenly Father is perfect" (Matthew 5:48). To grow in holiness, we must make conscious choices to respond to the Holy Spirit through prayer, reading the Sacred Scriptures, and receiving the Sacraments, the Eucharist in particular. But it is important to remember that the holiness of the Church and of each member is the result of God's grace, not of our human efforts. **Grace** is the free and undeserved gift of God's loving presence in our lives. It enables us to respond to his call to be his adopted sons and daughters. Grace enables us to participate in the life of the Trinity. Grace is **supernatural.** In other words, it transcends the power of human intellect and will. Because it is supernatural, grace cannot be known except by faith. We cannot rely on our feelings or experiences to recognize God's grace. We can, however, see the results or fruits of God's grace at work in us and in the lives of holy people.

It Is All about Grace

The Holy Spirit always makes the first move in our lives. If the Holy Spirit did not prepare us beforehand to receive and cooperate with his grace, we would never choose on our own to seek after him and his holiness. Recall that in creating us, the Father placed the desire for him alone in our hearts. The gift of grace, a response to this longing, enables us to cooperate with the Holy Spirit in order to grow in holiness and avoid things that separate us from God. Yet, we are given freedom along with grace, so how we respond to the gift of grace is up to us. When we choose in freedom to cooperate with grace, we are at our best, perfecting our God-given potential to form loving relationships with God and others. Grace brings with it the gifts we need to work with the Holy Spirit and to help in the sanctification of others and in the building of the Church.

Specific Types of Grace

The Holy Spirit gives the Church specific types of grace. **Sanctifying grace** is God's free and generous gift, sometimes called the "state of grace." It brings about a change in us that orients us to God and helps us to respond to his call. It is infused by the Holy Spirit into our souls to free us from sin and to make us holy. Through Baptism we receive sanctifying grace and a share in the divine life. Sanctifying grace is a habitual grace, meaning that it is a stable and supernatural disposition. It is always with us, helping us to live according to God's will.

Habitual grace therefore differs from another kind of grace called **actual grace.** Actual grace is the name for God's interventions that can come at the beginning of the conversion process and during the everyday moments of our lives.

There are other types of grace as well as those mentioned. There are **sacramental graces,** gifts that come from the particular Sacraments. Grace comes to us through the Sacraments because Christ instituted them and works through them. Each Sacrament gives us grace in a unique way. For example, the Sacrament of Matrimony gives couples the grace to love one another with the love with which Christ loved his Church, perfecting their human love and strengthening their unity. The graces of the Sacrament of Penance and Reconciliation enable us to have a peaceful conscience and increase our spiritual strength to resist temptation.

The charisms discussed in article 9, "The Holy Spirit Gifts the Church," are special graces of the Holy Spirit. All graces are at the service of love and building up of the Church. Graces of state accompany people in their specific vocations to live a Christian life and to minister within the Church. The Holy Spirit gifts parents as they do their best to raise their children. He inspires a hospital chaplain to know what to say or how to pray when ministering to someone who is dying.

sanctifying grace
The grace that heals our human nature wounded by sin and restores us to friendship with God by giving us a share in the divine life of the Trinity. It is a supernatural gift of God, infused into our souls by the Holy Spirit, that continues the work of making us holy.

actual grace
God's interventions and support for us in the everyday moments of our lives. Actual graces are important for conversion and for continuing growth in holiness.

sacramental grace
The gifts proper to each of the Seven Sacraments.

Types of Graces

- sanctifying grace
- habitual grace
- actual grace
- sacramental grace
- special graces (charisms)

God's grace will not automatically make us holy without our cooperation. We must make a real effort to work with God and to fight against the temptation to do things that separate us from God, such as going along with the crowd or doing things we know are wrong. It is a struggle to work toward holiness, but the end result—true peace and joy and everlasting life—makes the struggle infinitely valuable. ✝

John Paul II and Purifying Memories

Have you ever owned up to something you have done wrong? It can be difficult and humbling, but it is important. The Church realizes that her members have sinned in the past and desires that they honestly face up to those sins. Over a decade ago, Pope John Paul II called for a purification of memories, a process in which both Catholics and non-Catholics would study their shared past together, honestly admit wrongs, and ask one another for forgiveness. At a Day of Pardon Mass in the year 2000, the Pope asked for God's forgiveness for these wrongs over the last two thousand years:

- sins that have led to division in the Body of Christ
- sins against the people of Israel
- sins that have violated the rights of ethnic groups or not respected their cultures and religious traditions
- sins against the dignity of women

© PIZZOLI ORI/CORBIS SYGMA

Article 22 The Communion of Saints

When we recite the Nicene Creed at Mass, we profess
our belief in the Communion of Saints. This refers to the
Church. The Church is a communion of holy people, living
and dead (but alive with God). There is a second, closely
related, meaning of *Communion of Saints.* The English
saint can translate the Latin *sancti* ("holy people") and the
Latin *sancta* ("holy things"). The holy things are primarily
the Sacraments, especially the Eucharist. When we profess
belief in the Communion of Saints, we say something about
our relationships with all faithful people living now and in
the past, but that is not all. We are also saying that "holy
things"—especially the Eucharist—bind us to one another
and unite us to God. When we participate in the Sacraments,
particularly the Eucharist, we are nourished with the Body
and Blood of Christ, and we become the Body of Christ for
the world.

Love, by its very nature, brings communion to the
Body of Christ. Saint Paul says in his Letter to the Romans,

Purgatory
A state of final puri-
fication or cleansing,
which one may need
to enter following
death and before
entering Heaven.

"None of us lives for oneself, and no one dies for oneself"
(14:7). Every act of love, no matter how small, builds the
communion.

The Three Stages of Sanctification

The Church is a Communion of Saints who exists in one of
three stages of sanctification:

- the faithful, followers of Jesus, here on earth
- the faithful who have died and are being purified and made
  holy in **Purgatory** to join God in Heaven
- the faithful who have already attained the perfect holiness
  and glory of Heaven, seeing God as he is

The communion that Christ has given the Church through
the Body of Christ enables the boundaries between the living and the dead to be surpassed by life in the Holy Spirit.
The living and the dead benefit from each other spiritually
through their prayers. As we are drawn closer to the saints in
Heaven through our veneration of them, we are also drawn
closer to Christ.

We pray for those who have passed away from this life;
our prayers help them as they are purified of the effects of
earthly sin in their journey through Purgatory to the fullness
of the heavenly life. We especially remember the faithful
departed by offering the Eucharistic sacrifice of the Mass for
them. ✝

Pray It!

Praying in the Communion of Saints

It is good to have prayers by the saints nearby for different situations you may
face. You may at times find yourself at a loss for words and ready for an established prayer that you know is appropriate. Here is one from Saint Catherine of
Siena, a Doctor of the Church. You can use it when you are short on time or patience!

Lord, take me from myself and give me to yourself.

Connecting Heaven and Earth in the Mass

Next time you participate in the Mass, notice the strong connection between the saints in Heaven and the saints on earth in our Eucharistic prayers. We pray for our past loved ones: "Remember also our brothers and sisters who have fallen asleep in the hope of the resurrection and all who have died in your mercy: welcome them into the light of your face." (Eucharistic Prayer II). We know that our prayers and worship are joined with the prayers and worship of those in Heaven: "And so with the Angels and all the Saints we declare your glory" (Eucharistic Prayer II).

Article

23 The Saints: Models and Intercessors

Because the Church is holy, all members of the Church are saints or holy ones. So why does the Church give only certain people the official title Saint?

The Church recognizes the work of the Holy Spirit in certain people and holds them up as examples to the rest of us. These deceased people lived a life of extraordinary holiness or died for their faith. The holiness of the Church shines more clearly in their lives. Saints inspire us to grow in holiness and nourish our hope in good on earth and in eternal life.

Saints Are the Face of Christ in the World

Cardinal José Saraiva Martins, CMF, the Prefect (head) of the Congregation for the Causes of Saints at the Vatican, wrote a document that includes this excerpt, which summarizes why saints are so important in the Church:

> To understand the Church, we need to be acquainted with the saints who are her most eloquent sign, her sweetest fruit. To contemplate the face of Christ in the changing, diversified situations of the modern world, we must look at the saints who are "the living reflection of the face of Christ," as the Pope reminds us. The Church must proclaim the saints and she must do so

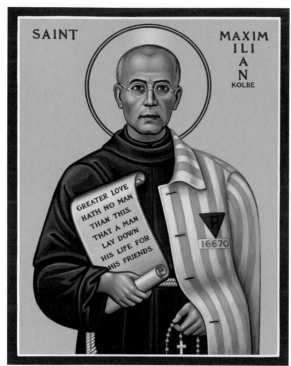

SAINT   MAXIM
                         ILI
                         A
                         N
                         KOLBE

GREATER LOVE HATH NO MAN THAN THIS, THAT A MAN LAY DOWN HIS LIFE FOR HIS FRIENDS.

16670

© Monastery Icons

Notice the concentration camp uniform draped over the shoulder of Saint Maximilian, recalling his loving sacrifice. Many people are inspired to live holier lives because of his example. Who are the saints that inspire you to live a holy life?

in the name of that proclamation of holiness that fills her and makes her, precisely, a means of sanctification in the world

> ("Reflection by Cardinal José Saraiva Martins," 2)

As we learn about saints or read their writings, we see holiness in action in real life. Those saints whose lives share common elements with our own may be particularly inspiring for us.

Saints Are Models of Holiness

As models of holiness, saints encourage others. Throughout history saints have been sources of renewal for the Church in difficult times. In the fourth century, for example, Saint Athanasius championed the orthodox Christian faith when many were led astray by the Arian heresy. Martyrs such as Saint Maximilian Kolbe, who took the place of another man about to be executed in a concentration camp, are great examples to us of people who were not afraid to lay down their lives for Christ's sake.

The Saints Intercede for Us

Saints are so closely united to Christ in his heavenly glory that they can intercede or pray to God on our behalf in a special way.

We honor or venerate the saints and ask for their prayers. The saints do not take the place of God, however. We do not pray to them. Nor does our honoring the saints suggest that we cannot pray directly to God or that we need the saints as intermediaries. We ask the saints to pray for us, just as we might ask a friend to pray for us when we are going through a difficult time.

We associate some saints with particular needs. If you have ever searched your room for something lost, you know that you wouldn't mind some help. Pray for the intercession of Saint Anthony of Padua for help in finding lost items! Pray for the intercession of Saint Blase when you have a sore throat and Saint Teresa of Ávila for help with headaches.

Learning about the saints can be very inspiring. Come February, everyone is talking about Saint Valentine, whose feast day is February 14. It may not surprise you that he is the patron saint of engaged couples and happy Marriages. Did you know, however, that he was a Roman priest martyred in the third century?

Honoring Saints through the Liturgical Year

The Church honors Mary, especially, because of her link to the saving role of her Son, on special days such as the Feast of the Assumption on August 15. The Church honors saints on fixed days of the year. Honoring the saints with the whole Church reminds us of the Paschal Mystery visible in their lives, exposes us to holy people, and unites us with the liturgy of Heaven, which is constant praise of God as is revealed in the Book of Revelation.

The examples of the saints inspire us, teach us, and help us to see what it means to live like Christ. At Confirmation you often choose a saint's name as your Confirmation name

Catholic Wisdom

Heavenly Intercession

Many saints have had a strong sense while they were living that they would still be able to help those on earth through their heavenly intercession. Saint Thérèse hoped to make a difference after death, and Saint Dominic shared the same thought with his brothers on his deathbed:

I want to spend my heaven in doing good on earth. (Saint Thérèse of Lisieux)

Do not weep, for I shall be more useful to you after my death and I shall help you then more effectively than during my life. (Saint Dominic)

because you feel drawn to the saint for some reason. Get to know a saint well by reading about him or her, especially one who particularly inspires you. ✝

Article

24 Mary: Perfect Model of Holiness

Marie, Mariam, Maureen, Moira, Mariah, Molly, Maria, Moya, Maryam, Maura, Mary. Do you have any friends with these names? Ask them if they know why their parents chose their name. Parents have named their children after the Virgin Mary for centuries, one way of honoring her special role in the Church. Perhaps this is true for your friends.

Mary's Holiness and Role in the Church

The Church honors Mary above all other saints. Mary is the holiest human being who ever lived. She was perfectly holy. We strive to become like her and ask her help in becoming

A Patron Saint for Teens

Saint Aloysius Gonzaga was born to a wealthy Italian family in the late 1500s. Inspired by the lives of the saints and his love of prayer, Aloysius gave up a life of luxury and comfort to join the Society of Jesus, the Jesuits. While Aloysius was studying in Rome, a great plague broke out. He went out into the streets, on a regular basis, to care for the plague victims, soon catching the disease himself. He died at the age of twenty-three.

© Zvonimir Atletic/Shutterstock.com

holier. The destiny of the Church is to be "holy and without blemish" (Ephesians 5:27). Mary has already reached that perfection. Mary's life is therefore a model toward which all members of the Church strive.

To consider Mary is to appreciate that she is the masterpiece of the mission of the Son and the Holy Spirit. Mary was born completely free of Original Sin and remained pure from all personal sin throughout her life.

The Holy Spirit used and uses Mary to bring people into communion with Christ. Grace alone, through Jesus, saves us. God willed that a human should take a real and active role in working out the divine plan. He chose Mary from among the descendants of Eve to be the Mother of Jesus. The Holy Spirit worked in Mary's life to prepare for the coming of the Son of God, Jesus Christ. Through the Holy Spirit's divine intervention, the Father gives the world Emmanuel, God-with-us.

Notice the scene on the far left of the picture. What is the connection between the Annunciation and the Fall?

© The Art Archive/Corbis

fiat
Latin for "let it be done."

Theotokos
A Greek title for Mary meaning "God bearer."

Mary's Yes

The Virgin Mary modeled the perfect response to God by saying "Yes" to him. When the angel Gabriel announced that Mary, though still a virgin, would give birth to Jesus, she cooperated freely and fully with the Father's plan, saying, "Behold, I am the handmaid of the Lord. May it be done to me according to your word" (Luke 1:38). Mary, by her **fiat**, by her acceptance of Gabriel's message, by her "yes," was cooperating in a real way in the Father's plan of salvation through Jesus.

Mary Is *Theotokos*

The word **Theotokos** means "God-bearer" in Greek. The Church uses this term for Mary because she is the Mother of Jesus Christ, the Eternal Son of God who became man and who is himself God. In order for Mary to have such an important role, some preparation was needed.

© Roca/Shutterstock.com

The Holy Spirit prepared Mary to be the Mother of God. In order to carry the Son of God within and then mother him, she needed to be sinless and humble, full of grace. She was thus prepared in her mother's womb to be the holy Mother of God. She was free of Original Sin and was redeemed at the moment of her conception. She is the first and best fruit of Jesus' coming to redeem us.

It was through Mary that the amazing work of the Holy Spirit in Christ and the Church first began to be seen. She showed

What does this image convey about Mary's relationship with Jesus?

others the Father's Son for the first time. The Son of God was revealed first to humble people and Gentiles and they were the first to accept him.

Mary said "yes" throughout her life, notably as she stood by her son, sharing in his suffering on the cross. When Mary's earthly life was over, she was taken up, body and soul, into Heaven, where she already shares in the glory of her Son's Resurrection. We call this wonder the **Assumption of Mary.** The Lord glorified his mother by making her Queen over all things.

In her lifelong obedience and openness to the Father's will, through her Son's work of salvation, and according to the guidance of the Holy Spirit, Mary is the Church's model of faith and love and the first to collaborate with Christ in his mission. Mary foreshadows the destiny of all the members of the Body of Christ—we all hope to be resurrected on the last day, perfected through God's grace, and accepted into the heavenly Jerusalem, where there is no sadness or death.

Assumption of Mary

The dogma that recognizes that the body of the Blessed Virgin Mary was taken directly to Heaven after her life on earth had ended.

Mary, Holy Mother of the Church and Intercessor

Because of her unique, active role in the Father's plan of salvation through his Son, Mary can be called our mother in the order of grace. Mary is thus the Mother of the Church because she actively participates in the divine plan of giving birth to believers.

Mary and Eve

The Church draws a parallel between Mary and Eve by calling Mary the New Eve. Just as Eve's disobedience signals humanity's fall into sin, Mary's obedience and cooperation with God's will reveals humanity's release from sin. Saint Irenaeus wrote, "The knot of Eve's disobedience was untied by Mary's obedience: what the virgin Eve bound through her disbelief, Mary loosened by her faith." Saint Jerome taught, "Death through Eve; life through Mary." Through her obedience Mary "became the new Eve, mother of the living" (*CCC*, 511).

We know we can pray for Mary's intercession. After Jesus' Ascension, she prayed with his other followers for the outpouring of the Holy Spirit. Through her intercession we receive gifts that help us to move spiritually toward eternal salvation. Because of this assistance, she is called Advocate, Helper, and Benefactress. ✝

Part Review

1. How is the Church both visible and invisible?

2. How is the Church holy when its members are sinful?

3. How is our holiness the result of God's grace?

4. What is sanctifying grace?

5. Explain the Communion of Saints as the communion of holy things.

6. Explain the Communion of Saints as the communion of holy people.

7. How do the saints model holiness for us?

8. How do the saints intercede for us?

9. Why is Mary a perfect model of holiness for other Church members?

10. What is the Assumption of Mary?

Part 3

The Church Is Catholic

You may be tempted to say: "Of course the Catholic Church is catholic. That is why it is called the Catholic Church." As easy as that might sound, in this case we are saying that the third mark of the Church is *catholic,* meaning "universal."

After learning the meaning of the word *catholic,* we will see how the One, Holy, Catholic, and Apostolic Church is present in the worldwide Church, in each particular church or diocese, and in each assembly gathered to celebrate the Eucharist. The Church in each of these references has the fullness of Christ and the full means of redemption if in fact she is in communion with the other bishops and the Pope.

We will learn that because the Church calls all people to unity in the People of God, she is in relationship with every person, Christian or not. She has a special bond with Judaism, and she shares a lesser bond with Islam. The Church is also in relationship with people who are Hindus, Buddhists, or of other traditions.

The universal Church is one, yet diverse, because instead of trying to erase differences, she embraces them. The communion between Eastern Catholic Churches who have different rites and practices than the Roman Catholic Church is an example of diversity's being unified into a common effort. The Church can also take different cultural traditions throughout the world and integrate them into her worship. Her catholicity is expressed in a variety of popular devotions and prayer forms that reflect the variety of cultures throughout the world.

The topics covered in this part are:

- Article 25: "The Meaning of the Word *Catholic*" (page 98)

- Article 26: "Catholicity: The Fullness of Christ in the Church" (page 100)

- Article 27: "The Church's Relationship with All People" (page 102)

- Article 28: "Universality and Diversity" (page 106)

Article 25 The Meaning of the Word *Catholic*

catholic
Along with One, Holy, and Apostolic, *Catholic* is one of the four marks of the Church. *Catholic* means "universal." The Church is catholic in two senses. She is catholic because Christ is present in her and has given her the fullness of the means of salvation and also because she reaches throughout the world to all people.

The word *catholic* comes from the Greek word *katholikos*, which means "universal." Notice that the word is not "Catholic" with a capital *C* as in the phrases "Roman Catholic," "Eastern Catholic," or "Catholic Church." The Church is **catholic** in two senses. First, she is Catholic because Christ is present in her. She possesses the fullness of Christ and has received from him the fullness of the means of salvation. Second, she has been sent on a mission by Christ to all people in the world to gather all into the People of God. Therefore, while the mark of the Church "one" refers to her indivisibility, the Church is "catholic" because she possesses the total means of salvation for all people.

To help you distinguish the two senses from each other, you might think of the first meaning as "The Church has it all," because she has the fullness or "all" of Christ and the fullness or "all" of the means of salvation. You might want to think of the second meaning as "The Church calls to all," because she invites "all" of humanity to the People of God.

Catholicity: The Church Has It All

The Church is catholic because Christ is fully present in her and because he has given the Church the full means of salvation. The means of salvation are free divine gifts given to the Church through the Holy Spirit and include the full-

Cyril of Jerusalem on the Word *Catholic*

The fourth-century Church Father Cyril of Jerusalem explained the connection between the Church and wholeness or totality (emphasis added):

> It is called Catholic then because it extends over *all the world* . . . and because it teaches *universally and completely* one and all the doctrines which ought to come to men's knowledge . . . and because it brings into subjection to godliness the *whole race of mankind* . . . and because it *universally* treats and heals the *whole class* of sins . . . and possesses it itself *every* form of virtue.
>
> (*Catechetical Lectures* 18.23)

ness of the faith, the fullness of the Seven Sacraments, and the fullness of the ordained ministry passed down from the Apostles.

Two Meanings of *Catholic*

Big 'C' =   the Catholic Church that was founded by Christ

Small 'c' =   The Church is catholic, meaning it contains the fullness of Christ and has a mission to all people

Catholicity: The Church Calls to All

The Church is also catholic in the sense that Jesus Christ has sent her out on a mission to the whole human race. Jesus commanded his Apostles, "Go, therefore, and make disciples of all nations" (Matthew 28:19).

Because all human beings share the same divine Creator and destiny with God, the Church's purpose is to gather all people from all times together as one. The Church is already a "sign" of this unity because she has unified people from all over the world in a common faith, but the perfect union of all people with one another and with God will not take place until the end of time. ✝

Catholic Wisdom

Thomas Aquinas and the Word *Catholic*

The thirteenth-century theologian Saint Thomas Aquinas had this to say about the third mark of the Church:

> The Church is Catholic, i.e., universal, first in respect to place, because it is everywhere in the world. . . . Second, the Church is universal with respect to the state of men, because no one is rejected, whether master or slave, male or female. . . . Thirdly, it is universal with respect to time . . . this Church began from the time of Abel, and will last to the end of the world.
>
> ("Exposition of the Apostles' Creed," in Avery Dulles, *The Catholicity of the Church*, page 181)

Article 26 Catholicity: The Fullness of Christ in the Church

Recall that the meaning of the word *church* is "the convocation or assembly of people whom God calls together to be in a special relationship with him." There are three distinct references for the word *church*. The first reference is to the entire community of God's People around the world; the second reference is to the local community, or diocese; the third reference is to the community assembled for liturgy, especially the Mass. In each of these three references, the Church is fully catholic in that she has the fullness of Christ and the means of salvation.

Which of these three references first comes to mind when you hear the word *church*? It seems logical that the first reference would be the fullest manifestation of the Church. But the Church is indivisible, as is Christ. The diocese of Winona, Minnesota, for example, is called a particular church. Each particular church, in union with Rome, has the full means of salvation within it.

When you gather together with others in your local community for the Mass, you hear the Gospel of Christ preached, and an ordained priest presides over the mystery of the Lord's Supper. When this happens, Christ is there, and, through Christ, the One, Holy, Catholic, and Apostolic Church is also present. That same Church is present at every Mass said throughout the world, no matter how small or poor the local community is.

It would be a mistake, however, to see the Church as simply the sum total of all of the dioceses worldwide like a federation with its global headquarters in Rome. The Church is fully present throughout the world but is also fully present in given locations, which differ from one another.

Catholicity and the Roman Catholic Church

Particular churches are fully catholic when they are in communion with the Church of Rome. Why is the Roman diocese so important?

In the early centuries of Christianity, Christians struggled with many misleading beliefs, so they turned to and relied on the apostolic churches, those established under the authority of the Apostles, for guidance. This was because these churches had preserved the full authentic apostolic teaching.

The Church of Rome had a special authority among these apostolic churches, because two great Apostles, Peter and Paul, had proclaimed the Gospel and were martyred in Rome. The Bishop of Rome is the successor of Peter, who was the leader among the Apostles. In the second century, Saint Irenaeus wrote this about the Roman Church: "It is a matter of necessity that every Church should agree with this Church, on account of its preeminent authority." When churches are in communion with Rome, they possess the fullness, or catholicity, of the apostolic faith as it is preserved in the Roman Church.

Churches in full communion with the Church of Rome recognize the authority of the Pope as the visible foundation for the unity of the college of bishops and of all members of the Church. Because the Pope is pastor of the whole Church, those in communion with the Pope share the fullness of Christ because they are united with the earthly, visible leader of the universal Church. ✝

Pictured is Vatican Square, in front of Saint Peter's Basilica. The Vatican is the seat of the Bishop of Rome, the Pope.

© Ugorenkov Aleksandr/Shutterstock.com

The Fullness of the Sacraments

The Church retains the fullness of the Sacraments by celebrating all Seven Sacraments that Christ instituted. Though many Christians recognize only Baptism and the Eucharist as Sacraments, the Catholic Church, with the Orthodox Churches, celebrates seven.

The Seven Sacraments express fullness in the sense that they touch the totality of a person's life, from Baptism at the beginning to Anointing of the Sick at the end. The Sacraments of Christian Initiation—Baptism, the Eucharist, and Confirmation—lay the foundation of Christian life. The Sacraments of Healing—Penance and Reconciliation and Anointing of the Sick—show us Christ's will that the Church continue his work of comprehensive, total healing, both physical and spiritual. The Sacraments at the Service of Communion and the mission of the faithful—Matrimony and Holy Orders—reflect the different aspects of the Church's universal mission to and in the world.

© The Crosiers/Gene Plaisted, OSC

Article 27 The Church's Relationship with All People

We have looked at the relationship between the Church and other Christian communities and the ecumenical movement that seeks to unify all Christians. In this article we look at the Church's relationship with the over four billion people belonging to non-Christian religions, such as Islam, Hinduism, and Buddhism, as well as those who do not affiliate themselves with a religion.

The Church and Non-Christian Religions

Recall that the catholicity of the Church can be seen as the Church calls all of humanity to unity in the People of God. She is open to having dialogue with people of other religions. The Church recognizes that non-Christian religions seek God and that goodness and truth can be found in them. She considers this goodness and truth to be a preparation for the Gospel. She has a duty to proclaim clearly that Christ is the way, the truth, and the life (see John 14:6).

The Catholic Church seeks dialogue with people of different religions, witnessing to her own faith while acknowledging and encouraging the spiritual and moral truths found in their religions. Note, however, that the Church does not support any religious groups that lead people astray or distort the image of God found in all humans.

The Church is in relationship with all people of non-Christian religions, but she is more closely connected to Jews and Muslims. Like Christians, Jews and Muslims acknowledge belief in one God.

This young man is celebrating his Bar Mitzvah at the Western Wall in Jerusalem. Jesus was raised in the Jewish tradition and participated in many of the Jewish rituals that continue today.

© Robert Mulder/Godong/Corbis

The Church's Relationship with Jews

The Church has a unique relationship with the Jewish people and religion; many links bind us together. Jesus himself was Jewish; God revealed himself to the Jewish people through the old Covenants, and the Jewish faith is a response to his Revelation. God irrevocably gifted the Jews with the promises, the Law, and the covenants and called them to be his People.

Although Christians are a people of the New Covenant, we should not assume that God has rejected or cursed the Jews and their Covenant with God. On the contrary, the Jewish people remain dear to God, "since God does not take back the gifts he bestowed or the choice he made" (*Declaration on the Relation of the Church to Non-Christian Religions* [*Nostra Aetate*, 1965], 4; see Romans 11:28–29). The Catholic Church warns its members not to blame Jewish people for the death of Christ, as has been done by some Christians. Although Jewish leaders were involved in Jesus' death, in no way can we blame the Jewish people as a whole, either in ancient times or today, for his death.

Live It!

Common Commitment to Peace

The participants at the Day of Prayer for Peace in the World held in Assisi, Italy, on January 24, 2002, concluded their gathering by proclaiming their commitment to promoting peace in the world. As part of this proclamation, the following commitment was read in various languages:

> Violence never again!
> War never again!
> Terrorism never again!
> In the name of God, may every religion bring upon the earth
> Justice and Peace,
> Forgiveness and Life,
> Love!

These words challenge us to work for peace in the world. They also challenge us to make justice, peace, forgiveness, life, and love central in our efforts to promote peace. Share this commitment with your family and friends and invite them to join you in praying for peace in the world.

The Church's Relationship with Muslims

God's plan of salvation also includes Muslims. Muslims acknowledge the one Creator, trace their faith back to Abraham, and worship the one God by praying, giving alms, and fasting (see *Relation of the Church to Non-Christian Religions,* 3). Though Muslims do not accept the divinity of Jesus, they do recognize him as a great prophet. They also honor Mary and believe that she gave birth to Jesus while still a virgin, and they acknowledge the resurrection of the dead and God's Final Judgment (see 3).

The Church's Relationship with Other Religions

The Church is also in relationship with people who participate in religions that do not share belief in the one God, creator of all. Two examples of these religions are Hinduism and Buddhism. Despite differences in belief, the adherents of these religions search for the one God.

Gathering for a World Day of Prayer for Peace

Pope John Paul II organized a World Day of Prayer for Peace in Assisi, Italy, on January 24, 2002, partially in response to the terrorist attacks of September 11, 2001. This was the second time that he had assembled representatives from different Christian communities and world religions to pray for peace.

At this event the Pope welcomed patriarchs from Eastern Catholic and Orthodox Churches, the Archbishop of Canterbury of the Anglican Church, the Secretary General of the Ecumenical Council of Churches, and representatives of other Christian communities. He greeted distinguished members of world Judaism; representatives of world Islam; Buddhist representatives; Hindu representatives; representatives of African Traditional Religion; Sikh delegates; Confucian, Zoroastrian, and Jain delegates; as well as others.

The Church recognizes that Hindus contemplate the divine mystery, which they express through mythic stories and philosophical insights. Buddhists have developed traditions of profound meditation and seek God in confidence and love. They recognize the temporary nature of this world and teach that humans can attain liberation from these limitations through their own efforts and with divine help (see *Relation of the Church to Non-Christian Religions,* 2).

The Church sees herself connected with all people, even those affiliated with no religion, because all people are made in the image and likeness of God.

The Church deeply respects people of different religious traditions as we can see in this excerpt from *Declaration on the Relation of the Church to Non-Christian Religions*:

> She regards with sincere reverence those ways of conduct and of life, those precepts and teachings which, though differing in many aspects from the ones she holds and sets forth, nonetheless often reflect a ray of that Truth which enlightens all men. (2) ✟

Article 28 Universality and Diversity

In article 16, "The First Mark of the Church," we saw that unity does not mean uniformity. We can also say that universality does not mean uniformity; rather, the Church encompasses great diversity.

The Church Reconciles and Embraces Diversity

Even though the Church of Rome is pre-eminent among particular churches, the Church is not Italian or even European. In Christ there is not an exclusively African or Asian or American Church. Saint Paul indicates that the Church is a place where differences can be reconciled:

> So then you are no longer strangers and sojourners, but you are fellow citizens with the holy ones and members of the household of God, built upon the foundation of the apostles and prophets, with Christ Jesus himself as the capstone. Through him the whole structure is held together and grows

into a temple sacred in the Lord; in him you also are being
built together into a dwelling place of God in the Spirit.
(Ephesians 2:19–22)

Communion with God requires reconciliation rather than
competition and rivalry where division exists. It can be
comfortable to associate primarily with people who are like
us, who think like us or act like us. For the Church to fully
realize its catholicity, however, differences of culture, race,
wealth, athletic ability, social class, or any other dividing
characteristic need to be embraced, not erased.

The Eastern Catholic Churches

The relationship between Roman Catholics and Eastern
Catholics is an example of unity in diversity. Though the
Eastern Catholic Churches have some rituals and prac-
tices that differ from those of the Roman Catholic Church,
Eastern Catholics are in full communion with Rome. There
are a total of twenty-one Eastern Catholic Churches. These
Churches refer to the Roman Catholic Church as the Latin
Church.

Most of the Eastern Churches separated from the
Roman Catholic Church as a result of the schism between
the Orthodox and Catholic Churches in the eleventh
century. As we have seen, the Eastern Orthodox Churches
are still not in full communion with the Catholic Church.

The Saints: The Sign of the Church's Catholicity

We also see the Church's catholicity in the saints themselves, who come
from various walks of life and from many different places in the world.
Thus the Church recognizes the Italian Thomas Aquinas, the great theologian and philosopher. She recognizes powerful kings and queens, such
as Saint Louis of France and Elizabeth of Hungary, but also poor farmers
such as Juan Diego of Mexico. Pope John Paul II canonized Saint Andrew
Dung-Lac and his companions, Vietnamese Catholics who suffered martyrdom during a time of persecution against the Church and her members. Saints have included the twelve-year-old Maria Goretti and the
105-year-old Anthony of Egypt. Saints include priests such as John
Vianney, popes such as Saint Leo the Great, abbots such as Benedict, as
well as married people such as Saint Elizabeth Ann Seton.

icon

Religious painting traditional among many Eastern Christians. Christian iconography expresses in image the same Gospel message that the Scriptures communicate by words.

This is an image of the front of an Eastern Catholic iconostasis. Notice the prevalence of the large icons. Can you identify who is pictured?

© Pascal Deloche/Godong/Corbis

Those Churches that did return to full communion with the Catholic Church are called Eastern Catholic Churches. Although they do share much in common with Orthodox Churches because of their origin in the Eastern part of the Roman Empire, the Eastern Catholic Churches should not be confused with the Eastern Orthodox Churches.

Eastern Catholic Churches have different liturgical rites, customs, laws, devotions, and theological interests than the Latin Church but enjoy equal dignity with her.

Here are some examples of the ways Eastern Catholic Churches differ from the Latin Church:

- The use of **icons** is central.
- An **iconostasis** (a wall, with doors, decorated with icons) separates the altar from the rest of the church.
- The Sign of the Cross is made by touching the forehead and the chest ("In the name of the Father and of the Son") and then touching the right shoulder ("and of the Holy Spirit").
- The tradition is to celebrate the Sacraments, called mysteries, of Baptism, Confirmation, and the Eucharist at the same time. Thus when infants are baptized, they are also confirmed and they receive the Eucharist by means of a few drops of the Blood of Christ.
- Married men can be ordained to the priesthood.

Additional Examples of Catholicity

Because the Church is universal, it enables her to integrate diverse cultural elements and popular devotions into her unity. At the same time, the Church purifies or transforms culture elements in the light of faith.

The Church's diversity is evident through the various pilgrimages, religious dances, and religious processions performed in various parts of the world. Pilgrims from all over the world travel to the shrine of Saint James in Santiago de Compostela, Spain. At Christmastime in Mexico, young people celebrate *La Posadas,* reenacting the story of Mary and Joseph seeking shelter in Bethlehem before Mary gave birth to Jesus. Throughout the world, believers dress in traditional clothing and join in colorful processions to celebrate the Feast of Corpus Christi.

iconostasis
A screen or partition with doors and tiers of icons that separates the bema, the raised part of the church with the altar, from the nave, the main part of the church, in Eastern Churches.

Pray It!

Words of Saint Josephine Bakhita of Sudan

Valuing the catholicity of the Church can include praying with saints from different parts of the world. Saint Josephine Bakhita of Sudan was sold as a slave several times. While working as the caretaker of an Italian girl, she traveled to Italy where she met Catholic sisters, converted to Catholicism, and entered the Canossian Sisters at the age of thirty-four. She was canonized on October 1, 2000. These are some of her words to mediate with:

© Vicki Shuck/Saint Mary's Press

- "I have given everything to my Master: He will take care of me. . . . The best thing for us is not what we consider best, but what the Lord wants of us!"
- "I received the Sacrament of Baptism with such joy that only angels could describe."
- "O Lord, if I could fly to my people and tell them of your Goodness at the top of my voice: oh, how many souls would be won!"
- "If I were to meet the slave-traders who kidnapped me and even those who tortured me, I would kneel and kiss their hands, for if that did not happen, I would not be a Christian and Religious today."

(From the National Black Catholic Congress Web site)

Often the devotions to saints and to Mary are closely tied to the history and culture of particular people. Among Slavic people Saints Cyril and Methodius are honored as the saints who evangelized the Slavs and helped to develop the Cyrillic alphabet in which Slavic languages are still written today.

The icon of Our Lady of Czestochowa (also known as the Black Madonna) has played an important role in Polish history. In Portugal Mary is especially honored through her appearance at Fátima. Our Lady of Lourdes has a particular devotion in France. ✞

Part Review

1. How is the Church catholic in two senses?

2. What are three free divine gifts the Holy Spirit has given to the Church?

3. How is the Church catholic in each of the three distinct meanings of the word *church*?

4. Why does the Church of Rome have special authority?

5. Why does the Church have a unique relationship with Judaism?

6. What are some beliefs shared by Islam and the Catholic faith?

7. What is a significant difference between the Eastern Catholic Churches and the Eastern Orthodox Churches?

8. Identify three ways the practices of Eastern Catholic Churches differ from the practices of the Latin Church.

Part 4

The Church
Is Apostolic

Thus far we have explored what it means that the Church is one, holy, and catholic. This part of the book treats the fourth mark of the Church: apostolic.

The Church is apostolic because she is founded on the Apostles. Jesus sent his Apostles to continue his Father's mission and gave authority and power to them. Because the Church is built on this apostolic foundation, she is indestructible. Christ governs the Church through the Pope and the bishops in communion with him—the successors to Peter and the Apostles. The Pope and the bishops in union with him form the Magisterium—the living, teaching office of the Church. The Magisterium is entrusted with transmitting and interpreting Divine Revelation. The Church's handing on of the Gospel message and transmission and interpretation of Divine Revelation are known as Sacred Tradition.

Bishops are the successors of the Apostles through the fullness of the Sacrament of Holy Orders, which conveys sacred power to the bishops through the laying on of hands. Just as Jesus gave Peter specific authority, the Pope has full, supreme, and universal power over the Church.

The laity also has a vocation to spread the Good News of the Kingdom of God. Union with Christ and regular celebration of the Eucharist is key for Church members to carry out her mission. The laity's apostolate can take various forms through their career or family life.

The topics covered in this part are:

- Article 29: "The Apostles Continue Jesus' Mission" (page 112)

- Article 30: "Apostolic Tradition" (page 114)

- Article 31: "The Successors to Peter and the Apostles" (page 117)

- Article 32: "The Apostolate of the Laity" (page 120)

29 The Apostles Continue Jesus' Mission

apostolic
To be founded on the Twelve Apostles.

Has someone you love and respected ever asked you to continue or to complete an important job? Did the job feel like an important responsibility? If so, then you have a small sense of the seriousness Jesus' Apostles gave their mission when Jesus sent them out.

The Church Is Apostolic in Three Ways

We say that the Church is **apostolic** because she is founded on Jesus' Apostles in three ways:

- She was and is built on the "foundation of the Apostles" (Ephesians 2:20), who lived with and were taught by Jesus.
- With the help of the Holy Spirit, the Church preserves and hands on the teaching of the Apostles and their successors.
- The Church continues to be taught, made holy, and led by the Apostles through their successors, who are the college of bishops, assisted by priests, in union with the Pope, the visible head of the Church.

Who Is an Apostle?

You know quite a bit about the Apostles. The Greek word *apostolos* literally means "one who is sent." Mark wrote, "He appointed twelve [whom he also named apostles] that they might be with him and he might send them forth to preach and to have authority to drive out demons" (3:14–15).

Jesus Sends His Apostles Just as the Father Sent Him

The Father sent his Son to offer us forgiveness of sin and everlasting life: "God so loved the world that he gave his only Son, so that everyone who believes in him might not perish but might have eternal life" (John 3:16). Jesus did not conduct his own mission apart from his Father. Though hidden from human eyes at that time, the Holy Spirit was intimately involved in the Father and the Son's mission.

Jesus then sent his Apostles to continue his Father's mission and united them to the divine mission. "As the Father

Paul's Weakness and Christ's Power

Apostles were not limited to Jesus' companions and witnesses of the Resurrection. We know that Saint Paul persecuted Jesus' followers, but then, after an encounter with Jesus while journeying to Damascus, Paul became a follower, too, and devoted his life to spreading the Good News (Acts of the Apostles 9:1–19; 22:3–21). Paul says: "Am I not an apostle? Have I not seen Jesus our Lord?" (1 Corinthians 9:1). Although Paul insisted that his authority as an Apostle was as great as that of any other Apostle (see 2 Corinthians 11:5), he also emphasized that all his strength and authority was based on God's grace only, saying: "I will rather boast most gladly of my weakness, in order that the power of Christ may dwell with me. Therefore, I am content with weaknesses, insults, hardships, persecutions, and constraints, for the sake of Christ; for when I am weak, I am strong" (2 Corinthians 12:9–10).

has sent me, so I send you" (John 20:21). Just as Jesus relied on the power of his Father, the Apostles relied on the power Jesus gave them.

Jesus gave his Apostles great power and authority to serve in his name and act in his person. The Apostles had the authority to:

- proclaim the Kingdom of Heaven (see Matthew 10:7)
- heal the sick and cast out evil spirits (see Mark 6:13)
- raise the dead (see Acts of the Apostles 9:36–42)
- forgive sins in Jesus' name (John 20:22–23)

The Apostles could do all these things by the power of Christ. Peter said to the man who was crippled, "In the name of Jesus

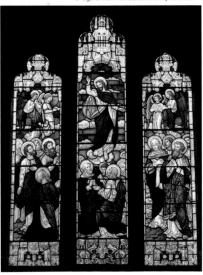

© Ugorenkov Aleksandr/istockphoto.com

Jesus commissioned the Apostles to continue his work on earth. How do you see the Church continuing Jesus' mission in the world today?

Sacred Tradition
From the Latin *tradere*, meaning "to hand on." Refers to the process of passing on the Gospel message. It began with the oral communication of the Gospel by the Apostles, was written down in the Scriptures, and is interpreted by the Magisterium under the guidance of the Holy Spirit.

bishop
One who has received the fullness of the Sacrament of Holy Orders and is a successor to the Apostles.

Christ the Nazorean, [rise and] walk" (Acts of the Apostles 3:6). (Here, the "name" of Jesus refers to Jesus' authority and power.)

After Jesus' Ascension the Apostles, with Peter as their leader and spokesman (see Acts of the Apostles 1:15–26, 2:14–21), led the first church in Jerusalem and held authority over other new churches. When a debate arose in some churches about whether it was necessary for all followers of Jesus to be circumcised in accordance with Jewish law, the Apostles made the final decision (see 15:1–34). ✝

Article 30 Apostolic Tradition

The Church is very aware of her past, present, and future. She is very conscious of her responsibility to honor the gifts received from successors of the Apostles in the past and is also conscious that she must prepare leaders and all members of the Church for the future.

Appointing Successors

Jesus Christ, the fullness of Divine Revelation, commanded and entrusted the Apostles to herald to all people and all nations what they had heard and seen regarding salvation. The teachings of Jesus have thus been transmitted from generation to generation and are proclaimed not only in word but also in action. As they moved from village to village, city to city, the Apostles, under the inspiration of the Holy Spirit, helped more and more people believe in Jesus Christ. This handing on, or transmission, of the truths Jesus Christ taught is known as **Sacred Tradition** and will continue "under the inspiration of the Holy Spirit, to all generations, until Christ returns in glory" (*CCC*, 96).

Recall that Apostolic Succession is a source of unity in the Church. Let's look at it more closely. Once the time had come to finish their work on this earth, the Apostles chose their successors, who are given the title **bishop.** To these successors the Apostles passed on the authority to teach and interpret the Scriptures and Tradition. This process is known as Apostolic Succession. In this way the bishops and the entire Church, in "her doctrine, life, and worship"[2] (*CCC*, 78), proclaim the redemption found in Jesus Christ. It is through the doctrine, life, and worship of the Church that she "perpetuates and transmits to every generation all that she herself is, all that she believes"[3] (78).

The Faith of the Church

Sometimes when we use the word *faith,* we speak of faith as a personal act—"the free response of the human person to the initiative of God who reveals himself" (*CCC,* 166). We might say, "She is a woman of great faith." Any faith-filled person, however, has received the faith from others, as she could not give it to herself. She, in turn, must share the faith with others.

Though faith or believing is a personal act, its source is the Church, who teaches each one of us. The faith of the Church precedes, supports, and nourishes the faith of

© 2010 Monastery Icons

Jesus entrusted the Apostles to continue his earthly mission. They in turn chose successors and passed on the authority to teach and interpret the Scriptures and Tradition.

Live It!

Combining the Subjective and the Objective in Our Worship

Our Catholic faith is both "subjective" and "objective." The objective part is God's Revelation, which is transmitted through the Scriptures and Tradition. The subjective part is how we respond to God's Revelation. We need both dimensions of faith.

Reciting the Nicene Creed at the Mass is a great opportunity for us to live out both aspects. Challenge yourself to more fully understand the Creed by studying the words and then apply to your life the truths expressed in the Creed.

ecclesial
Of or relating to
church.

individuals. Faith is both personal and **ecclesial.** If it were not for the Church's carefully preserving and passing down the faith, we would have no solid basis for our beliefs at all.

Passing Down the Apostolic Tradition

The Apostles handed on the Gospel message in two ways:

- **Orally.** Prior to the written Scriptures, the Apostles handed on the faith to the earliest Christians through preaching, providing examples of how to live, and establishing institutions. The Apostles shared what Jesus had taught them, what he had done, what they had learned from the Holy Spirit.
- **In writing.** The Sacred Scriptures have divine authorship because the Apostles or their associates wrote them under the inspiration of the Holy Spirit. Because of this we know that the inspired books teach the truth. The Scriptures are living rather than static.

Some might question why the Church cannot just use the Bible as the source of authority. Although the written Scriptures and the living Tradition have one common source, God's Revelation in Jesus, some of these elements of Tradition are not found in the Scriptures alone:

- the exact list of books that should be regarded as the Sacred Scriptures. The early bishops, guided by the Holy Spirit, identified the writings that were inspired and therefore should be part of the official canon. The canon includes 46 Old Testament books and 27 New Testament books.

Clement of Rome and Apostolic Succession

Clement, Bishop of Rome, describes the process of Apostolic Succession in a letter written around the year 96:

> The Apostles received the Gospel for us from the Lord Jesus Christ, Jesus the Christ was sent from God. The Christ therefore is from God and the Apostles from the Christ. . . . [The Apostles] appointed their first converts, testing them by the Spirit, to be bishops and deacons of the future believers. . . . If they should fall asleep, other approved men should succeed to their ministry. (*To the Corinthians,* 42, 44)

- the word *Trinity*, which is not used in the Bible
- many contemporary questions, such as how to use genetic information, use technology, share resources, and so on

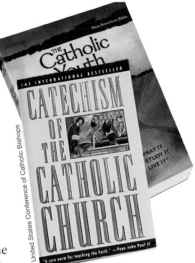

In order to present the faith without error, the Magisterium authentically interprets the Word of God and applies it to new questions. The Church does this especially through the official proclamations of the bishops in union with the Pope. (See article 49, "The Magisterium," for more about this body.)

   Together "Sacred Scripture and Sacred Tradition make up a single sacred deposit of the Word of God (*Dei Verbum* 10)" (*CCC*, 97). This deposit of the Word of God enables the Church to contemplate God, who is "the source of all of her riches" (97). The Scriptures and Tradition never contradict one another, and we need both. Each helps us to understand the other more fully. ✝

God's Revelation is present in both Sacred Scripture and Sacred Tradition. Together they provide the fullness of revelation that is present in the Church.

^{Article}
31 The Successors to Peter and the Apostles

Let's look more closely at the bishops, the men who have succeeded the Apostles and are responsible for the Apostolic Tradition. Bishops have central roles in their own dioceses but also share a global responsibility for the Church with fellow bishops in communion with the Pope.

The Apostles and the Bishops

The **Sacrament of Holy Orders** is an essential element of Apostolic Succession. Jesus specifically gave authority to his Apostles through the Gift of the Holy Spirit. Appearing to his disciples, Jesus breathed on them and said: "Receive the holy Spirit. Whose sins you forgive are forgiven them, and whose sins you retain are retained" (John 20:22).

   Jesus' Apostles passed on the Gift of the Holy Spirit to their successors through the laying on of hands. Thus Paul

Sacrament of Holy orders
The Sacrament by which members of the Church are ordained for permanent ministry in the Church as bishops, priests, or deacons.

episcopal
Of or relating to bishops.

reminds Timothy "to stir into flame the gift of God that you have through the imposition of my hands" (2 Timothy 1:6).

Bishops, who are already priests, receive the fullness of the Sacrament of Holy Orders, known as the high priesthood in the early Church. The **episcopal** consecration confers the office of sanctifying, teaching, and ruling on the bishop. The Sacrament of Holy Orders gives a Gift of the Holy Spirit, conveying sacred power from Christ onto the man being consecrated as bishop. The laying on of hands by the bishop who is celebrating the Ordination resembles the process of the early Church. Priests and deacons receive the Sacrament of Holy Orders, but this does not make them successors to the Apostles nor does it give them the authority of the bishops. The ordination of deacons, priests, and bishops is conferred by the laying on of hands followed by a consecratory prayer asking God to pour forth upon the newly ordained the graces of the Holy Spirit he needs for his ministry. Ordination imprints a sacramental character on the deacon, priest, or bishop.

We will learn more about the bishops in article 41, "The Role of the Bishops in the Church Hierarchy."

Pictured is a cardinal conferring the Sacrament of Holy Orders on a new bishop. Why is the laying on of hands a vital part of the Sacrament of Holy Orders?

© ALESSIA PIERDOMENICO/Reuters/Corbis

Peter and the Pope

Just as the office of the Apostles continued in the office of the bishops, so too the office of Peter as the head of the Apostles continued in the role of the Pope as head of the college of bishops.

Jesus entrusted a specific authority to Peter: "I will give you the keys to the kingdom of heaven. Whatever you bind on earth shall be bound in heaven; and whatever you loose on earth shall be loosed in heaven" (Matthew 16:19). This power of the keys signifies Peter's authority to govern the Church; the power to bind and loose refers to Peter's special authority to absolve sin, make judgments about official doctrines, and make disciplinary decisions in the Church. This authority is also given to the Apostles as a whole, with Peter as the head.

The Pope is the Bishop of Rome. He is the source and foundation of the unity in the Church and especially in the college of bishops. As Vicar of Christ, and pastor of the global Church, the Pope has full, supreme, and universal power over the Church. This is covered more thoroughly in article 40, "The Pope: Visible Head of the Church." Unlike the United States' political check-and-balance system, the college of bishops cannot veto the Pope or act apart from him. They have no authority without him. The college of bishops acts in communion with the Pope. ☨

Pray It!

Intercessory Prayers on the Feast of Peter and Paul (June 29)

© Christie's Images/CORBIS

The following is from the Liturgy of the Hours:

> The Lord Jesus built his holy people on the foundation of the Apostles and the prophets. In faith let us pray:
> Lord, come to the aid of your people.
> You once called Simon, the fisherman, to catch men,
> —now summon new workers who will bring the message of salvation to all peoples.
> You calmed the waves, so your followers would not be drowned,
> —guard your Church, protect it from all dangers.
> You gathered your scattered flock around Peter after the resurrection,
> —good Shepherd, bring all your people together as one flock.
> You sent Paul as Apostle to preach the good news to the Gentiles,
> —let the word of salvation be proclaimed to all mankind.
> You have the keys of your kingdom into the hands of your holy Church
> —open the gates of that Kingdom to all who trusted in your mercy while one earth.

(Christian Prayer: The Liturgy of the Hours, pages 1180–1181)

Peter's Leadership Despite His Weaknesses

Despite his leadership role, Peter very clearly had human failings. Jesus criticized Peter for having little faith (see Matthew 14:31) and rebuked him sharply for thinking in human terms, not in God's terms (see Mark 8:33). Peter's greatest failing occurred when he denies three times that he knows Jesus (see Luke 22:55–62).

Yet, despite his fallibility, Jesus chose Peter to be the solid rock of the Church. If God can make use of Peter, with all his weaknesses, that should give hope to the rest of us less-than-perfect humans!

Article

32 The Apostolate of the Laity

apostolate
The Christian person's activity that fulfills the apostolic nature of the whole Church when he or she works to extend the Kingdom of Christ to the entire world. If your school shares the wisdom of its founder, its name-sake, or the charism of the religious order that founded it, it is important to learn about this person or order and his or her charism, because as a graduate you will likely want to incorporate this charism into your own apostolate.

Every member of the Church has a vocation to the **apostolate.** The apostolate describes the Christian's activity that fulfills the apostolic nature of the whole Church when he or she works to extend the reign of Christ to the entire world.

We Are Sent

The whole Church is apostolic in that she is in communion of faith and life with the Apostles and because she is sent out into the world on a mission to spread the Good News of the Kingdom of God over all the earth.

The source of the apostolate for all members of the Church is Christ. Our relationship with Christ affects our ability to spread the Good News. Whether ordained or lay, a person who wants to engage in the apostolate must be in union with Christ. Participating in the celebration of the Eucharist is the soul of the apostolate.

Catholic Wisdom

Encouraging Advice

Saint Francis de Sales shares this simple advice: "Be who you are and be it well."

The apostolate can take many forms for **laypeople (laity),** specifically because we live in the world, sharing the varied gifts given to us by the Holy Spirit. Every morning when we get up, we are sent out into the world, whether that is through school or work or taking care of family. The essential nature of the apostolate is love. Every day we face small and big decisions that could result in a choice to love or not.

laypeople (laity)
All members of the Church, with the exception of those who are ordained or in consecrated life. The laity shares in Christ's role as priest, prophet, and king, witnessing to God's love and power in the world.

What Does a Lay Apostolate Look Like?

What is the difference between a career understood as an apostolate and one that is not? A professional baseball career as an apostolate will lead the player to become involved with the community, to use his time and money to improve the lives of others. We have all encountered receptionists, some who clearly do not view their work as an apostolate, and others who try to improve the day of every patient or client who comes in their door. How about a doctor who spends several weeks a year in a third-world country, using her skills to help people who do not have access to good medical care? How about a lawyer who takes on a good number of pro bono cases for clients who cannot pay him?

Your life as a student can be an apostolate if you choose to make it so. How can you spread the Good News of Jesus Christ? How can you choose love in your life today? ✝

© Liba Taylor/CORBIS

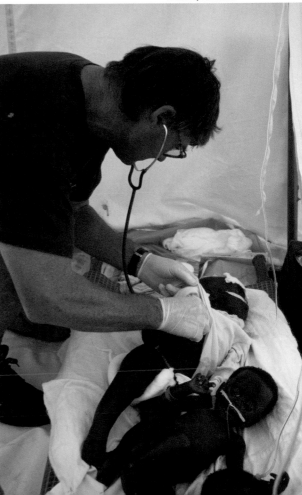

This doctor is treating orphans in a refugee camp in Zaire. Currently your apostolate is to live out your Christian faith as a student. What might you envision your apostolate to be in the future?

The Apostolate of Catholic Schools

The apostolate of Catholic education that was almost exclusively the work of priests or consecrated religious in the first half of the twentieth century has become a primarily lay apostolate. Some schools were founded by a religious order or named after an inspiring Catholic. It is important for lay or religious leaders to continue to promote the charism of the school.

If you attend a Jesuit school, you may be familiar with the charism of Saint Ignatius of Loyola and the Jesuits and have learned to do things for the greater glory of God. If you go to a high school operated by the De La Salle Christian Brothers, you may have learned that you are always in the presence of God, a gift from Saint John Baptist de La Salle. Visitation schools are run by Sisters of the Visitation, founded in France in 1610 by Saint Jane de Chantal and Saint Francis de Sales.

Here is a well-known quotation from Francis de Sales: "There is nothing so strong as gentleness and nothing so gentle as real strength." On a more humorous and practical note, he said, "You can catch more flies with a spoonful of honey than with a barrel of vinegar."

Part Review

1. In what three ways is the Church apostolic?

2. Describe how Jesus joined the Apostles to the mission the Father had sent him on.

3. Define "Apostolic Succession." Why is this Apostolic Succession necessary?

4. How is faith both personal and ecclesial?

5. Who is a bishop?

6. What specific authority did Jesus give Peter as the head of the Apostles?

7. What is a vocation that every member of the Church shares?

8. Why is Christ the source of the apostolate?

The Church's Salvation and Mission

Part 1

The Church and Salvation

There is a sense among some people in our society today that all religions are generally the same. With this in mind, we consider the question, Why be a Catholic? We discover that Christ established the Church as the means of salvation. We also address that although other faith traditions do have elements of sanctification and truth, the Catholic Church alone has the fullness of these means.

These truths lead to a second question: Does someone have to be Catholic to be saved? We learn that God offers salvation to all people, including those who, through no fault of their own, have never heard of Christ or his Church and that salvation can be attained in non-Catholic Christian churches, but only through these churches' relationship to the fullness of the Catholic Church.

We then consider a final question: Why belong to any organized religion? We find that because humans are social by nature, so too human salvation is social—God offers us salvation through the community of the Church.

The topics covered in this part are:

- Article 33: "The Fullness of Truth and Salvation" (page 126)

- Article 34: "Salvation for Those Outside the Church" (page 129)

- Article 35: "Who Needs Organized Religion?" (page 132)

Article 33 The Fullness of Truth and Salvation

It is comforting to assume that most people will go to Heaven, regardless of their religion. According to this way of thinking, it doesn't really matter if we are Catholic, as long as we try to be good. This idea can seem very open-minded and tolerant, but before accepting it, we should ask a deeper question: Is this assumption true, or is it just based on wishful thinking?

The Scriptures tells us that God loves all people and "wills everyone to be saved." The verse goes on to say that God wills everyone "to come to knowledge of the truth" (1 Timothy 2:4). It is through knowledge of the truth that we are saved. The truth is in fact a person, Jesus Christ, who is the one true path to salvation. Salvation begins with God's loving initiative. The Father sent his only Son to atone for our sins. Jesus freely gave himself so that salvation would be possible for all people. God has entrusted that truth to the Church, and thus the Church has the obligation to proclaim that truth to the world, an obligation that inspires and gives life to the Church's missionary activity.

The Fullness of the Church of Christ

In the previous section of this book, we explored the four marks of the Church: one, holy, catholic, and apostolic. As we look at what these marks tell us about the Church, we must keep in mind that the fullness of Jesus Christ's Church is found only in the Catholic Church. This means the Catholic Church, led by the Pope and the bishops in communion with him, is the only Church with the fullness of the four marks. However, when we express our belief that the Church is one, holy, catholic, and apostolic, we do so with humble hearts. We pray knowing the members of the Church struggle with sin. We pray also with the knowledge that holiness and truth can be found outside the visible organization of the Catholic Church.

This fullness includes:

- the fullness of Revelation, which is transmitted through the Scriptures and Tradition
- the fullness of the Sacraments
- the fullness of the ordained ministry

The Catholic Church alone has retained the fullness of these means of salvation.

The Church Is Necessary for Salvation

Christ is the one path to salvation (see John 14:6), and he is present to us in the Church. Jesus established the Church as a visible organization through which he communicates his grace, truth, and salvation. Jesus himself spoke of the necessity of joining the Church through Baptism

When an infant is baptized, what are the parents hoping for and promising to do for their child?

Returning to the Fullness of the Catholic Church

The Englishman John Henry Newman, an Anglican priest, was a brilliant intellectual closely associated with Oxford University. Along with other influential Anglican leaders, Newman launched the Oxford Movement, an effort to recover the roots of the Anglican Church in the earliest Church and the Apostolic Succession. Newman's intense study of the early Church history, however, eventually led him to conclude that it was only the Catholic Church that had preserved the fullness of the Apostolic Tradition. Despite discouraging social pressure, Newman followed his convictions, and was received into the Catholic Church in October of 1845.

sacramentum
The visible sign of the hidden reality of salvation.

mysterium
The hidden reality of God's plan of salvation.

in order to be saved: "Whoever believes and is baptized will be saved; whoever does not believe will be condemned" (Mark 16:16). He also said, "No one can enter the kingdom of God without being born of water and Spirit" (John 3:5). Thus salvation comes from Christ, who is our head, through the Church, which is his body.

The Church as Sacrament

The Church in this world is the Sacrament of salvation, the sign and instrument of the saving union between God and humans. You might be asking, How can the Church be a sacrament—aren't there only Seven Sacraments? Yes, there are seven official Sacraments of the Church, but the idea of sacrament is bigger than that. A sacrament is a visible sign of God's invisible grace. There are two Latin terms that can help us to understand the mystery of the Church as sacrament: **sacramentum** and **mysterium.** Both terms originally translated the Greek *mysterion.* Over time the term *sacramentum* came to refer to the visible sign of the hidden reality of salvation, while the word *mysterium* came to refer to the hidden reality. The first or primary sacrament is Jesus Christ. This is because he, more than anyone or anything else, makes visible God's presence in the world. He himself is the mystery of salvation and his saving work is made visible to us through the Seven Sacraments. It is through the

Live It!

Why Are You Catholic?

Has anyone ever asked you why you are Catholic? How did you respond? Answering this question can be a daunting task if you are not familiar with your faith and the teachings of the Church. There are several ways you can prepare for this question:

- Consult the *Catechism of the Catholic Church.*
- Reflect on what you have learned in this class.
- Talk with your pastor.
- Pose the question to adults who are committed to the Church.

Each one of us is called to be able to share our faith in a true and meaningful way. The best way to share your Catholic faith with others is to know your faith. If you prepare you will be able to explain to others, in a way that can help them to come to love and appreciate the Church, why you are Catholic.

Sacraments that the Holy Spirit spreads the grace of Christ throughout the Church. "The Church, then, both contains and communicates the invisible grace she signifies" (*CCC*, 774). She is a sacrament because she makes visible the invisible communion we share with God—Father, Son, and Holy Spirit. When we call the Church the "sacrament of salvation," we emphasize that it is through the Church that we come to know God and to be saved. Because the Church shows us God's love for all people everywhere, we can add *universal* to the description: The Church is the "universal sacrament of salvation" (*Lumen Gentium*, 48).

The Church is a sacrament of communion with God and unity among people. The Church is a sign of this communion with God and people and also brings this communion about. The primary focus of the Church is union with God for all its members. Union with God for the Church also brings unity among people. The Church is the instrument Christ uses for the salvation of the whole world. Because the Church is a sign of God's grace and redemption, and because the Church brings God's grace and redemption, it is possible to say that the Church herself is a sacrament. ♱

Article 34 Salvation for Those Outside the Church

Church leaders such as Saint Cyprian have taught that "outside of the Church there is no salvation." Does this mean only Catholics can be saved? Although in a way that seems like a logical conclusion, the actual answer is no. Let's consider why this is so.

Salvation Is Offered to All People

God desires that all people be saved. His Son Christ died for the sake of all people. Because of this, salvation in Christ is a real possibility for all people, including those who are not Christian. Think of all the millions of people, both now and in the past, who never had the chance to join the Church or who never heard the Gospel message. If the Church is necessary for salvation, how could such people be saved?

The Church has answered this question. If people, through no fault of their own, do not know the Gospel of Christ or his Church, but nevertheless sincerely seek God, and, moved by God's grace, try to do God's will as they know it in their conscience, they may still be saved. They are offered salvation in a way that is fully known to God alone. We can say, therefore, that salvation is available to those outside the Church through God's grace.

The missionary work of the Church extends to everyone whether or not they are Catholic. What are examples of the missionary work of the Church?

Grace and Truth Outside the Visible Boundaries of the Church

Because of God's great mercy, saving grace is also available outside the visible boundaries of the Church. This grace outside the Church, however, still comes from Christ as a result of his sacrifice, and is communicated by the Holy Spirit. It is mysteriously connected with the Church of Christ, in a way that is not fully clear to us.

As we have said, many elements of sanctification and truth can be found outside the visible boundaries of the Church. The Holy Spirit works through non-Catholic churches and ecclesial communities to offer salvation to their members. For example, if someone is baptized in another Christian

© Philippe Lissac /Godong/Corbis

Catholic Wisdom

Saint Cyprian on the Necessity of the Church for Salvation

Thus too the Church bathed in the light of the Lord projects its rays over the whole world. . . . She extends her branches over the whole earth in fruitful abundance; she extends her richly flowing streams far and wide; yet her head is one, and her source is one. . . . By her womb we are born; by her milk we are nourished; by her spirit we are animated. . . . He cannot have God as a father who does not have the Church as a mother.

("The Unity of the Catholic Church")

denomination in the name of the Father, Son, and Holy Spirit, the Catholic Church recognizes that Baptism as valid. If that person converts to Catholicism, he or she is not "re-baptized" in the Church. At the same time, however, the ability of these communities to offer salvation ultimately depends on the fact that the fullness of Christ's grace and truth has been preserved in the Catholic Church.

The Church's Continuing Mission

Although salvation is possible outside the visible boundaries of the Church, should the Church give up her missionary activity and assume that God will offer all people salvation through their own religious traditions? Not at all. The Church still has the sacred duty, and the right, to preach the Gospel to all people. This task is from Jesus himself: "Go, therefore, and make disciples of all nations" (Matthew 28:19). The Church has been given this missionary mandate to share the fullness

Jesuit Volunteer Corps

The missionary mandate of the Church has been lived out throughout her history, and it continues today. One group that has embraced the missionary work of the Church is the Jesuit Volunteer Corps (JVC). JVC is made up of men and women twenty-one years of age or older who make a yearlong commitment (two years if working internationally) to serve those in need and to live in community with other JVC members. Currently, over three hundred volunteers are serving across the United States and in eight countries internationally. Volunteers work with people who are elderly, homeless, abused, and mentally ill, as well as others who are marginalized by society. All of their work is grounded in the teachings of the Catholic Church. The Jesuit Volunteer Corps is committed to four core values: social justice, simple living, community, and spirituality. JVC volunteers live out the missionary mandate of the Catholic Church by sharing God's love in both action and example.

of truth that has been entrusted to her with all people. This missionary mandate is part of who the Church is. In regard to non-Catholic Christians, the Church's missionary efforts should help to lead us to the goal of Christian unity. Her mission also involves a respectful dialogue with non-Christian religions, allowing Church members to better appreciate the elements of holiness and truth in those religions, and allowing those elements in turn to be raised up and completed in the full light of the Christian Gospel. ♱

Article 35 Who Needs Organized Religion?

Have you ever heard people say they feel closer to God when they are alone with nature than when they sit in a church? Others might say they don't like all the rules of organized religions and feel they have the right to worship God in their own personal way. The best response to such beliefs is a simple question: "Is this how God wishes to be worshipped?" God desires that we know him in all aspects of our lives. The Scriptures and Tradition, though, teach us that God wishes to be worshipped by people joined together in communities, not just by isolated individuals.

The Social Nature of Humans and of Salvation

Each one of us is created to live in community and to build relationships. We all share a longing for true friendship and love. The reality is that we cannot attain true happiness in isolation. We need one another to offer support and encouragement and to provide an example for following Christ. Our social nature is a gift from God; therefore, it is one essential reason why God saves us by calling us together as one group, one family—the Church. In fact, the goal of salvation itself is ultimately about relationship. The goal is communion with God and unity among all people.

It is important to know that as individual human beings, we cannot save ourselves. We depend completely on Christ's free gift of grace. Christ distributes this gift through the community of the Church. It is in community where we

encounter Jesus when we hear the Gospel proclaimed. In fact, Christ assured that we encounter him in community when he said, "Where two or three are gathered together in my name, there am I in the midst of them" (Matthew 18:20).

Communal and Individual Worship

When we participate in the Mass, or the Eucharist, we are part of a community at many different levels. We are part of the liturgical assembly, those who gather throughout the **Liturgical Year** to celebrate the **Paschal Mystery**. We are part of the local church or diocese. And we are part of the People of God throughout the world. The liturgical celebration itself is essentially communal rather than individual. It is the work of the whole Christ, the head in union with the body. In the sacrifice of the Eucharist, the whole Church offers herself in union with Christ's sacrifice. The liturgy unites us with not only Christ and the Church on earth but also the worshippers in Heaven, both angels and those humans who have attained Heaven.

Liturgical Year

The annual cycle of religious feasts and seasons that forms the context for the Church's worship. During the Liturgical Year, we remember and celebrate God the Father's saving plan as it is revealed through the life of his Son, Jesus Christ.

Paschal Mystery

The work of salvation accomplished by Jesus Christ mainly through his Passion, death, Resurrection, and Ascension.

Gatherings like World Youth Day can strengthen and renew our faith. National and diocesan gatherings of Catholic youth can be equally moving. Take advantage of the opportunity to participate in one of these gatherings.

© Bill Wittman/www.wpwittman.com

Of course it is also true that we can, and indeed should, worship God through our own individual devotions, whether inside or outside a church building. As we have said, God desires to know us in all parts of our lives. Our personal, private worship should both draw us to communal prayer and complement the communal worship of the Church (see Matthew 6:5–6). In other words, even when we pray on our own, we should be preparing for communal prayer and keeping in mind the needs of the larger community.

We are social in nature. Think of how we came into existence and how we are dependent on one another to both survive and thrive in this world. Our need for community extends beyond our relationships with other human beings, however. We were created by God, and we are constantly being called into communion with him. This communion with God and unity with all people is the goal of God's plan for us, and the Church is the means through which the goal will be accomplished. We all need organized religion, but more specifically we need the Church. It is through the Church that we can achieve our God-given destiny. ✝

Pray It!

See the Body of Christ

Have you ever taken time to look around at everyone gathered with you when you go to the Mass? Of course you see the people you know—possibly friends from school, relatives, or a former teacher or catechist. More than likely, you also see many people you don't know. An elderly couple might be sitting in the front pew, possibly a family with a crying baby, maybe a teenager who looks your age but whom you've never met, and possibly a young adult by himself or herself. All the people gathered with you are a part of the Body of Christ. Each one of them brings their own gifts, troubles, joys, and pains. This Sunday when you go to the Mass, take a moment to notice the wonderful and diverse Body of Christ and offer a prayer for the needs of those gathered with you. You might even consider introducing yourself to someone you don't know and thanking her or him for being a part of your community.

Communal Worship in the Book of Revelation

The Book of Revelation offers many different scenes of heavenly communal worship. It begins by portraying the communion of the Persons of the Trinity: God the Father sitting on his throne; the Son, portrayed as the Lamb, standing near him; and the Holy Spirit as a stream of water flowing from God's throne.

The Book of Revelation goes on to depict all of creation's being involved in the worship of God. The four living creatures represent all of nature (see 4:6–8), the twenty-four elders represent both the old (Twelve Tribes) and new (Twelve Apostles) Covenants (see 4:10–11). Angels worship alongside the elders and the creatures (see 7:11–12). The 144,000 worshippers (the number is based on the symbolism of the Twelve Tribes) represent the new People of God (see 7:1–9). Finally, "a great multitude, which no one could count, from every nation, race, people, and tongue" stand before God's throne and worship (see 7:9).

Part Review

1. In what sense is the Church necessary for salvation?

2. What does it mean to say that the fullness of the Church of Christ is found in the Catholic Church?

3. Can a person who has never heard of Christ or his Church still be saved? If so, in what way?

4. Can the Holy Spirit be active outside the visible boundaries of the Catholic Church? Discuss examples.

5. How are the social needs of human beings related to the way God offers us salvation?

6. In what ways is the Church's worship communal?

Part 2

The Church and the World

In this part we begin deepening our understanding of Apostolic Tradition and how the Church applies the Scriptures and Tradition to the changing conditions of the world. Subsequently, we explore in more depth what it means for the Church to "read the signs of the times" and interact with the modern world. Finally, we turn our attention to evangelization, the primary focus of the Church's purpose and mission. Evangelization is the proclamation of Christ through both word and deed, and it requires active engagement with modern life and culture. This means both utilizing resources that assist in the sharing of the Gospel message and working to transform modern culture when it stands counter to that message.

The topics covered in this part are:

- Article 36: "Engaging the World" (page 138)

- Article 37: "Engaging Modern Culture" (page 140)

- Article 38: "The Church and Evangelization" (page 141)

Article 36 Engaging the World

As we discussed in section 2, the Church was entrusted with the task of handing down the Apostolic Tradition, the truths of the Catholic faith transmitted through the Scriptures and in Church teachings. Together Sacred Tradition and the Sacred Scriptures are a single deposit of the Word of God where the Church encounters God. Through her teaching, life, and worship, the Church gives to each generation all that she is and all that she believes. One of the ways she does this is through the Apostolic Succession: the Apostles' handing on the tradition to their successors, the bishops in union with the Pope.

Reading the Signs of the Times

The Church has the responsibility of looking at the particular circumstances of each generation and of interpreting them in the light of the Scriptures and Tradition. As

The Church in the Modern World

Interpreting the signs of the times in light of the Gospel brings the Church into dialogue with different cultures. *The Church in the Modern World* offers the following insight on how the Church interacts with different cultures in changing times and how the Church also remains constant in her mission:

> There are many links between the message of salvation and culture. In his self-revelation to his people, fully manifesting himself in his incarnate Son, God spoke in the context of the culture proper to each age. Similarly the Church has existed through the centuries in varying circumstances and has utilized the resources of different cultures to spread and explain the message of Christ in its preaching, to examine and understand it more deeply, and to express it more perfectly in the liturgy and in the life of the multiform community of the faithful. [...] The Church is faithful to its traditions and is at the same time conscious of its universal mission; it can, then, enter into communion with different forms of culture, thereby enriching both itself and the cultures themselves. (58)

expressed in the Vatican II document *Pastoral Constitution on the Church in the Modern World* (*Gaudium et Spes,* 1965), "In every age, the church carries the responsibility of reading the signs of the times and of interpreting them in the light of the Gospel, if it is to carry out its task"(4). Thus it is not enough for the Church to proclaim the Gospel message. She must be able to apply that message to the issues each generation faces. Additionally the Church must speak to each generation in a manner that is understandable and that answers the questions people have about this life and the life to come.

© amanaimages/Corbis

What opportunities do new technologies offer us to share the love of Christ?

In our generation the Church must apply a Gospel perspective to issues such as international conflicts, health care reform, economic justice, and technology. The essential Gospel message does not change, but it requires wisdom and discernment to understand how it applies to these and other particular issues. In the next article, we further address how the Church engages and interacts with the world. ✝

Pray It!

Saint Joseph

Did you know that Saint Joseph, along with Saint Peter, is the patron saint of the Church? Joseph, who was the husband of Mary and the adoptive father of Jesus Christ, was named the patron saint of the Church in 1847 by Blessed Pope Pius IX. During his life on earth, Joseph helped to raise and protect Jesus. As the patron saint of the Church, Joseph continues to help the Body of Christ, the Church. The next time you pray, ask Saint Joseph to continue his prayers and protection of the Church.

Article 37 Engaging Modern Culture

The Catholic Church has a responsibility to be active in the modern world, promoting and proclaiming the truth that has been entrusted to her. This proclamation of the Church must take advantage of the latest technologies and cultural developments. The Church, however, must not only utilize the appropriate development of modern society but also transform the culture when it comes in conflict with the Gospel message. As part of its prophetic mission, the Church often finds itself in the position of standing counter to the developments in our modern society.

Confronting the Culture of Death

One of the most pressing issues the Church must work to transform in the world is what Pope John Paul II called the "culture of death." The prevalence of abortion and the growing acceptance of euthanasia are elements of this culture of death. The Church recognizes that from the moment of conception to natural death, all human life is sacred and should be treated with care and dignity. For this reason the Church stands firm in promoting a culture of life. At the heart of this is an effort to educate people to have a profound respect for the sacredness of every human life. The Church also called for new programs to care for the sick and elderly, and for political action against unjust laws that do not respect the right to life of innocent persons.

The Church has a responsibility to engage modern culture and promote the teachings of Christ. What issues in the world today stand counter to the truth and love of Christ?

© Mark Peterson/CORBIS

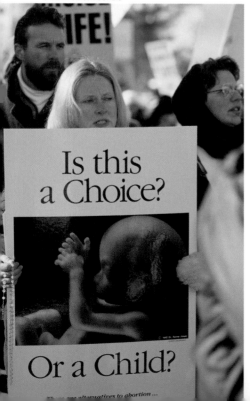

Is this a Choice?

Or a Child?

The Church and Politics

The prophetic mission of the Church also extends to the arena of what can be referred to as political issues. You have heard the concept of the separation of Church and state, which means that the government does not support a particular religion or establish a national religion.

The Church, however, still has both a right and a responsibility to bring Christian values into the public debate on various social, political, and economic issues. The Church is careful not to advocate for specific political candidates or parties; instead she addresses specific issues that affirm or stand counter to the Gospel message. This activity does not conflict with the separation of Church and state; rather, it strengthens the public debate and dialogue.

© Bettmann/CORBIS

Pope John Paul II called Catholic youth to share their faith with their peers who did not know Christ. How is your life a witness to your faith in Christ?

The most pressing issue the Church addresses in the public arena is the value and dignity of every human life. When any public group promotes social or political policies that threaten God-given human rights, the Church has a responsibility to speak out publicly. Thus the Church works to address poverty, environmental issues, and other issues that threaten the dignity of the human person. ✞

Article 38 The Church and Evangelization

As mentioned earlier the Church has a missionary mandate to help all people to share in the communion of the Holy

Catholic Wisdom

Pope John Paul II's Message to Young People at World Youth Day in 1989

You young people are the first apostles and evangelizers of the world of youth. . . . So many of those of your own age do not know Christ, or do not know Him well enough. So you cannot remain silent and indifferent! You must have the courage to speak about Christ, to bear witness to your faith through a life-style inspired by the Gospel. . . . Christ needs you!

Faithful Citizenship

Every four years since 1976, the United States Conference of Catholic Bishops has issued a statement on the responsibilities of Catholics to society. The 2012 edition of this statement, entitled *Forming Consciences for Faithful Citizenship*, summarizes the consistent and challenging message found in Church teachings. The United States bishops remind all members of the Church of their responsibility to promote the dignity and sacredness of the human person and the common good. One way we do this is by being active in the political arena. *Forming Consciences for Faithful Citizenship* provides guidance on how parishes and individuals can do this in a way that respects the political process and is consistent with the teachings of the Church.

Trinity. Evangelization is the primary way we accomplish this mission. It means proclaiming Christ both by our words and by the witness of our lives. In his encyclical *Redemptoris Missio* (1990), Pope John Paul II identified three situations in which the Church is to evangelize in the world today. The first is in cultures, communities, and groups where Christ and the Gospel message are not known or where the people lack the ability to adequately proclaim the faith. The Church has a responsibility to actively share the Gospel message in these situations. The second situation is in places where there are active and vibrant Christian communities. The Church evangelizes in this situation by continuing to carry out "her activity and pastoral care" (33). The third situation involves circumstances in which individuals or groups who have been baptized in the faith no longer actively live the faith or even consider themselves members of the Church "and live a life far removed from Christ and his Gospel. In this case what is needed is a 'new evangelization' or a 're-evangelization'" (33).

Examples of Evangelization

It was the evangelizing activity of Jesus and the Apostles that bore the Church in the world, and their evangelizing activity continues in the Church today. Therefore everyone in the Church has a responsibility to share the Good News of Jesus Christ. The laity are called upon to evangelize both at home and at work; this ordinary setting can help to make their witness particularly effective. Married couples can evangelize within the family by witnessing the faith and love of Christ to one another and to their children.

Young people are some of the best evangelists for other young people, especially if they evangelize by the witness of their lives. The witness of a teen committed to living a chaste life is a powerful witness to Gospel values in our age. The witness of a young man who has earned a reputation for always telling the truth when others easily rely on convenient "white lies" is equally striking.

The religious orders play an important role in the evangelical mission of the Church. Among the most notable efforts in history have been those of the Franciscans and Dominicans in the Spanish colonies of Mexico and California and the missions of the Jesuits in the Far East. Today the evangelical efforts of religious can take many forms. For example, some evangelize through the witness of their special love of God as expressed by their dedicated lifestyle. Other religious, such as Mother Teresa's Missionaries of Charity, do not attempt to actively convert to Christianity the poor whom they serve, but through their selfless acts of

Live It!

Taking Part in the Evangelization

How can you participate in the Church mission to evangelize? Consider the following:

- **Recommit to personal holiness.** Nothing turns people away from faith faster than someone who preaches the faith but doesn't practice it. While you share your faith, make sure that every day you take opportunities to grow in holiness. Mother Teresa, for example, spent four hours daily in prayer.
- **Respect other traditions.** All people, including non-Christians, are God's children. Proclaim Christ, but also listen to the truth that exists in other traditions, and then explore how that truth relates to Christ.
- **Recommit to evangelization.** It is difficult and a little scary to proclaim the truth of our own faith these days. But, deep down, people are hungry for the truth and most often will respond positively to your own witness if they see that it genuinely brings you peace and joy.

service, they evangelize by witnessing to their love of Jesus. Blessed Teresa said: "I'm evangelizing by my works of love. . . . That's the preaching that we are doing, and I think that is more real."

The ordained—deacons, priests, and bishops—share in the evangelical mission of the Church in a special way. Bishops "are directly responsible, together with [the pope], for the evangelization of the world, both as members of the College of Bishops and as pastors of the particular churches" (*Redemptoris Missio,* 63). Priests are entrusted with both the pastoral care of a specific community and the evangelization of those who do not yet know Christ. They evangelize through their example of a life devoted to the Christ, through their ministry of preaching, and especially through their role in the celebration of the Sacraments.

The Sisters of Charity put love into action through their care of those who are most in need. What are ways you show love through action?

© SUCHETA DAS/Reuters/Corbis

Elements of Evangelization

Redemptoris Missio presents three conditions in which the Church is to be active in evangelization in the world today, so how do we evangelize in these situations? There are numerous elements or principles we can each embrace, be it in the situation of evangelizing those who have never heard the Gospel message, those who are active in their faith, or those who have moved away from the Church:

- **Boldness and respect.** Christians should respect religious freedom and local cultures, seeking to inculturate the Gospel message, but should not be afraid of proclaiming the truth of Christianity, even if some see this as narrow minded or intolerant (see 2–3).

- **Technological developments.** We have the ability to communicate in ways that were not possible even fifteen years ago. We have to have a willingness to use the latest technologies in proclaiming the Gospel.

- **Commitment to personal holiness.** The earliest Christian missionaries were successful not because of new techniques of preaching, but because of the holiness of the preachers (see 90).

- **Reaching out to people of all ages.** The Gospel message applies to everyone, no matter what age, so there must be an effort made to evangelize all people. As a young person, you have the unique ability to share the Gospel message with your peers and to challenge them to live according to Gospel values.

As we have said, evangelization is central to the mission of the Church and is the responsibility of all her members. It is important for us to continually recommit ourselves to this mission and to be willing to expand the tools we utilize to reflect the changing times in which we live. ✝

What Is Inculturation?

Through her evangelization the Church seeks to inculturate the Gospel message. So what is inculturation? Inculturation involves a respectful encounter between the Christian faith and a particular culture. The process is a two-way street: (1) it takes up particular cultural values and integrates them into the life of the Church, and (2) it proclaims the Gospel message in different cultural contexts, allowing it to "take flesh" in each people's culture. One of the challenges of inculturation is the assimilation of the Gospel message into different cultural contexts without betraying the fundamental truths of that message. A few examples of the inculturation of the Gospel message are these:

- Pope John Paul II suggested that traditional African ancestor worship was a preparation for the African people to understand and accept the Christian belief in the Communion of Saints.

- Lakota Catholics such as Black Elk saw traditional Lakota ceremonies as a preparation for Christianity. He thought the Lakota were better prepared to understand Christ's sacrifice through their experience of the Sun Dance, a ceremony in which participants voluntarily endure suffering for the benefit of their people.

- The Church allows different liturgies, popular devotions, prayer forms, and devotions to various saints and to Mary to express the unique cultural conditions of areas throughout the world.

© Elke Stolzenberg/CORBIS

Part Review

1. What does it mean to say the Church reads the signs of the times?

2. Explain the difference between the "culture of death" and the "culture of life."

3. What should be the role of Catholics in public policy debates?

4. What are some specific ways a layperson might evangelize in her or his home or workplace?

5. What are the characteristics of evangelization as presented in *Redemptoris Missio?* How might you live out some of them in your own life?

6. What is inculturation?

The Lived Mission of the Church

Part 1

The Leadership Structure of the Church

Like any organization the Church needs clear and well-defined leadership. This leadership is provided primarily through the clergy of the Church. The Church's leadership is a visible, hierarchical structure. The Pope, the bishop of Rome, is the one leader of the whole Church, the successor to Peter. He symbolizes the Church's unity. The bishops of the Church, together with the Pope, are responsible for the spiritual welfare of the entire Church. But bishops are also the leaders in their own dioceses, where they are assisted by their coworkers, the priests and the deacons.

The ordained ministers of the Church, through the grace of Holy Orders, use Christ's authority to govern, teach, and sanctify the Church. They make Christ present to us through the Sacraments. Following Christ's example, they exercise leadership by service to the Body of Christ.

The topics covered in this part are:

- Article 39: "The Church and Hierarchy" (page 150)

- Article 40: "The Pope: Visible Head of the Church" (page 153)

- Article 41: "The Role of the Bishops in the Church Hierarchy" (page 156)

- Article 42: "The Priesthood" (page 160)

- Article 43: "The Diaconate" (page 163)

Article 39 The Church and Hierarchy

The Church comprises two distinct but interconnected groups, the hierarchy and the laity. The hierarchy is the Apostles and their successors, the Pope and bishops of the Church, along with their coworkers, priests and deacons. They are called hierarchy because the leadership of the Church, as established by Christ, is hierarchical, meaning that her leaders and institutions are organized in a specific order. Any group needs organized leadership; otherwise chaos would result.

This does not mean that bishops are more important than priests or that bishops and priests are more important than the laity. All members of the Church are equal in dignity, but they are called to different roles and ministries, each contributing to the building up of the Body of Christ. The articles in this part focus on the role of the hierarchy. The articles in the next part focus on the role of the laity.

Hierarchical Leadership: Divine Authority and Service

The hierarchy consists of the ordained ministers of the Church: bishops (including the Pope), priests, and deacons. From the beginning of the Church, there have always been these three orders, or degrees, of ordained ministers. Only bishops confer these three degrees of ordained ministry through the Sacrament of Holy Orders. These orders are absolutely necessary for the Church to exist, for without the hierarchy, the Church is without the leadership instituted by Christ that makes Christ present in the Church through the Sacraments.

At the top of the Church hierarchy is the Pope, who is a bishop with supreme power over the whole Church. Next are the bishops, whose authority depends on their union with the Pope. Priests are the next level, and they are the bishop's coworkers. Deacons are at the lowest level of the hierarchy.

The Latin name for the bishop's chair is *cathedra*. This is why the church where the bishop is the pastor is called a cathedral.

© Bill Wittman / www.wpwittman.com

The Church is hierarchical because Christ himself set up this structure. Christ established the bishops as the successors to the Apostles, and the Pope as the successor to Peter, the head of the Apostles. The bishops and the Pope represent Christ (the Pope in a unique way) and thus Christ's own divine authority flows through this hierarchical structure. Because of this the hierarchy has the spiritual authority necessary to govern, teach, and provide pastoral care for the Body of Christ.

We as Americans value equality and democracy, and thus are naturally suspicious of hierarchies. However, we must remember that the hierarchy's order was established by Christ and the authority of those within the hierarchy is not to be expressed in a domineering way. Christ defines how they must exercise their leadership: "You know that those who are recognized as rulers over the Gentiles lord it over them, and their great ones make their authority over

The Vatican Curia

The Pope leads the Church through the Roman Curia located in Rome. The Curia is a complex of offices that administer Church affairs. They include a Secretariat of State, nine Congregations, three Tribunals, eleven Pontifical Councils, and seven Pontifical Commissions. Following are a few examples of these to give you some sense of the Curia's activities:

- *Secretariat of State.* Coordinates the Curia's offices and maintains diplomatic ties with foreign nations.
- *Congregation for the Doctrine of the Faith.* Oversees Catholic doctrine, publishes statements to clarify Catholic teaching.
- *Congregation for Bishops.* Coordinates the appointment of bishops worldwide.
- *Apostolic Signatura.* The highest Church court.
- *Pontifical Biblical Commission.* Issues instructions on biblical interpretation.

© Saint Mary's Press/Brian Singer-Towns

Holy See

This term is a translation of the Latin *sancta sedes*, which literally means "holy seat." The word *see* refers to a diocese or seat of a bishop. The Holy See is the seat of the central administration of the whole Church, under the leadership of the Pope, the Bishop of Rome.

them felt. But it shall not be so among you. Rather, whoever wishes to be great among you will be your servant; whoever wishes to be first among you will be the slave of all" (Mark 10:42–44). Beginning with Pope Gregory I (590–604), and continuing with Pope John Paul II and Pope Benedict XVI, popes regularly refer to themselves as the "Servant of the Servants of God," following the example of Christ.

Organizational Structure of the Church

The Church is generally organized into parishes and dioceses, with the spiritual center of the Church in Rome. This reflects the ascending hierarchy of priests, bishops, and the Pope. Here is a brief description of the different organizational levels in the Church's structure:

> **The Holy See.** This term is a translation of the Latin *sancta sedes,* which literally means "holy seat." The word *see* refers to a diocese or seat of a bishop. The **Holy See** is the seat of the central administration of the whole Catholic Church, under the leadership of the Pope, the Bishop of Rome.

Live It!

The Hierarchy and You

Most of us have little direct contact with the hierarchy of our Church. But there are some concrete things you can do to establish a closer connection with them that would enrich your own life:

- Pray for the Pope and the bishops. We pray for them at each Mass, but you could include them in your daily prayers as well. These leaders bear great responsibilities, and our prayers can help them.
- Pray the Holy Father's prayer intentions for each month. You can easily find these online.
- Read the teachings of the bishops. A great place to start is with *Stewardship and Teenagers: The Challenge of Being a Disciple* (United States Conference of Catholic Bishops, November 14, 2007). It has some good, practical advice on how to share your talents with others and how to grow more deeply in your personal relationship with Christ.

Diocese. A diocese is usually a certain geographic area governed by a bishop. There are over twenty-eight hundred dioceses worldwide, with 194 dioceses in the United States. The universal Church is the communion of these dioceses worldwide.

Parish. A parish is a distinct community within a diocese. The bishop typically appoints one or more priests to care for each parish, although there are some exceptions.

Family. Because the family is where the faith is first taught and practiced, it can be thought of as the most basic level of the Church, sometimes call the **domestic church.**

As you can see, the number of Catholics increases at each level, culminating with the Holy See's responsibility for the spiritual care of all the world's Catholics. This responsibility would be overwhelming were it not for the Holy Spirit, who guides and strengthens the leaders in their important roles. ✝

domestic church
Another name for the first and most fundamental community of faith: the family.

40 The Pope: Visible Head of the Church

Article

Is the Pope Catholic? People sometimes use this question as a reply to a question whose answer is obviously yes. This question works because the Pope and our Catholic faith fit so naturally and obviously together. When we see the Pope, we see the Catholic Church, as the Pope is the visible head of the Church.

Who Is the Pope?

We start with the fact that the Pope is first a bishop. That means he has all the rights and authority of a bishop, a successor of the Apostles. But the Pope is not just a bishop; he is the leader of all the bishops. Let's review and consider his chief titles to help clarify his unique identity and role as leader of the Church:

- **Successor to Peter.** Christ established his Apostles as a permanent college with Peter at the head. The Pope is the successor to Peter, just as the bishops are the successors of the Apostles. Christ gave Peter the "power of the keys"—

college of bishops
The assembly of bishops, headed by the Pope, that holds the teaching authority and responsibility in the Church.

vicar
Someone who serves as a substitute or agent for someone else. As the Vicar of Christ, the Pope acts for Christ, his human representative on earth.

The Pope is the Bishop of Rome and holds a special responsibility and authority to lead the Church.

that is, the authority to govern the Church. This authority is passed down to each new Pope.

- **Bishop of Rome.** During the lifetime of the first Apostles, the city of Rome was established as the spiritual center of the Church. The Apostles Peter and Paul, the two great leaders of the early Church, both ended up in Rome and were eventually martyred there. With rare exception, all the popes since Peter have lived in Rome. As the Bishop of Rome, the Pope is leader of the spiritual center of the Church.

- **Head of the College of Bishops.** All the bishops of the world are united with one another, with the Pope as their head. As previously explained, this body is called the **college of bishops**, another name for the hierarchy. The Pope has the responsibility for providing leadership to the college of bishops. In addition, the college of bishops has no authority unless united with the Pope. As head of the college of bishops, the Pope has the authority to appoint the bishops throughout the world.

- **Vicar of Christ.** The Pope is the **Vicar** of Christ, meaning that he acts for Christ as Christ's human representative on earth. It is true that bishops are also called vicars of Christ, but when this phrase is used in the singular, it refers to the Pope. Just as Christ himself is the single head of his Body, the Church, so too the Pope is the visible and juridical head of the Church. The Pope is the visible sign of Christ's pres-

© OSSERVATORE ROMANO/Reuters/Corbis

ence on earth. He is a personal sign and guarantee of the Church's unity in its belief, its Sacraments, and its authority that has its origins with Peter and the Apostles. Catholics all over the world, as well as many world leaders, look to the Pope for guidance and inspiration.

- **Pastor of the Universal Church.** The Pope has the responsibility for the big picture, to minister to Catholics throughout the world. To carry out this tremendous responsibility, Christ gives the Pope full, supreme, and universal power over the entire Church.

As you can see from these titles, the Pope has a key role in the hierarchy of the Church. We look to him in a unique way for guidance and inspiration on our common journey as disciples of Christ. ✝

Newman and the Development of Papal Supremacy

If the Bishop of Rome is the supreme head of the Church, you might wonder why we do not see this teaching more clearly in the New Testament, or in early writers, like Ignatius of Antioch. John Henry Newman argued that this early silence was only natural, as the conditions necessary for revealing this teaching had not yet arisen.

Specifically, Newman argues, the early Churches were too scattered and too concerned with local issues, such as poverty and the threat of persecution, to be led by one clearly identified pastor of the whole Church. During the fourth and fifth centuries, however, conditions changed. Persecutions came to an end and Christianity had become the official religion of the empire. Bishops could gather in Ecumenical Councils to clarify theological beliefs, and it was natural for the authority of a clearly identifiable, single head of the Church to grow stronger and function more openly.

Jesus' appointment of Peter as the head had established the principle of papal supremacy from the beginning, and the Church of Rome and its bishop were accorded special recognition from the early days of the Church. However, the universal authority of the Bishop of Rome, the Pope, emerged clearly only later, when the time was right.

Article 41 The Role of the Bishops in the Church Hierarchy

ministry

Based on a word for "service," a way of caring for and serving others and helping the Church fulfill its mission. Ministry especially refers to the work of sanctification performed by those in Holy Orders through the preaching of God's Word and the celebration of the Sacraments. The laity helps the Church fulfill its mission through lay ministries, such as that of lector or catechist.

province

A grouping of two or more dioceses with an archbishop as its head.

Hopefully you have had a chance to meet the bishop of your diocese, perhaps at your Confirmation or at a parish or school liturgy. A bishop's life is a busy one, with a calendar that is very full. Bishops are frequently on the road to be with their people. This is because the hierarchy—the bishop in communion with the Pope—has the task of teaching, sanctifying, and governing the Church.

Some Facts about Bishops

Let's review some basics about bishops. When Christ first called his Twelve Apostles, he formed them as a permanent group, or "college," with Peter as their head. The bishops, as successors to the Apostles, receive this same apostolic authority through the fullness of the Sacrament of Holy Orders. Together they form a college, with the Pope at their head. As the successors to the Apostles, they are entrusted with faithfully passing down the Apostolic Tradition. They do this by authentically teaching the faith, celebrating divine worship—especially the Eucharist—and acting as the pastoral leaders in their own dioceses. The bishops are assisted in these responsibilities by the priests and deacons of the diocese.

Each bishop is the visible head of a particular church, or diocese. Within his diocese, a bishop is the visible source and foundation of unity. In other words, the bishop is a living symbol that his particular church is unified with the universal Church. This unity comes through Apostolic Succession, through sharing the same truths, and in celebrating the same Sacraments. The *episcopacy* or *episcopate* is another term for the bishop's governance of his church.

All bishops are ordained as priests before they become bishops. When a position for a new bishop arises, the Pope appoints a priest or bishop to fill this position. These men are recommended by local bishops, a papal representative, and the Curia's Congregation for Bishops. If the newly appointed leader is a priest rather than a bishop, then he is consecrated as a bishop, usually by an archbishop.

You may have wondered about some related terms. An archbishop governs a particularly important diocese (including large cities such as New York or Los Angeles) and presides over meetings and gatherings of the other bishops in his **province**. A cardinal is a senior Church official, usually a bishop, appointed by the Pope to serve as a member of the college or body responsible for electing the Pope. The major offices responsible for governing the Church are headed by cardinals.

Sanctifying Office of the Bishops

As the representative of Christ and the Church, the bishop sanctifies, or makes holy, the Church by overseeing the administration of the Sacraments in his diocese. He is especially responsible for the Eucharist: notice how his name is mentioned in the Eucharistic Prayers of every Mass. Every priest's authority to celebrate the Sacraments flows from the sacramental authority of the bishop.

© Sébastien Désarmaux/Godong/Corbis

The bishop also plays a special role in celebrating other Sacraments. You most likely have been, or will be, confirmed by a bishop; they are the ordinary celebrants of Confirmation in the Latin rite. The bishop is the only person who can ordain priests and deacons, because the Sacrament of Holy Orders continues the **ministry** of the Apostles.

Local bishops have the authority to ordain new priests and deacons. Why is it important for a bishop to ordain the priests and deacons who will serve in his diocese?

collegial

Characterized by the equal sharing of responsibility and authority among the members of a group who form a college. The bishops of the Church together with the Pope at their head form a college, which has full authority over the Church.

The Governing Office of the Bishops

As a vicar of Christ, a bishop has the authority to govern his particular church. He sets guidelines and establishes procedures for things such as the requirements for receiving the Sacraments or how the priests and deacons of the diocese are prepared for their ministries. The bishop does this with the help of many other people, including the priests, deacons, and lay ecclesial ministers of the diocese. However, he has the final authority and responsibility for all decisions affecting the spiritual and corporal welfare of the diocese. He serves the People of God, promotes their true interests, and helps them to reach the goal of salvation. In this he follows the example of Jesus, who came to serve, not to be served (see Mark 10:45).

Even though a bishop has the ultimate governing authority in his own diocese, he is not completely free to make whatever decisions he wants. He must use his authority in communion with the whole Church under the guidance of the Pope.

In his governing, a bishop shows a special concern for the poor, for those who are persecuted for their faith, and for missionaries throughout the world. The Catholic Campaign for Human Development, for example, is an initiative of the United States bishops that empowers the less fortunate to help themselves.

The Collegial Nature of the Bishops

A bishop is primarily responsible for his own diocese, but he also is concerned for churches throughout the world, especially those most in need. In this regard a bishop's relationship with other bishops is **collegial,** meaning they share equally in the authority to make decisions affecting the Church in a particular country or region or even the Church worldwide. These decisions are always made in union with the Pope.

The collegial nature of the episcopate is especially clear when bishops gather together with the Pope in an Ecumenical Council to settle, after careful and open discussion, questions of major importance for the entire Church. Bishops also meet in synods or provincial councils at a more local level. In October 2009, for example, Pope Benedict XVI convened a synod of African bishops. The bishops in the United States meet twice a year. We see a powerful symbol of their collegiality when bishops gather together to consecrate a new bishop. ✝

The Bishop in Ignatius of Antioch's Letters

The letters of Ignatius of Antioch, written around the year 100, are a particularly important witness to the hierarchical structure of the early Church, as well as the crucial role of the bishop in passing down the faith. Ignatius of Antioch lived at a time when there was much debate and confusion about Christian belief. He insisted that Church members follow closely the teachings and authority of the bishops and thus of Christ himself. Following are some quotations from his letters. These were written as he was being escorted to Rome for execution, due to his refusal to renounce his faith in Christ.

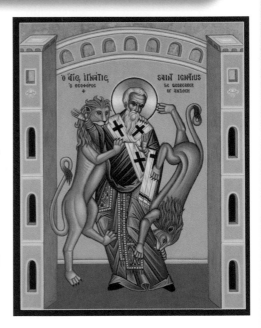

"Do nothing without the bishop and the presbyters."

"We should look upon the bishop even as we would upon the Lord Himself."

"Do all things in harmony with God, with the bishop presiding in the place of God."

"All of you should follow the bishop as Jesus Christ follows the Father."

(Quotations from Bart D. Ehrman, editor and translator, *The Apostolic Fathers*, pages 247, 225, 247, and 303)

Article 42 The Priesthood

presbytery, presbyterate
The name given to priests as a group, especially in a diocese; based on the Greek word *presbyter*, which means "elder."

vocation
A call from God to all members of the Church to embrace a life of holiness. Specifically, it refers to a call to live the holy life as an ordained minister, as a vowed religious (sister or brother), in a Christian Marriage, or in single life.

The Church leader you are probably most familiar with is the priest (or priests) of your parish. He shares in your bishop's authority; he is the bishop's wise coworker in service to your parish. He and the other priests of the diocese are in union with your bishop and together are responsible for the spiritual and temporal welfare of the whole diocese.

In the early Church, the term *presbyter* was more commonly used for the ordained ministers we now call priests. In Greek it literally means "elder," a term that originally referred to the older, more experienced community leaders. That is why you will sometimes hear the priests in your diocese referred to as the **presbytery** or **presbyterate.**

The Priest's Authority and Responsibility

The bishops, who share the authority of the Apostles and thus of Christ, in turn share their authority with the priests as coworkers. Together with their bishop, priests are responsible for a particular diocese. The bishop gives individual priests the authority over a specific parish community or another office within the diocese.

All the baptized participate in Christ's priestly office, called the common priesthood of the faithful. But the priesthood of the ordained priest, sometimes called the ministerial priesthood, differs in its essence from the priesthood of the faithful. The Sacrament of Holy Orders confers a sacred power on the priest, which is to be used in service to the faithful. He represents Christ to the community, serving in the name and in the person of Christ within the community.

Catholic Wisdom

The Heavenly Vocation of the Priest

[A priest is] the defender of the truth, who stands with angels, gives glory with archangels, causes sacrifices to rise to the altar on high, shares God's priesthood, refashions creation, restores it in God's image, recreates it for the world on high, and, even greater, is divinized and divinizes.

(Saint Gregory of Nazianzus)

He exercises his service to the People of God through his teaching, divine worship, and pastoral leadership.

The priest's primary role is that of sacramental minister. He presides over the celebration of the Eucharist in his parish on Sundays and weekdays. He also offers the faithful the grace of the Sacraments of Baptism, Penance and Reconciliation, Anointing of the Sick, Matrimony, and Confirmation. (Only priests and bishops may celebrate the Eucharist, Penance and Reconciliation, Anointing of the Sick, and Confirmation.) But priests also have many other responsibilities. They oversee the religious education in their parish and Catholic school if there is one. They visit the sick and offer spiritual care to those who need it. They oversee the work of the parish staff and make sure the parish buildings are taken care of. In many ways their work is never done!

Yet just as the bishop is concerned not for his diocese alone, but also for the universal Church, the priest's mission is not restricted to his parish. He also participates (through the Sacrament of Holy Orders) in the universal mission of

The laying on of hands by a priest or bishop is a part of the Sacrament of Anointing of the Sick. What other Sacraments have the action of the laying on of hands?

© Bill Wittman / www.wpwittman.com

the Apostles, whom Christ sent out "to make disciples of all nations" (Matthew 28:19).

As bishops in union with the Pope have a collegial relationship with one another, so too do the priests of a particular diocese, in union with their bishop, have a collegial relationship with one another. We see a sign of their collegi-

How Does One Become a Priest?

Have you ever wondered how a person becomes a priest? First, a person does not choose to become a priest— rather, he is called by God. He must be a baptized man. Any man who feels God might be calling him to the priesthood must submit his desire to the authority of the Church, who

then determines whether he should in fact be called. Only Church authority has the responsibility and the right to call someone to receive the Sacrament of Holy Orders.

Someone who feels called to the priesthood typically goes through an unofficial process of **discernment,** praying, gathering information, seeking advice from wise and trusted people. If he then still believes he has a vocation to the priesthood, he begins the formal process outlined in general terms here:

- **Candidacy.** This is a formal period of discernment with other men who are considering the priesthood. Also known as pre-theology, this generally lasts for two years.
- **Seminary study.** Sponsored by his diocese, a candidate then enters seminary for priestly formation and theological studies. This generally lasts for four years, and then the candidate works for one year in a parish of the diocese.
- **Transitional Diaconate.** About a year before ordination to the priesthood, a seminarian is ordained to the Transitional Diaconate (different from the Permanent Diaconate). He makes vows of celibacy and obedience to the bishop at this point.
- **Priesthood.** When the bishop determines he is ready, the transitional deacon is ordained to the priesthood by the bishop.

ality when priests, after the bishop, place their hands on the priest candidate during the Rite of Ordination.

The authority of a priest also has a personal character. Through the Sacrament of Holy Orders, a priest receives the sacred power to act as Christ's representative. This power is seen most clearly when the priest offers the Eucharist in the person of Christ, making present again in our time Christ's offering of his life on the cross. ✝

discernment

From a Latin word meaning "to separate or to distinguish between," it is the practice of listening for God's call in our lives and distinguishing between good and bad choices.

Article 43 The Diaconate

You may or may not be familiar with the ministry of deacons (also called diaconal ministry). Shortly after the close of Vatican II, Pope Paul VI restored the diaconate as a permanent order in the Church. The number of deacons is growing as more men are called into this ministry of service.

Most deacons are not full-time Church ministers. They earn their living by working in the world, just as most of the laity does. And unlike priests they can be married and raise families. This may seem confusing, but it is very similar to the way deacons ministered in the early Church. Today's deacons are examples of service to the Church and the world, just as the deacons of the early Church were.

What Is a Deacon?

A deacon is ordained for ministry and service. *Diakoinia* is the Greek word for "service" used in the New Testament writings. This indicates the primary role of the deacon, to be of service to the Church and to the world. Their Ordination by the bishop confers on them the grace to serve in the ministry of the Word, in the Church's worship, in pastoral governance, and in acts of charity. In these works of service, the deacon is directly responsible to the bishop of the diocese.

Deacons share in Christ's mission and grace in a special way. The Sacrament of Holy Orders leaves an "imprint," which shapes their lives to the life of Christ, who was himself a deacon in the sense that he humbled himself to become a servant of all (see Philippians 2:7–8, Mark 10:45).

Service of the Deacons

As previously mentioned, deacons serve the Church in three primary areas: the liturgy, the Word, and charity.

In Service of the Liturgy

A deacon is an ordinary minister of the Sacrament of Baptism, along with a priest or bishop. He also blesses Marriages in the Sacrament of Matrimony. He assists with the Eucharist and distributes it.

In Service of the Word

Deacons give homilies and may lead celebrations of the Liturgy of the Word. They also fulfill various catechetical and other teaching positions. A deacon may lead a Bible study at your parish or offer religious instruction to children, youth, or adults. Through these activities deacons play a part in the new evangelization and contribute to the missionary activity of the Church.

In Service of Charity

Deacons also dedicate themselves to various ministries of charity, including pastoral ministry to families. Other tasks might include assisting with administering church finances or coordinating various social services.

Deacons, though ordained, often are married, have children, and have careers outside of the Church. How is this a gift in their service of the Word as preachers and teachers?

© Bill Wittman / www.wpwittman.com

History of the Diaconate

How did the diaconate begin? The title deacon is used in the New Testament (see 1 Timothy 3:8–13), although it is unclear what the precise functions of the deacons were at that time. The diaconate can be traced back to the Apostles' selection of seven men to assist them, as told in Acts of the Apostles 6:1–7. Saint Stephen, the first Christian martyr, was one of these seven and is the patron saint of deacons. Saint Ignatius of Antioch, writing around the year 100, refers to deacons, along with bishops and presbyters, as a distinct group.

Saint Lawrence, Deacon

Saint Lawrence was a deacon martyred at Rome around the year 250. One tradition tells us that during a time of persecution, Roman authorities demanded that Lawrence give up the Church's treasures to the emperor. Lawrence replied that he would need three days to collect them. During that time, Lawrence gathered together the poor and the sick of Rome, and presented them to the authorities, calling them the treasures of the Church. Lawrence died a martyr; the authorities put him to death by slowly roasting him over a fire.

© Nicolo Orsi Battaglini / Art Resource, NY

**Latin Church,
Latin Rite**

That part of the Catholic Church that follows the disciplines and teachings of the Diocese of Rome, especially the liturgical traditions. It is called the Latin Church or Latin Rite because Latin has been the official language since the fourth century. The majority of the world's Catholics belong to the Latin Rite.

Over the centuries the importance of the diaconate as a separate ministry declined in the **Latin Church,** until by modern times it was only a transitional stage in preparing for the priesthood. The Churches of the East have always maintained the Permanent Diaconate. The Second Vatican Council, however, restored the Permanent Diaconate in the Latin Church.

A 2007 survey commissioned by the United States Conference of Catholic Bishops estimated that there are some 16,500 deacons in the United States, thirteen thousand of them actively engaged in service. Ninety-three percent are married and 90 percent are over the age of fifty.

Deacons Are Called to a Life of Holiness

In his 1967 apostolic letter on the Permanent Diaconate, Pope Paul VI called on deacons to devote themselves to a

Pray It!

Prayer for Deacons

During the Ordination of deacons, the bishop prays over them as part of the Ordination liturgy. The following is a selection from that prayer. You can pray it in support of the ministry of deacons around the world.

Lord,
send forth upon them the Holy Spirit,
that they may be strengthened
by the gift of the sevenfold grace
to carry out faithfully the work of the ministry.
May they excel in every virtue:
in love that is sincere,
in concern for the sick and the poor,
in unassuming authority,
in self-discipline,
and in holiness in life.

. . . .

May they in this life imitate your Son,
who came, not to be served but to serve,
and one day reign with him in heaven.

(English translation of *Ordination of Deacons, Priests, and Bishops*, 18)

special holiness of life. The Pope called them to commit themselves to the following activities:

- Carefully study and meditate on Scripture.
- Frequently attend the Mass; if possible, on a daily basis.
- Receive the Eucharist frequently and participate in Eucharistic Adoration.
- Frequently receive the Sacrament of Penance and Reconciliation.
- Examine your conscience daily.
- Develop a special devotion to Mary, Mother of God.
- Participate in the Liturgy of the Hours.

(Adapted from *The Sacred Order of Deacons*
[Sacrum Diaconatus Ordinem], 26)

Part Review

1. What does it mean to say that the Church is hierarchical? Why is it necessary for the Church to be hierarchical?

2. In what way are the Holy See, the diocese, the parish, and the family related in the hierarchy?

3. In what way is the Pope the visible sign of the Church's unity?

4. In what way is the Pope the successor to Peter?

5. In what specific ways does a bishop sanctify the Church?

6. What are some examples of the collegial nature of the bishops?

7. Describe the relationship between a bishop and a priest.

8. Describe the responsibilities of a priest.

9. Explain what a deacon is and describe three of his primary areas of service.

Part 2

Many Vocations to Holiness

Christ calls all of us to a life of holiness, not just the hierarchy. In order to live holy lives, we are called to follow the evangelical counsels of obedience, chastity, and poverty, each of us in our own way. In addition to living the evangelical counsels, the laity shares in Christ's priestly, prophetic, and kingly offices. Laity who are called to the vocation of Marriage also have the responsibility of raising children in the faith. This is why the family is often called the domestic church.

When a person makes a public profession of the evangelical vows, he or she enters the consecrated life. Life in a religious order or community is a common form of the consecrated life; these communities are characterized by the rhythm of daily prayer. Religious communities have their origin in the spirituality of the desert of hermits in Egypt, a form of the consecrated life that still exists. New forms of consecrated life are also emerging, including secular institutes and a revival of consecrated virgins.

The topics covered in this part are:

- Article 44: "The Evangelical Counsels" (page 169)

- Article 45: "The Mission of the Laity" (page 172)

- Article 46: "The Work and Vocation of the Laity" (page 176)

- Article 47: "The Consecrated Life: Religious Orders" (page 179)

- Article 48: "Other Types of Consecrated Life" (page 182)

44 The Evangelical Counsels

Article

You might be aware that Roman Catholic diocesan priests make promises of **celibacy** and obedience to the bishop as part of the Sacrament of Holy Orders. And religious priests, brothers, and sisters make lifelong **vows** of poverty, chastity, and obedience. But did you know that every Christian is called to make a commitment to these virtues?

On our path to holiness, all Christians are called to follow the **evangelical counsels** of chastity, obedience, and poverty. However, men and women who publicly profess these vows and commit to a stable state of life have a vocation to the consecrated life. In this article we take a closer look at what it means to live the evangelical counsels.

Poverty

Jesus told the rich young man, "Go, sell what you have, and give to [the] poor and you will have treasure in heaven; then come, follow me" (Mark 10:21). Most of us, however, are not literally called to give up all our possessions. The evangelical counsel of poverty calls us to focus on spiritual riches, not material wealth. We must not become attached to money and material things, because it is all too easy for these to become the focus of our lives. As Jesus warned his disciples, "Amen, I say to you, it will be hard for one who is rich to enter the kingdom of heaven"

© The Crosiers / Gene Plaisted, OSC

Jesus told the rich young man, "Go, sell what you have . . ." (Mark 10:21). Why do you think Jesus told the rich young man that he had to sell everything to have treasures in Heaven?

vow
A free and conscious commitment made to other persons (as in Marriage), to the Church, or to God.

celibacy
The state or condition of those who have chosen or taken vows to remain unmarried in order to devote themselves entirely to the service of the Church and the Kingdom of God.

evangelical counsels
The call to go beyond the minimum rules of life required by God (such as the Ten Commandments and the Precepts of the Church) and strive for spiritual perfection through a life marked by a commitment to chastity, poverty, and obedience.

chastity
The virtue by which people are able to successfully and healthfully integrate their sexuality into their total person; recognized as one of the fruits of the Holy Spirit. Also one of the vows of religious life.

(Matthew 19:23). It is easy to fall into the trap of focusing on having the newest clothes or getting the newest gaming system. Christ calls every Christian to be "poor in spirit" and to use money and possessions in a moderate and healthy way.

When a person in the consecrated communal life takes a vow of poverty, however, she or he literally does give up the right to individual possessions, promising to share possessions in common with the community. For example, if religious sisters or brothers receive pay for a job, some or all of the paycheck usually goes to their community, not to the individual. Diocesan priests do not take a vow of poverty, but they are called to live a simple lifestyle.

Chastity

Chastity is the healthy integration of our sexuality into our whole person; it is a virtue that is also one of the fruits of the Holy Spirit. Every baptized person is called to lead a chaste life according to our state of life, with Jesus as our model. To be chaste does not mean denying or suppressing our sexuality, but rather ordering it in the right way. We are all called to control our sexual desires, rather than having them control us.

Even married couples are called to chastity. Most obviously this means that the husband and wife must be sexually faithful to each other—that is, they must not commit acts of adultery or even engage in nonsexual romantic relationships with someone who isn't their spouse. But it also means that a husband and wife must practice sexual control with each other. If the couple is using natural family planning, for example, in order to space out the birth of children for serious reasons, they must abstain from sexual relations for certain periods of the month. This allows a couple to develop self-discipline and a healthy respect for each other's bodies. It also encourages them to discover nonsexual ways of intimacy.

As a young person, you are called to complete abstinence before Marriage. You are called to a purity of heart, keeping away from sexual fantasies and pornography. In our sexually permissive society, living a chaste life is a huge challenge, but this virtue can be developed with daily effort and with the help of God's grace, including the sacramental graces of Baptism and the Eucharist. The results are worth it. Chastity helps you to develop a greater respect for the beautiful gift of your own sexuality and will allow you to share that gift in a full and joyful way when the time for Marriage arrives.

Those who are called to the ordained priesthood and to the consecrated life live chaste lives through their vow of celibacy. This means that they commit to not getting married, to not having sexual relations with anyone for the rest of their lives. This is a major life commitment, and those who make it spend years discerning if this is their call. But living a celibate life allows people to dedicate themselves to God and to their ministry in a very special way. And through this commitment, they give living example to all people of the importance of living a chaste life.

We can all take part in fun activities that respect our call to live chaste lives. What activities do you and your friends like to do that help keep you pure of heart?

Commitment to Celibacy

Before taking the vow of celibacy, the bishop gives these instructions to the men preparing for priesthood. They give us insight into the call to celibacy.

By your own free choice you seek to enter the order of deacons [the Transitional Diaconate before priestly Ordination]. You shall exercise this ministry in the celibate state for celibacy is both a sign and a motive of pastoral charity, and a special source of spiritual fruitfulness in the world. By living in this state with total dedication, moved by a sincere love for Christ the Lord, you are consecrated to him in a new and special way. By this consecration you will adhere more easily to Christ with an undivided heart; you will be more freely at the service of God and mankind, and you will be more untrammeled in the ministry of Christian conversion and rebirth. By your life and character you will give witness to your brothers and sisters in faith that God must be loved above all else, and that it is he whom you serve in others.

(English translation of *Ordination of Deacons, Priests, and Bishops*, 10)

Obedience

All Christians are called to obey Christ; this is the very definition of being a disciple. But this also means that we have a duty to obey the Church's Magisterium. The Pope and bishops are the vicars of Christ; they are Christ's representatives to the Church and the world. They have been given divine authority from Christ to teach us God's revealed truth, and it is our duty to obey their teaching. This idea might seem strange, because in our democratic society we highly value our independence. We basically do not like others telling us what to do. But Jesus himself gave us the example of this type of obedience by his obedience to his Father's will: "He humbled himself, / becoming obedient to death, / even death on a cross" (Philippians 2:8).

Ordained ministers and those in the consecrated life make special, lifelong vows of obedience. Priests and deacons promise obedience to the bishop of the diocese. They commit to being the bishop's representatives, teaching and administering as directed by their bishop. If they are in a religious community, people in consecrated life promise special obedience to their religious superiors. ✝

Article 45 The Mission of the Laity

As a young person, you are part of the laity. And as a lay person, you should realize that not only do you belong to the Church, but as a member of the Body of Christ, you have a very important role in God's plan of salvation.

The laity are all the members of the Church except for those who have been ordained. We have already seen how the various ordained ministers participate in the hierarchy. The hierarchy's primary role is to provide leadership for the Church. But the laity's primary role is in witnessing to God's love to the whole world. You are to be Christ's hands and feet and voice and ears in sharing the Good News of the Gospel with your friends, classmates, family members, and people in your community. You are in a unique position to help influence the world's social, political, and economic realities to reflect God's will. You have both the right and the duty to make known to others the saving message of Christ. At times it is only through the laity that certain people will hear the Christian message. Your ministry and the ministry of the hierarchy work together in continuing Christ's mission in the Church and the world.

So even though you are not ordained to holy orders, in your own way you participate in the priestly, prophetic, and kingly functions of Christ as a layperson. In this article we explore some of what this means.

The Priestly Office of the Laity

The laity share in Christ's priesthood. Through the graces of Baptism and Confirmation, they are united with him in serving the world, fulfilling their call to holiness. Just as the priest offers the sacrifice of the Mass to God, the laity too can offer their daily work, family life, and leisure activities—if they are done in the Spirit—as a spiritual sacrifice to the

Live It!

Praying with Your Family

Getting along with family members isn't always easy. One way to get our family relationships to where they should be is by learning to pray together. Consider some of these suggestions:

© Don Hammond/Design Pics/Corbis

- Pray at mealtimes. Beginning a family meal by thanking God is a great way to turn our thoughts away from the busyness of the day and to focus for a few moments on how our Creator blesses and sustains us. Praying before meals at a restaurant can be a powerful witness of our faith to others.
- Pray before leaving on a trip.
- Pray for family members in your own private prayer.
- Pray the Rosary or Angelus together with family members.
- Pray at bedtime. This can be a wonderful opportunity to instruct younger siblings in some of the basics of the faith. Bedtime prayers help to instill habits of being grateful for the day's blessings and of turning over worries and problems to God before going to sleep.

© Bill Wittman / www.wpwittman.com

There are many ways young people can contribute to the liturgical life of the Church. What opportunities do you have to serve in your school or Church liturgies?

Father. Developing a life of prayer and offering intercessions for the needs of others is a way we participate in Christ's priestly office.

The ministerial priesthood is clearly different from the common priesthood of the faithful. The Ordination of priests confers on them a sacred power for the service of the faithful, which only they can exercise through their teaching, sacred liturgy, and pastoral leadership. The laity may also assist in the more specific ministries of the Church, including lectoring, serving, and singing in the choir. Have you taken the opportunity to serve your church in any of these ways?

The Laity's Role in Establishing a Culture of Life

In his 1995 encyclical *The Gospel of Life*, John Paul II challenged us to take part in the ongoing battle between a culture of death and a culture of life in our society today. He discussed several ways laypeople are and can be involved in promoting the culture of life:

- caring for the weak in our society, including AIDS patients, the elderly, and the disabled
- teaching and promoting methods of natural family planning
- supporting single mothers
- encouraging health care personnel, including doctors, pharmacists, and nurses, to resist the temptation to manipulate lives or be agents of death
- influencing political and legislative processes to pass laws that respect the dignity of every life
- rethinking labor or other social policies so as to give families adequate time to care for babies or the elderly

The Prophetic Office of the Laity

Christ fulfills his prophetic office not only through the priests and bishops but also through the laity, using them as witnesses and providing them with the sense of faith (*sensus fidei*)—their readiness to accept the true teaching of the Church in faith and morals. To be a prophet means to share God's Word with those who need to hear it. The laity are called to be witnesses to Christ in every circumstance of their lives and with every person they meet, thus bringing the Good News of salvation to all corners of the world. Here are some ways the laity can participate in the prophetic office of Christ:

- Laypeople are involved in evangelization, proclaiming Christ through words and through the witness of their lives.
- Capable and trained laity may also collaborate with the hierarchy as catechists and religion teachers.
- Laypeople are playing an increasingly important role in providing a Catholic voice on television, radio, Internet sites and blogs, and other various new media.
- The laity also have the right and duty to make their opinions known, in a respectful manner, to their pastors on matters relating to the good of the Church.

The Kingly Office of the Laity

The laity are also called to share in Christ's kingly office. What does it mean to do this, to be a leader from God's point of view? It starts with self-discipline, to consistently choose what is good and right. It continues with our commitment to follow God's call with all our strength and soul for our entire lives. And it means always serving those most in need. The laity are called to lead others by the example of their moral choices, by commitment to God's will in their lives, and by following Christ's example of leading through service.

The laity can also assist the hierarchy in governing the Church, in the parish through membership on various committees and at a higher level by playing a role in councils and synods. How have you exercised Christian leadership in your school, parish, and community? ✝

Article 46 The Work and Vocation of the Laity

domestic
Relating to household or family.

In what specific ways do you live out your call to holiness? Each of us has unique opportunities to share Christ's love with the world, to continue his saving mission. As a layperson, you have relationships with people who may have never gone to church or met a priest. Because of this the laity's work and vocation is very important. In this article we look at some of the ways the laity participate in Christ's mission.

The Work of the Laity

We are all called to bring Christ into the work we do. What careers are you considering in your life? How can you show the love of Christ through those careers?

A primary way laypeople participate in Christ's mission is through their work. All laypeople are called to seek the Kingdom of God by doing God's will within their chosen work, whether it is as a parent, a nurse, a lawyer, or a computer programmer. This also includes being a student! By doing their work well, by being honest, friendly, caring and joyful in schools and workplaces, the laity give witness to the Kingdom of God.

© Rob Marmion/Shutterstock.com

Another primary way laypeople participate in Christ's mission is through the vocation of Marriage. The vocation of Marriage is natural to human beings. A married couple has a natural vocation to have children and to raise their children in a way that respects their own child's vocation to follow Jesus.

From the beginning of Christianity, some laypeople have chosen to renounce the great good of Marriage in order to follow Christ as a single, celibate person. Both the call to Marriage and the call to virginity for the sake of the Kingdom come from the Lord himself. The call to renounce Marriage may take the form of a dedication to the consecrated life, a topic covered in the next article. Yet many laity live as single people without consecrating themselves to that choice. These single people are often especially close to Jesus' heart and serve God and neighbor with great dedication.

It is the duty of all Christians to work with their civil authorities to create a society where truth, freedom, solidarity, and justice reign. The work of those laity called to political office or other influential positions in society is of special importance in accomplishing this. Because their decisions influence the lives of so many other people, they have a special responsibility to work for the common good, to act in harmony with Church teaching, and to be witnesses and agents of peace and justice.

The Family: The Domestic Church

Did you know that you woke up in church this morning? A believing family is called a "**domestic** church." Raising a

Pray It!

Prayer Honoring Saint Gianna Molla

Gianna Berreta Molla (1922–1962) was an Italian pediatrician, wife, and mother. Facing a difficult delivery of her baby, she made clear that if the doctors could only save one person, they should save her child. The baby was delivered, but Gianna died from the complications. Gianna was canonized as a saint in 2004.

© Society of Saint Gianna Beretta Molla

You, Lord Jesus, were for Gianna a splendid example. She learned to recognize you in the beauty of nature. As she was questioning her choice of vocation she went in search of you and the best way to serve you.

Through her married love she became a sign of your love for the Church and for humanity. Like you, the Good Samaritan, she cared for everyone who was sick, small or weak. Following your example, out of love she gave herself entirely, generating new life. Holy Spirit, Source of every perfection, give us wisdom, intelligence, and courage so that, following the example of Saint Gianna and through her intercession, we may know how to place ourselves at the service of each person we meet in our personal, family and professional lives, and thus grow in love and holiness. Amen.

Christian family is a unique and special way the laity participate in Christ's mission. The Christian home is the place where children first hear the Word of God and the call to faith. In families we learn how to share in the Trinity's communion of love through prayer, moral living, and serving others. The Christian family is the first and best teacher of human virtues and Christian charity.

The family as a type of Church has always been significant in Christian history. In the earliest days of Christianity, when the head of a household converted to Christianity, his or her household also converted (see Acts of the Apostles 16:15,31–33; 18:8). The early Church literally met in people's houses (see Romans 16:5, 1 Corinthians 16:19).

Parents have a special role in the family. Obviously they have a duty to provide for the physical and spiritual needs of their children as much as humanly possible. But in our culture, it is very easy to focus on the physical needs—maybe even too easy to focus on material things—and neglect the spiritual needs. Parents must remember that they are the first proclaimers of the faith to their children. They teach their children the virtues and set a good example by their own lifestyle. They further evangelize their children by bringing them into the life of the Church from their earliest years. Parents should teach their children to pray and to discover their vocation as a child of God; always teaching their

Third Orders

Third Orders are associations of laypeople connected to a particular religious order in the Church. As laypeople they do not take public vows of chastity, obedience, and poverty. The laity who belong to a Third Order practice the religious order's spirituality and are typically involved in assisting with the ministries to which the order is committed.

Three of the best known are the Franciscan Third Order, the Dominican Third Order, and the Carmelite Third Order.

There are other lay associations connected with religious orders that are not called Third Orders. For example, laity associated with the Christian Brothers are called Lasallian associates. Maryknoll, the missionary institute, has lay associates who serve as lay missioners.

children that our first duty and responsibility as Christians is to follow Jesus, our Lord and Savior.

Children in turn can help parents to grow in holiness. Living in a family, we can learn from one another the joys of work, love, forgiveness, and self-sacrifice. ☩

Article 47 The Consecrated Life: Religious Orders

Hopefully you have had the good fortune of having known a priest, brother, or sister who is a member of a religious order, at times also called religious communities. The names of these orders are sometimes based on the name of the person who inspired or founded the order: Franciscans (Saint Francis), Dominicans (Saint Dominic), and Benedictines (Saint Benedict) are a few examples. The members of these orders have made a formal public profession to live out the evangelical counsels of poverty, chastity, and obedience in a stable state of life recognized by the Church, thus entering into the **consecrated life.** Religious orders are the most widely known form of the consecrated life, but they are not the only form. Other forms of the consecrated life are discussed in the next article.

The Beginning of Religious Orders

Members of religious orders live communal lives, publicly profess the evangelical counsels, share a liturgical character, and belong to **institutes** recognized by the Church. By their desire to more closely follow Christ, they witness to the union of Christ with the Church.

In the first centuries of the Church, there was a great monastic movement involving **hermits** who went to the desert to dedicate themselves to following Christ more closely. These were people whom God had called to withdraw from the world for a life of prayer and solitude. Some hermits gradually formed communities; Saint Pachomius is usually credited with founding the first monastic community around the year 320 (*monastic* is derived from the Greek word for "alone"). People belonging to these communities were called **monks** and nuns. Religious life first developed in Syria and Egypt out of these monastic movements.

consecrated life
A state of life recognized by the Church in which a person publicly professes vows of poverty, chastity, and obedience.

institute
An organization devoted to a common cause. Religious orders are a type of religious institute.

hermit
A person who lives a solitary life in order to commit himself or herself more fully to prayer and in some cases to be completely free for service to others.

monk
Someone who withdraws from ordinary life, and lives alone or in community, in order to devote oneself to prayer and work in total dedication to God.

(religious) brother
A lay man in a religious order who has made permanent vows of poverty, chastity, and obedience.

(religious) sister
A lay woman in a religious order who has made permanent vows of poverty, chastity, and obedience.

Eventually these communities became known as religious orders. A religious order can have both consecrated lay members (religious brothers and sisters) and consecrated ordained members (priests) who live communal lives and follow a common religious rule. The consecrated lay men in religious orders are called **brothers,** and the consecrated lay women are called **sisters** (sometimes nuns). Religious orders in the Roman Catholic Church must be approved by the Pope.

Variety of Religious Orders

New religious orders have responded to changing conditions. In the Middle Ages, the Dominicans responded to a need for teachers and preachers, and the Franciscans were established due to Saint Francis's desire to restore a life of simplicity to the Church. The Jesuits responded to the need to reform the Catholic Church after the upheaval of the Protestant Reformation.

The founders of religious orders impart a certain charism to their community. The Christian Brothers follow

Presentation Sisters

Nano Nagle (1718–1784) was born to a wealthy Irish family and was educated in France. Drawn to the religious life in France, she eventually chose to return to serve her Irish people. At that time the English penal laws prohibited Catholic schools in Ireland, so Nano secretly set up schools for poor children. She also ministered to the elderly and sick at night, earning her the nickname Lady of the Lamp. She eventually established a religious order that became known as the Presentation Sisters of the Blessed Virgin Mary.

Today the Presentation Sisters have ministries on every continent. Following Nano's charism, they are involved in education, health care, and the promotion of social justice. In South Dakota, for example, the Presentation Sisters have established three hospitals and sponsor one college. They continue to advocate on social justice issues, including calling for the abolition of the death penalty.

© "Image Courtesy of the Sisters of the Presentation of the Blessed Virgin Mary (PBVM)"

John Baptist de La Salle's emphasis on the education of the young, particularly those in greatest need. The Dominicans focus on preaching and teaching, following the example of their founder, Saint Dominic.

Religious orders took a leading role in the evangelization of non-Christian lands, including the Jesuit missions in the Far East, and the Dominican and Franciscan efforts in the Americas. Many religious communities today continue to do missionary work throughout the world, including working for justice in places where there is a great deal of injustice.

There are also religious orders and congregations that are devoted primarily to prayer and contemplation. Rather than being actively engaged in the world, these communities follow the ancient monastic path of separating from the world so their members can avoid the world's distractions and more fully commit themselves to the pursuit of holiness through prayer and study.

© Bill Wittman / www.wpwittman.com

Prayer is an integral part of the life of vowed religious. Through their continual prayer, they both pray for the needs of God's children and model a devotion to prayer for all the members of the Church.

Prayer as the Rhythm of the Religious Life

The daily life of all religious orders is characterized by regular prayer, especially the prayers of the Liturgy of the Hours (also known as the Divine Office). The Hours are designed to make the whole course of the day and night holy by the praise of God, and thus to fulfill Saint Paul's exhortation to "Pray without ceasing" (1 Thessalonians 5:17). Priests are required to pray the Hours daily; other consecrated people, permanent deacons, and the laity can also join in praying the Hours, as it is the public prayer of the Church. The Office focuses heavily on Psalms, and also includes hymns, Scripture readings, prayers, and responses.

The Liturgy of the Hours in the Roman Rite includes seven "hours." Morning prayer (also referred to as Lauds) and evening prayer (also referred to as Vespers) are the primary hours. ✝

Article 48 Other Types of Consecrated Life

Thomas Merton was a well-known spiritual writer and Trappist monk who chose to spend the last years of his life as a hermit.

© Photograph of Thomas Merton by John Howard Griffin courtesy of the Merton Center and used with permission of the Griffin Estate.

In addition to life in religious orders, there are several other forms of the consecrated life. The variety of possibilities is a testimony to the work of the Holy Spirit in the Church, calling people to different ways of living out the evangelical counsels.

Hermits: The Eremitic Life

Do you sometimes feel a need to be alone, to find some peace and quiet away from the constant busyness of life? If so, perhaps you can relate somewhat to the life of the hermit.

Hermits, without necessarily publicly professing the evangelical counsels, separate themselves from the world in order to focus on prayer and

Catholic Wisdom

A Story from the Desert Fathers

The devil appeared to a monk disguised as an angel of light and said to him, "I am Gabriel, and I have been sent to you." But the monk said, "Are you sure you weren't sent to someone else? I am not worthy to have an angel sent to me." At that the devil vanished.

(Benedicta Ward, *The Desert Fathers: Sayings of the Early Christian Monks*, page 165)

penance. The degree of separation varies; even though some hermits live very secluded lives, virtually all have had some degree of human contact. Essentially hermits are a witness to the interior aspect of the mystery of the Church; the hermit's focus on being completely in union with God reflects the Church's perfect union with Christ.

eremitic
Having to do with hermits.

The **eremitic** tradition began around AD 250 with men who lived in the Egyptian desert. (The term *eremitic* is derived from the Greek word for "desert.") Saint Anthony (died around 350) is the most well known of the Desert Fathers who lived and prayed alone in the desert. Some women, such as Sara and Syncletica, who lived in the fourth century, were also called to this vocation.

The spirituality of the hermits is a spirituality of the desert—a life of solitude and purification. Models for this spirituality are Israel's forty years of wandering in the desert, the prophet Elijah's time in the desert, and John the Baptist and Jesus' forty days in the desert. However, the life of a hermit is not centered on himself or herself only. Though the hermit is alone, his or her prayer life is universal: he or she prays for the good of the whole world.

Consecrating a Bride for Christ

Therese Ivers, a canon lawyer who works for the Diocese of Sioux Falls, South Dakota, became a consecrated virgin on August 15, 2009, in a rite conducted by Bishop Paul Swain. Therese wore a white wedding dress and carried a golden lamp to symbolize Jesus' parable of the wise virgins who keep their lamps ready for the coming of the Bridegroom (see Matthew 25:1–12). She was given a wedding ring and a volume of the Liturgy of the Hours.

secular
Relating to worldly concerns; something that is not overtly religious.

Consecrated Virgins and Widows

Consecrated virgins and widows are women who were widowed or who never married who dedicate themselves to a life of celibacy for the sake of the Kingdom of God. Such a person is betrothed mystically to Christ and is an image of the Church and a sign of the Church's love for Christ. She is consecrated by the bishop of her diocese but remains fully in the world, working in her **secular** job. She often supports the Church through her prayers and volunteer work but is not required to take on specific duties.

Secular Institutes

Secular institutes are communities of people living consecrated lives but whose daily work is within the world. They are thus a powerful witness to Gospel values in society and share in the work of evangelization. Members of secular institutes share annual retreats, meetings, and daily common prayer.

Charitas Christi, for example, is an organization of single Catholic women who desire to follow Christ more closely while still continuing to work in their secular jobs. Their inspiration is Saint Catherine of Siena, who desired to serve the Church while remaining in the world. Pope Pius XII officially recognized such groups in 1947.

Societies of Apostolic Life

Societies of Apostolic Life, also called apostolic societies, are not strictly speaking a form of the consecrated life, but they are similar to religious orders. These societies are composed of laity or clergy who usually live in community for a particular purpose but do not make public religious vows. Maryknoll, also called the Catholic Foreign Mission Society of America, is an apostolic society dedicated to foreign missions. The Oratory of Saint Philip Neri, a congregation of priests and lay brothers founded in the late 1500s at Rome, fosters a greater devotion to prayer, preaching, and the Sacraments. The mission of the Paulist Fathers is to evangelize North America in ways appropriate to the distinct cultures. ✞

Part Review

1. What are the three evangelical counsels and how are they applied by different groups in the Church?

2. What is the special mission of all laypeople?

3. Describe how the laity shares the prophetic, kingly, and priestly functions of Christ.

4. In what ways is the family the domestic church?

5. Describe how the work of the laity participates in the mission of Christ.

6. What are two things the individual members of a religious order have in common?

7. What are some of the needs that have been fulfilled by religious orders throughout history?

8. How does the Liturgy of the Hours help fulfill Paul's admonition to pray without ceasing?

9. Define the terms *hermits, consecrated virgins, secular institutes, Third Order,* and *Societies of Apostolic Life.*

Part 3

The Magisterium: The Teaching Office of the Church

We have seen that the bishops have the duty of celebrating divine worship, especially the Eucharist, and guiding their churches in the role of pastor. In this part we examine their duty as the Magisterium to authentically teach the faith.

The Church's Magisterium has an obligation to interpret the Word of God, whether it is in the form of the Scriptures or the Tradition. The Magisterium also ensures that the Church remains faithful to the teaching of the Apostles. The work of the Magisterium helps Church members to grow in their understanding of the faith. The Church's teaching allows her members to be confident that they will not be led astray. The *Catechism of the Catholic Church* is one very helpful resource for learning about what the Church teaches.

The Church has the gifts of indefectibility and infallibility. The Church's indefectibility means she will remain faithful to Christ's teaching until the end of the world. If you remember, *infallibility* means that her pastors, the Pope and the bishops in union with the Pope, can definitively proclaim a teaching related to faith or a teaching related to the moral life.

The Church has many teachings. It is possible to identify, however, which of these truths are the most central, because there is an order or hierarchy to them. The Church's emphasis on truth challenges relativism, a philosophy that says that truth depends on a person's opinion or viewpoint.

The topics covered in this part are:

- Article 49: "The Magisterium" (page 187)

- Article 50: "Indefectibility and Infallibility" (page 190)

- Article 51: "The Magisterium and Truth" (page 193)

Article 49 The Magisterium

The Church perpetuates and transmits to all generations all that she is and all that she believes through her doctrine, life, and worship. The Holy Spirit helps all members of the Church as they grow in their understanding of the Church's heritage of faith contained in the Scriptures and Tradition. This understanding is able to grow through the following means:

- **Theological inquiry.** "Theological inquiry should pursue a profound understanding of revealed truth; at the same time it should not neglect close contact with its own time that it may be able to help these men skilled in various disciplines to attain to a better understanding of the faith." (*Pastoral Constitution on the Church in the Modern World* [*Gaudium et Spes*, 1965], 62)

- **Contemplation and study.** "There is a growth in the understanding of the realities and the words which have been handed down. This happens through the contemplation and study made by believers, who treasure these things in their hearts (see Luke, 2:19,51) through a penetrating understanding of the spiritual realities which they experience, and through the preaching of those who have received through Episcopal succession the sure gift of truth." (*Dogmatic Constitution on Divine Revelation* [*Dei Verbum*, 1965], 8)

- **The teaching of bishops.** When all the bishops in union with the Pope, called the Magisterium, speak on faith and morals, their teachings are guided by the Holy Spirit and are without error. This is called infallibility, and assures us that the teaching of the bishops represents the truth of salvation.

Sacred Tradition, the Sacred Scriptures, and the Magisterium are so closely connected that one cannot stand apart from the others. Through the action of the Holy Spirit, all three work together to help bring about salvation.

What Is the Magisterium?

Let's review our basic knowledge of the Magisterium. The Magisterium is the name given to the official teaching authority of the Church, whose task is to interpret and

© MAX ROSSI/Reuters/Corbis

preserve the truths of the faith transmitted through the Scriptures and Tradition. The bishops in communion with the Pope form this body. They are responsible for preserving and passing on the faith handed on by the Apostles.

What Does the Magisterium Teach?

The Magisterium has the right but also the duty to preserve and share the Church's teaching, and serves us by ensuring us we will not be led astray. We can be confident we have received the truth that allows us to have a relationship with God and that leads to our salvation.

Changing Guidelines for Changing Circumstances

The Magisterium interprets and preserves the heritage of faith contained in the Scriptures and Tradition, but it does not change it. Various disciplinary, liturgical, and devotional traditions, however, can be changed under the guidance of the Magisterium. For instance, disciplinary rules on fasting and abstinence have changed over the years.

Your grandparents, for example, may remember when Catholics abstained from meat every Friday. For centuries, the Church had taught the faithful to abstain from eating meat on Fridays in order to commemorate Jesus' suffering and death. In 1966, however, in his "Apostolic Constitution on Penance," Pope Paul VI adjusted the law on fasting and abstinence. He spoke of the danger of purely external practices and stressed that acts of penitence, such as abstinence and fasting, be intimately related to inner conversion, prayer, and works of mercy. He called for new penitential practices well-suited to the times and to the goal of inner conversion and asked that all the faithful voluntarily adopt penitential practices that turn them away from sin and prepare them to encounter God.

The *Catechism of the Catholic Church* is one tool the Church uses to present the faith. The *Catechism* describes itself as "an organic synthesis of the essential and fundamental contents of Catholic **doctrine,** as regards both faith and morals, in the light of the Second Vatican Council and the whole of the Church's Tradition" (11). If we look to the *Catechism,* we can see that its presentation of the faith, like that of many earlier catechisms, is built on four pillars:

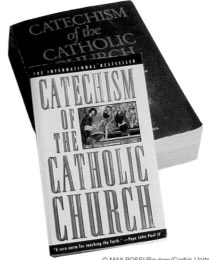

© MAX ROSSI/Reuters/Corbis United States Conference of Catholic Bishops

- **Pillar I: The profession of faith (the Creed).** Based on the Nicene Creed, this first part of the *Catechism* expands upon the Creed by exploring related concepts. The content of the book you are reading comes in large part from this section of the *Catechism.*
- **Pillar II: The sacraments of faith.** This second part explains how God's salvation was brought about through Jesus Christ and the Holy Spirit. It shows how salvation is made present in the sacred actions of the Church's liturgy, especially in the Seven Sacraments.
- **Pillar III: The life of faith (the Commandments).** The third part presents the ways human beings can achieve eternal happiness through freely chosen right conduct with the help of God's grace and law. Right conduct fulfills the commandments to love God and neighbor as explained through the Ten Commandments.

doctrine

An official, authoritative teaching of the Church based on the Revelation of God.

Catholic Wisdom

Pastoral Constitution on the Church in the Modern World

These are the opening words from Vatican II's *Pastoral Constitution on the Church in the Modern World:*

The joys and the hopes, the griefs and the anxieties of the men of this age, especially those who are poor or in any way afflicted, these are the joys and hopes, the griefs and anxieties of the followers of Christ. Indeed, nothing genuinely human fails to raise an echo in their hearts. (1)

- **Pillar IV: The prayer of the believer (the Lord's Prayer).**
  The last part of the *Catechism* presents the meaning and
  significance of prayer in the lives of Church members.
  It also examines in depth the Lord's Prayer, the Church's
  quintessential prayer, which was given to us by Jesus.

When you want to know what the Church teaches, the *Catechism of the Catholic Church* is a good place to start.

Because God created us with a longing for him, we have
the obligation to search for the truth about God and his
Church. We are then also obliged to embrace and assent to
the truth preserved by the Magisterium. ✝

Article 50   Indefectibility and Infallibility

Why do you think
Jesus used keys as
a symbol of spiritual
authority?

The Church is both indefectible and infallible—incorruptible and without error. The Church as a whole possesses
these charisms despite the reality that individual members of
the Church have faults and make mistakes.

© Arte & Immagini srl/CORBIS

Indefectibility

The **indefectibility of the Church** means that the one Church established by Jesus will remain, uncorrupted and faithful to Christ's teachings, until the end of human history. Jesus gave this promise of indefectibility to the Church when he said to Peter, "You are Peter, and upon this rock I will build my church, and the gates of the netherworld shall not prevail against it" (Matthew 16:18). Jesus promised that not even the powers of death would be able to overcome the Church. The gift of indefectibility belongs to the Church alone, and not to any individual member of the Church.

The First Vatican Council declared that under the leadership of Peter and his successors as popes, the Church will remain "indestructible until the end of time" ("The Bishop of Rome Is Peter's Successor"). The Second Vatican Council taught that by "the power of the Holy Spirit the Church is the faithful spouse of the Lord and will never fail to be a sign of salvation in the world" (*Church in the Modern World,* 43). The Church remains faithful to Christ's teaching until the end of time in order for all people to achieve salvation and communion with the Trinity. Even during the time of the final tribulation, the Church will remain firm.

indefectibility of the Church
The Church's remaining uncorrupted and faithful to Christ's teachings, until the end of human history.

A Church of Saints and Sinners

The Church has the gift of indefectibility, but individual members of the Church still have defects. The early desert monks and nuns had a favorite saying, from the Book of Proverbs: "The just man falls seven times and rises again" (24:16).

These men and women went to the desert to dedicate themselves to a life of holiness, yet they knew they would often fall short. By God's grace, however, they would rise again and go on trying.

Even the Pope sins: he has a father confessor and receives the Sacrament of Penance and Reconciliation. Knowing that we are all sinners, we nevertheless trust in Christ's promise that his Church, the Bride of Christ, will always remain faithful to him.

Infallibility

There is a relationship between indefectibility and infallibility. If the Church is without defect, it must also be without mistake, or not fallible, in her teachings. Recall that infallibility is the Gift of the Holy Spirit to the whole Church by which the leaders of the Church—the Pope and the bishops in union with him—are protected from fundamental error when teaching on a matter of faith and morals. This includes all elements of doctrine. The gift of infallibility ensures that the truths of the faith are preserved for all generations, correctly taught, and properly observed by the faithful. The gift of infallibility can take more than one form.

The Pope, as the supreme pastor and teacher of all the faithful, may proclaim infallible teaching on his own authority. When a pope makes such a definitive teaching, it is known as being *ex cathedra*. *Ex cathedra* is a Latin term meaning "from the chair." The term refers to the Pope's authority as the successor to Peter, an authority symbolized by the image of the Pope sitting in Peter's chair. The Pope's gift of infallibility applies in only very specific circumstances, when the Pope expressly acts in his position as the supreme pastor and with the authority of the Apostles to define a specific matter of faith or morality for the belief of the whole Church. When the Pope makes such a pronouncement, he is speaking as the supreme teacher of the universal Church rather than as a private individual.

The worldwide body of the bishops also has this gift of infallibility when, in union with the Pope, they agree

Pray It!

Praying for the Church

Eucharistic Prayer I of the Mass includes a prayer that the Lord protect and guide his Church, as well as those who lead it:

To you, therefore, most merciful Father, we make humble prayer and petition through Jesus Christ, your Son, our Lord: that you accept and bless these gifts, these offerings, these holy and unblemished sacrifices, which we offer you firstly for your holy catholic Church. Be pleased to grant her peace, to guard, unite and govern her throughout the whole world, together with your servant N. our Pope and N. our Bishop, and all those who, holding to the truth, hand on the catholic and apostolic faith. (*Roman Missal*)

that a certain doctrine regarding faith and morals is to be definitively held by the faithful. This infallible authority is most clearly expressed when the bishops are gathered in an **Ecumenical Council,** a gathering of all Catholic bishops, convened by the Pope and under his authority and guidance. The last Ecumenical Council was Vatican Council II, opened by Pope John XXIII in 1962.

An example of the first form of infallible authority occurred when Pope Pius XII proclaimed *ex cathedra* the Assumption of Mary to be a **dogma** of faith. An example of the second form of infallibility, exercised by the bishops in union with the Pope, was the teaching of the Council of Chalcedon (AD 451). At the time, Christians debated the exact relationship between Christ's human and divine natures. Using the teaching of Pope Leo I as one of its guidelines, the Council stated that the two natures exist "without confusion, change, division, or separation" *(Christ, the Eternal King [Sempiternus Rex Christus], Encyclical of Pope Pius XII on the Council of Chalcedon, 23).* ✝

Ecumenical Council
A gathering of the Church's bishops from around the world convened by the Pope or approved by him to address pressing issues in the Church.

dogma
Teachings recognized as central to Church teaching, defined by the Magisterium and accorded the fullest weight and authority.

Article 51 The Magisterium and Truth

The Church's teachings can seem overwhelming to someone approaching them for the first time. We might want to ask, "Of these teachings and truths, which ones are the ones I *really* need to know?" Luckily the Church has a hierarchy or order of truths, making it possible to identify the most fundamental truths and to see how other truths are connected to them.

Hierarchy of Truths

The hierarchy of truths does not mean that some truths are less relevant to our faith but rather that some truths are more fundamental and illuminate other truths. The Trinity, for example, is the central mystery of the Christian faith and "the source of all the other mysteries of faith, the light that enlightens them" (*CCC*, 234).

It is important for the believer to see that all of the Church teachings are interconnected and that it would be impossible to isolate one teaching and disregard it without

also disregarding other truths of the faith associated with it.

Dogmas are those doctrines that are recognized as central to Church teaching, defined by the Magisterium, and accorded the fullest weight and authority. Dogmas express the truths we need to know for our salvation. They do not involve intellectual belief alone, however. Their truth contributes to our spiritual and ethical growth. Conversely, if we are growing in our spiritual and ethical lives, we will understand dogmas better.

Truth and Relativism

Truth of any type can seem suspicious to some people today. Because of this it can be tempting to look at a Church teaching as simply one viewpoint among many. Some people in our culture intend to be tolerant and inclusive by hesitating to say what is true and what is not. Without realizing it, however, those people may come to think that truth is actually relative, that it depends on a person's opinion or viewpoint. This way of thinking is called relativism.

Live It!

Making Friday Special Again

Our bishops teach us to make every Friday a special day of penance and spiritual discipline in order to commemorate the suffering and death that Jesus underwent for our sakes. They encourage us to choose something that is personally meaningful. Consider some of these options:

- Continue the ancient tradition of abstaining from meat on every Friday. This can be a great weekly reminder (for yourself and others) of your Catholic identity, as well as a reminder not to become too attached to the things of this world.
- Commit to saying extra prayers.
- Commit to a "spiritual fast" from music, television, or computer time to focus better on growing in your spiritual life.
- Commit to volunteer work that helps the less fortunate.
- Commit to extra acts of kindness or thoughtfulness at home or school.

One indicator that relativism cannot be an accurate philosophy is that it is built on the premise that there is no absolute truth. Well, of course, this premise needs to be truly true for relativism to work. Relativism inherently contradicts itself.

"God is Truth itself, whose words cannot deceive. This is why one can abandon oneself in full trust to the truth and faithfulness of his word in all things" (*CCC*, 215). Remember from your study of the Genesis stories of Creation and the Fall that the first sin came out of a lack of trust in God, the suggestion by the serpent that the all-loving God was keep-

The Galileo Controversy

In 1633 Church officials condemned the Italian scientist Galileo Galilei for teaching that the earth revolved around the sun, because this idea appeared to contradict biblical statements that the earth stands still while the sun moves (see, for example, Joshua 10:13).

In his reflections on the affair, Pope John Paul II concluded that Church officials mistakenly confused scientific and revealed knowledge, using the Scriptures to make a judgment about a scientific fact, something that it is not competent to do.

ing something good from the first humans. God wants all good things for us, and these good things include Truth.

Be aware, though, of the opposing philosophy of relativism as you talk about your faith. You may need to differentiate between respect and acceptance of persons with contradictory beliefs and acceptance of the contradictory beliefs themselves. ✝

Part Review

1. Define *Magisterium* and explain its significance for the Church.

2. What are believers required to do in response to the teachings of the Magisterium?

3. What does it mean that the Church is indefectible?

4. What does it mean that the Church is infallible?

5. What is the central mystery of the Christian faith?

6. Explain the hierarchy of truths.

The Church and Young People

Part 1

You Have Been Called

In this section we look at some implications of what you've learned about Church for your own life. Recall that Jesus called his Apostles to follow him, built a relationship with them, and sent them out into the world to further his mission. You too have been called to follow Christ. You are free to choose your response as were the Apostles. If you respond and come to him, your relationship with him will grow.

To first hear our call and then to keep our relationship with Christ alive, we need some gifts and skills. We need to learn how to read the Scriptures in a prayerful way. We need to receive grace from the Sacraments. We need to know how to pray in various ways. The Scriptures, along with the Tradition, help us to understand God's Revelation, which, as you learned in an earlier course, is essential for our lives as Christians. If you are like most Catholic teens in the United States, God called you to new life in the Christ through the Sacrament of Baptism and since then you have received graces from other Sacraments.

God constantly calls all of us into communion with himself and others. The Church's call means that we will come to know God more intimately and come to have significant relationships with others who are his disciples. You are called to be part of this convoked assembly, the Church. Finding friends who can support your growth in faith is important. There are various opportunities at your Catholic school and in your parish to meet these friends.

The topics covered in this part are:

- Article 52: "Called by God to Belong to the Church" (page 199)

- Article 53: "Christ Enriches Us through Participation in the Life of the Church" (page 202)

- Article 54: "Called to Community" (page 206)

Article 52 Called by God to Belong to the Church

Perhaps at some point in your life, you received a wonderful gift. It could have been something material, something you had wanted for a long time but could never have asked for, or a relationship like a great friend or new sister or brother. When you look back at that moment, you might think: "Why me? I would never have expected that I would be given such a gift or that something so wonderful would have happened to me!"

Recall that the Church is the convocation or assembly of people whom God calls together to be in a special relationship with him. God calls everyone to the unbelievable gift of the Church. God's desire to be in relationship with us is extraordinary. The additional gifts we receive as members of the Church are due to God's love. He created the world, and all of humanity, out of love. He created us and gives us free will. We must freely respond to his call because he will not force us to come to him and receive his gifts. In addition to receiving gifts from the Church, we need to give the gift of ourselves to God and the Church.

Your Call from God

People can think that being called by God would be a dramatic, startling experience involving angels or a cloud or a trumpet in the background followed by God's instructions about what to do next. Saint Paul did have a spectacular call

Catholic Wisdom

A Christmas Greeting from the Pope

In a 2008 Christmas greeting, Pope Benedict XVI made the following remarks:

> We take too much for granted in our daily lives: the fact that God speaks, that God answers our questions; the fact that, with human words, he speaks to us personally. We can listen to him, come to know him and understand him. We can also realize that he can enter our life and shape it, and that we can emerge from our own lives to enter into the immensity of his mercy.
>
> ("Address of His Holiness Benedict XVI to the Members of the Roman Curia for the Traditional Exchange of Christmas Greetings")

that caused him to fall off his horse and be blinded, but for many people God's call is more subtle.

Most Catholic teens began the Christian life through the Sacrament of Baptism as infants. Perhaps this is the case with you. If you were baptized as an infant, you weren't able to knowingly respond to God's call, but your parents and godparents were able to do so. Your parents brought you to Baptism as their parents may have brought them. As Jesus said, parents "know how to give good gifts" to their children (Matthew 7:11). Think of all the good things parents do for their children, such as providing them with an education as well as the basics of food, clothing, and shelter. At the Baptism of infants, parents promise to do an additional good thing. They promise to help their children come to know God and to participate fully in the Church.

Receiving the Eucharist for the first time is a special experience. How did your family celebrate this event?

Your Life in the Sacraments

Through the Sacrament of Baptism, you were incorporated into the Church. You were immersed in the waters of Baptism, or the waters were poured over your head, as you died

and rose with Christ and were freed from Original Sin in the name of the Father, and of the Son, and of the Holy Spirit. You were anointed with **Sacred Chrism**, incorporated into the Body of Christ as priest, prophet, and king. Your white garment symbolized that you had "put on Christ," and your candle, lit from the Easter candle, symbolized that Christ has enlightened you as "the light of the world."

At about age seven or eight, the **age of reason,** many of you received the Sacraments of Penance and Reconciliation and the Eucharist for the first time. In the Sacrament of Penance and Reconciliation, you were able to receive God's mercy for sins you had committed against God and his Church. You learned how to examine your conscience, confess sins to the priest, and complete your penance.

When you received your First Communion, the Eucharist, you received the Sacrament that is at the center of our

Sacred Chrism

Perfumed olive oil that has been consecrated. It is used for anointing in the Sacraments of Baptism, Confirmation, and Holy Orders.

age of reason

The age at which a person can be morally responsible. This is generally regarded to be the age of seven.

Getting Involved in Your Faith

If you get involved in your parish's youth ministry or your school's campus ministry, you are likely to encounter teens who share a desire to grow in faith. Many may be seeking a break from some of the social pressure they feel in other settings. They may also want to make good friends with whom they can explore the life God calls us to. Parish-based youth ministries and school-based campus ministries provide opportunities to understand the Gospel message and discern how to apply its truths in daily life today. These ministries can also help teens to get more involved in practices of faith such as praying, serving others, and participating in the Sacraments.

faith. You were able to be in a special communion with Jesus and, through him, with the Father and the Holy Spirit as well. Weekly this Sacrament nourishes your spiritual life, protects you from sin, and unites you more fully with the Body of Christ.

You may have already received the Sacrament of Confirmation, or maybe you are still waiting to receive it. Through this Sacrament you receive the Gifts of the Holy Spirit. Baptism, Confirmation, and the Eucharist together are called the Sacraments of Christian Initiation.

Learning More about God and His Church

Your parents are also giving you the gift of a Catholic education. You will learn more about God and his Church through religion classes, books like this, retreats, liturgy experiences, and the positive examples of adults and older students who are serious about their faith. These adults, particularly, are there to answer your questions about the faith, to direct you to additional information about the Church, or to help you to apply a teaching to a real-life situation. It is difficult to realize that one is called, actually live out that call, and share the Good News with others if one does not know what the Church is all about.

God calls everyone throughout their lives. When God call us, he calls us to the Church. Part of what is exciting about the Church is that it is an assembly of people whom God has called and who have responded with a yes. With all those others who have responded to God's call, we are one family through faith and Baptism. We are united in love by the Holy Spirit. We are the Body of Christ in the world. ☩

Article 53 Christ Enriches Us through Participation in the Life of the Church

God wants to gift you with his love, and your parents have provided you with opportunities to gain the skills and knowledge you need to grow in faith. To get to know Christ better and receive his grace, take advantage of the opportunities. The Scriptures, the Sacraments, and personal prayer are three important ways Christ offers us the opportunity to get to know him and to receive his grace.

The Sacred Scriptures

We are inundated by words. We are in constant communication with one another. Cell phones are seemingly a necessity. We can text and tweet to our heart's content—at times ignoring the person next to us!

So when we call Jesus the Word of God, are we saying that he is one word among many in our lives? No. We are saying that he is the unique Word through which God has chosen to speak to us. "Christ, the Son of God made man, is the Father's one, perfect, and unsurpassable Word. In him he has said everything; there will be no other word than this one" (*CCC*, 65).

In reading and praying with the Scriptures, we not only learn more about Jesus and his life, death, Resurrection, and Ascension, but also encounter Jesus himself. Reading and praying with the Scriptures is a skill as well as a grace. It takes time and involves patience and commitment. But if we listen, we will hear him, offering us hope and encouragement in our lives. If some particular words speak to you, hang on to them! Repeat them in your mind. Take them along with you. The Sacred Scriptures are a gift from God, right there in the Bible, but in order to appreciate the gift, we need to open it up.

The Scriptures are an essential element of our lives as Christians, for as Saint Jerome said, "Ignorance of the Scriptures is ignorance of Christ"[1] (*CCC*, 133).

"The Church 'forcefully and specifically exhorts all the Christian faithful . . . to learn "the surpassing knowledge of Jesus Christ," by frequent reading of the divine Scriptures'" (*CCC*, 133).

© Kelly Redinger/Design Pics/Corbis

aspiration

A short prayer meant to be memorized and repeated throughout the day. The word comes from the Latin *aspirare*, "to breathe upon." In this way we can heed Saint Paul's injunction to pray without ceasing and continually turn our thoughts toward God.

The Sacraments

We are called to the Sacraments because they are gifts from Christ that bring us face to face with God. We don't literally see God visually, but we know he is with us and loves us. We encounter grace most fully in the Sacraments, and through grace we participate in God's divine life, the life of the Trinity. When we celebrate the Sacraments with the required disposition, an attitude of openness to God's love, we are able to recognize his presence more clearly. The Sacraments are efficacious signs of grace that truly make the graces proper to each Sacrament present.

The Gospels show us how Christ instituted the Sacraments, established the meaning of each Sacrament, and commissioned his disciples to celebrate them.

The Sacraments fall into three categories:

1. **Baptism, Confirmation, and the Eucharist** are the Sacraments of Christian Initiation, because they are the foundation of Christian life. Baptism is the first Sacrament celebrated, because it makes us members of Christ and part of the Church. Confirmation strengthens us and is necessary to complete baptismal grace. The Eucharist nourishes us with Christ's Body and Blood in order to transform us into the image of Christ and enable us to live as his dis-

One Monk's Favorite Prayer

What is your favorite prayer?

John Cassian (AD 360–435) was a monk who wrote that his own favorite kind of prayer was called "arrow prayer." It was prayer that was short, direct, and focused. It flew straight and true to God. These prayers were somewhat like what we call **aspirations** (breathings) today. Perhaps you have heard of these: "My Jesus, mercy" or "Jesus, Mary, Joseph." The name of Jesus, prayerfully repeated, is a prayer. Cassian's favorite prayer was: "O God, come to my assistance. O Lord, make haste to help me." He maintained that this prayer was always necessary and helpful. If we are sad, we need God's help to overcome our sadness. If we are happy, we need God's help to express and share our happiness.

Centuries later this prayer is still said by the Church at the beginning of the Liturgy of the Hours. You might like to choose or make up your own "arrow prayer" and pray it often.

ciples. The Eucharist is the high point of Christian life and all the Sacraments are oriented toward it.

2. **Anointing of the Sick and Penance and Reconciliation** are the Sacraments of Healing because through them the Church continues Jesus' mission to heal and forgive sins.

3. **Holy Orders and Matrimony** are the Sacraments at the Service of Communion. These Sacraments contribute to the Church's mission primarily through service to others.

© The Crosiers / Gene Plaisted, OSC

Our response to God's call means having an active liturgical life and, in turn, God calls us through this life. We should also witness other people as they receive the Sacraments. Attending ceremonies of the Sacrament of Matrimony, being present during Baptisms, or attending a friend's Confirmation strengthens our own faith and relationship to the Body of Christ.

You will be able to study the Sacraments in greater depth in a subsequent course.

Prayer

Through the Church, God calls us to be people of prayer, yet another gift. Notice the picture of Jesus knocking on a wooden door on this page. Strangely, this door does not have a handle on the outside. Jesus cannot open the door from his side. The person on the inside has to open the door to Jesus.

Pray It!

Saint Ignatius's Prayer for Generosity

We usually need to ask God's help to grow in holiness. This prayer is a good model:

> Lord, teach me to be generous.
> Teach me to serve you as you deserve;
> to give and not to count the cost,
> to fight and not to heed the wounds,
> to toil and not to seek for rest,
> to labor and not to ask for reward,
> save that of knowing that I do your will.
> Amen.

Prayer is something like that picture. Prayer is a door to Christ that can be opened at any time, but it must be opened from the inside. Only you can open the door of your life to Christ, through prayer.

Learning prayers or learning how to pray takes practice and guidance, and people pray in many different ways. Luckily there is no "one size fits all" way of praying. To begin, choose a time when you can say a short prayer asking Jesus to bless your day. Ask his help for the things that did not go so well. Ask him to be with you tomorrow. And he will be— right behind that door that only you can open.

Prayer is a vital necessity. Without it we fail to follow the lead of the Holy Spirit and we fall into sin. Prayer cannot be separated from our lives. God calls the Church to pray constantly, "giving thanks always and for everything in the name of our Lord Jesus Christ to God the Father" (Ephesians 5:20). We can accomplish this when we unite prayer with the things that we do. It is always possible to pray because the Risen Christ is always with us. ✝

Article 54 Called to Community

We know that God created both a woman and a man in Genesis because, as he declared, "It is not good for the man to be alone" (2:18). Through the account of the Fall, God teaches us that he wants his people to live in harmony with him, with creation, and with one another.

God wants his people to be in communion with him and others, and he wants us to have friends that bring us closer to him. The desire to be in relationship with others is wired into us. Even as infants, we are most drawn to the image of a human face. We have all experienced loneliness, an indicator of our need for others and for God.

The people in our lives are also gifts from God and ways God can communicate with us. You may have heard someone say, "He is such a Godsend," or found that you feel much better about yourself after you talk an issue through with a friend than if you stewed about it on your own. Friends can help us to learn about God just by who they are and how they care about us.

True Friends Help Us to Grow in Faith

The Book of Proverbs has this to say about friendship: "Some friends bring ruin on us, / but a true friend is more loyal than a brother" (18:24). True friends help us to grow in faith and as members of the Body of Christ. Even if we have experienced betrayal by friends before, each of us will find companions who meet us where we are and help us to be all we can be. True friends do the following:

- They build us up and encourage us in our gifts and talents rather than envy them.
- They support us and do not put us down, especially in front of others.
- They tell us the truth and do not make false promises.
- They keep confidences, as breaking confidences is one of the quickest ways to lose a friend.
- They share our values.
- They support us as we grow in faith.

Friends in Mission: Ignatius of Loyola and Francis Xavier

Saint Ignatius Loyola (1491–1556) studied for the priesthood. Then, in Paris, he met Saint Francis Xavier (1506–1552), and they became friends. Saint Ignatius founded the Society of Jesus, the Jesuits. Saint Francis was a member of the first group to take their vows.

When a missionary was needed in India, Ignatius chose Francis. Ignatius knew he would never see his friend again; there was no phone, no Internet, no text messaging, but only letters spanning the long distance from India to Italy. Even so, their friendship survived, for they shared the same ideal: to do all "for the greater glory of God." Wherever Francis was, Ignatius was there too. They were both canonized in 1622.

Some people have a lot of friends. Others are happier with two or three good friends. Of course, in order to find good friends, one has to be a good friend.

Of Sock Hops and Bobby Socks

Where can you find a true friend who can help you to grow as a Catholic?

Your grandparents may tell of gathering with their Catholic friends at weekly sock hops. These "hops" were usually held in the parish or school gymnasium, and everyone wore socks so that the hard leather heels and soles of their shoes would not scratch the gym floor.

Weekly sock hops may be a thing of the past, but there are plenty of opportunities to meet Catholic friends today. Your school is a primary example! You may have already encountered friends in class, at lunch, or in extracurricular activities. Many parishes offer activities for teens and have other ministry opportunities for adults and teens together. Parish or school retreats provide opportunities for socializing and for deeper discussion with other teens. You may find a friend who shares your values and interests through volunteering with parish- or school-sponsored service groups whose members may tutor, coach, serve at food kitchens, or visit people who need company.

In what service projects have you participated? How does service bring us closer to God and to other members of the Body of Christ?

© Bill Wittman / www.wpwittman.com

There are service opportunities in the Church related to each of its three meanings, which were discussed in article 1, "The Meaning of Church": the assembly gathered for liturgy, particularly for the Eucharist; the diocese; and the world-wide Church. Service in your own parish may take the form of helping in a food bank, working at a social event for older people or children, or participating in a service event outside the parish with other parishioners.

Body of Christ
A term that when capitalized designates Jesus' Body in the Eucharist, or the entire Church, which is also referred to as the Mystical Body of Christ.

Service opportunities occur on a diocesan level too. Sometimes teens from several parishes will gather for a larger service opportunity. A diocese may then send teens from different parishes on projects. Some service groups that work at the local parish or diocesan level have national or even global outreaches. Teens travel to other parts of the country to help people recover from natural disasters or may even go to other countries and build homes. How exciting it would be to participate in activities at your parish and then, someday, be one of the thousands of young people participating with the Pope in World Youth Day! It is very possible.

We Are Members of the Body of Christ

God has called us to a big family of faith, the People of God. As members of the **Body of Christ,** we are never alone. Even

Live It!

Catholics Are Not All the Same, Thank God!

As human beings we want to belong. Yet in everyday life we can find ourselves defining ourselves and others by our differences rather than by what unites us. This can sound like: "They dress differently. They listen to different music. They play (or don't play) sports. They are just not like us."

Recall the image of the Church as the Body of Christ. Each person who belongs to the Body offers something unique, and each person's gifts are important. Instead of defining yourself and others by your differences, and seeing these differences as negatives, try to see these very differences as gifts, evidence of God's creativity touching your life. If every snowflake is different, why shouldn't every human being, including you, be different as well?

If you are confident in your giftedness, you will all the more welcome and accept the uniqueness you find in others. If you do, you will not lose anything, but you will gain more understanding of the infinite diversity of God's creative power. Each one of us is gifted in different ways, yet we are all God's children.

hermits are intimately connected with the rest of the Body of Christ. The Church is diverse, its members coming from every nation and people. We can rejoice in what we have in common—our Catholic faith and relationship with God— and also the diversity of gifts we exchange with our brothers and sisters in the faith.

When God calls to us, he provides us with many opportunities to learn about him and different ways to respond to him. We can come to know him through reading the Scriptures, receiving the Sacraments, praying, and spending time with the people in our lives. As we take advantage of the gifts he has given us, we learn more about the Church and what it means to be a disciple. In the next several articles, we examine what being a disciple involves in daily life and how the Holy Spirit will support us as we are sent to share the Good News of Jesus Christ. ✞

Part Review

1. Explain why God's call to us is a gift.

2. How did Jesus call his Apostles?

3. Why are Baptism, Confirmation, and the Eucharist called the Sacraments of Christian Initiation?

4. What are the effects of the Sacrament of Baptism?

5. Why does Saint Jerome say that if we are ignorant of the Scriptures, then we are ignorant of Christ?

6. What is the relationship between the picture on page 205 and the life of prayer?

7. How do we know that God created us to be in community with others?

8. Why is a member of the Body of Christ never alone?

Part 2

Sent with the Holy Spirit

In the last part, we looked at how you are called to the Church, to Christ. Once you have gotten to know him, Christ sends you out into the world as a disciple with the help of the Holy Spirit. Although discipleship is an ongoing call and brings you closer to Jesus, discipleship does not simply mean following Jesus in an abstract way; it also means following him as a servant.

Being a disciple of Jesus means being part of his mission. It means being salt and light for the world and sharing your God-given talents for the sake of others. Many of your ordinary skills can make a big difference in the world.

Discipleship takes place in daily life, and it sometimes means acting in a way that is counter to the values of the culture. Prayer and the sacramental life are key aspects of discipleship. Good everyday choices resemble "the little way" of Saint Thérèse.

Our study of the Church has focused on the contributions of the Holy Spirit to the Church even though each Divine Person of the Trinity contributes to her well-being. Christ does not send you out alone but with the Holy Spirit. Making good choices involves living with our goal, life in communion with the Trinity, in mind.

The topics covered in this part are:

- Article 55: "Sent as a Disciple" (page 212)

- Article 56: "Discipleship in Daily Life" (page 215)

- Article 57: "Empowered by the Holy Spirit" (page 219)

Article 55 Sent as a Disciple

The Apostle John wrote to the earliest Christian disciples, "Children, let us love not in word or speech but in deed and truth" (1 John 3:18). This section presents some ways you as young people take these words to heart and live out your discipleship, not in words or speech, but in actions from the heart.

Salt and Light

When Jesus said to his disciples, "You are the salt of the earth" (Matthew 5:13), what did he mean? Why would he compare his disciples to salt rather than another spice? Why would Jesus say, "You are the light of the world" (Matthew 5:14)? Let's explore these metaphors.

Of all the spices, salt may be the most necessary and the tastiest. On its own it has a very strong bite. But when mixed with other foods, its zest enhances the other flavors in the foods. Christ calls us to bring out the true flavor and goodness of the world not only in ourselves but in others.

When Jesus said, "You are the light of the world," he went on to explain that people do not hide light under a bushel basket but put it on the lampstand "where it gives light to all in the house" (Matthew 5:15). In this way Jesus told us we each have talents and gifts to share with others and we should not hide them or keep them to ourselves.

The Church Needs You

Pope Benedict XVI reminded a stadium of thirty thousand young people that they are an important part of the Church:

> My appeal to you today, young people . . . is this: do not waste your youth. Do not seek to escape from it. Live it intensely. . . . You, young people, are not just the future of the Church and of humanity, as if we could somehow run away from the present. . . . The Church needs you, as young people, to manifest to the world the face of Jesus Christ, visible in the Christian community. Without this young face, the Church would appear disfigured.
>
> ("Meeting with Youth: Address of His Holiness Benedict XVI," 7)

Being Salt and Light for the World

What skills do you have? Can you read and write and solve math equations? Are you learning how to drive? Maybe you speak more than one language or have played the violin for a time. Perhaps you play basketball, tell great jokes, or are a good listener.

Read the quotation from Pope Benedict XVI in the sidebar. He says not to waste your youth; the Church needs you now. If you were to use your God-given abilities only for yourself, imagine how the metaphor about the bushel basket and light would relate to your life. Would the basket be covering the light?

How Are You Needed?

You may have a particular talent that gives joy to others, like a talent for music, art, writing, or mechanics. If so, work on it! Share it with others! Don't hide it under a basket, but take it as far as it will go. It will enhance your life and the lives of many other people.

If you can bake, you can hold a bake sale to raise money for people in need. If you can listen, you can visit a lonely older person who wants to share years of wisdom with you.

Service can take many forms. You can help out at a homeless shelter, visit a nursing home, or hold a fundraiser, like a car wash, to raise money for a charity.

© Bill Wittman / www.wpwittman.com

© Used with permission of Place of Grace; La Crosse, WI

The Catholic Worker movement has homes around the country run by volunteers that provide assistance for men, women, and children in need. Is there a Catholic Worker house in your community?

If you can do simple math calculations and read, you can tutor a younger child. If not you, then who?

Your gifts and talents are needed by the Body of Christ around the world. Catholic Relief Services (CRS) is an international relief and development agency of the Catholics in the United States, helping people in need all over the globe. Young people have raised money for this worthy cause by sponsoring car washes or running mini-marathons. The world needs your gifts.

The Catholic Campaign for Human Development (CCHD), sponsored by the bishops of the United States to increase the standard of living for people in the United States, has a yearly call for donations that are put to use in projects for good in our own country. The Body of Christ needs your gifts.

In your own parish, why not volunteer to share your singing talent in the choir or offer your services as a musi-

Catholic Wisdom

Change Love

Dorothy Day (1897–1980) was one of the founders of the Catholic Worker, a movement dedicated to the principles of nonviolence and to helping the poor in a practical way. The first Catholic Worker house and soup kitchen was founded in New York City, and many others have since been established in our country and around the world. This is a quotation from Dorothy's writings:

> We can, to a certain extent, change the world; we can work for the oasis, the little cell of joy and peace in a harried world. We can throw the pebble in the pond and be confident that its ever widening circle will reach around the world. We repeat, there is nothing we can do but love, and, dear God, please enlarge our hearts to love each other, to love our neighbor, to love our enemy as our friend.

("Love Is the Measure," in *The Catholic Worker*, June 1946)

cian? Does your parish need greeters? altar servers? sacristy help? catechists? ushers? Your parish needs your gifts.

Your local town or city needs you too. A coach working with younger children learning to play basketball could use your help to run drills and praise the kids for their improvement. Notice how being salt can help other people to shine.

If you can bag a lunch, you can help at a soup kitchen. In one town the teens from several parishes joined forces to go door-to-door collecting cans of food for a neighborhood food pantry. Two girls' volleyball teams, from rival high schools, played a volleyball game for premature babies in their local hospital. Admission proceeds went to the families of the hospitalized babies. If you investigate your own area, you might find a need that calls you to serve. Your community needs your gifts.

When we consider national and worldwide issues of importance, we find even more ways to serve. Is there an issue that impacts your city or state? Write your local representatives or those in the U.S. Congress. Many young people participate in right-to-life marches each year, traveling to their local capitol or to Washington, D.C., to do so. Let your voice be heard on these issues of national importance. Let the world taste a little of your salt! Let your light shine! ✝

Article 56 Discipleship in Daily Life

Discipleship is countercultural. Our culture so often says, "Me first!" but in the Church, we serve one another. Our culture so often says, "You are on your own," but in the Church, we are one in Jesus Christ. Our culture so often has many little rules: "Be this! Do this! Wear this! Act like this!" In the Church we adhere to the Gospel, where Jesus gives us this rule: "Do to others whatever you would have them do to you" (Matthew 7:12).

A Day in Your Life as a Disciple

Let's look at a school day to see practical ways we can live it as a disciple of Jesus. Notice the opportunities to love others that arise in your own schedule.

Morning

For some people morning is the hardest part of the day. It is more difficult to be kind when tired and stressed because you are running late. Preparing ahead of time can head off family conflicts. Going to bed earlier can lessen your fatigue.

Try to get things like books and lunch ready the night before. Use any down time, such as waiting for or riding a bus or sitting in traffic, to center yourself and to ask God's blessing on your day. Sometimes choosing love means creating the opportunity for loving interactions with other people and avoiding situations in which you are not at your best.

School

Most of your days are spent dealing with people at school. The desire for good grades is laudable, but it can also create temptation. Many students want to go on to specific colleges and universities, which can at times make grades seem more important than learning. Worrying excessively about grades can get you into trouble as a disciple. To keep your grade point average up, you might hear yourself asking, "Can I copy your homework?" Or you might be tempted to ask, "Can you get me the answers for the geometry test?"

As a student, you can live as a disciple by striving to fully utilize the gift of intellect that God has given you and by acting with integrity in all your studies.

© michaeljung/Shutterstock.com

If you experience this temptation, try to put your goals into proper perspective. More important than grades is who you are as a child of God. You are in charge of the person you become. Ask God for help with schoolwork if it becomes challenging. Go to your teachers for extra assistance rather than compromising your integrity.

Thoughts and Feelings

All day long, thoughts and feelings come into our consciousness or, in some cases, dominate it. It is natural to be distracted by the guy or girl you met last weekend, a problem with a friend, tensions at home, or your least favorite class. Amid these distractions also come thoughts such as, "I am too fat, skinny, tall, short, stupid, or smart."

Make a choice. Which thoughts or feelings will you take with you in your life? Will you accept negative thoughts? Will you internalize put-downs or rejections? Or will you discipline yourself by calmly turning your thoughts and feelings in a more positive direction or by praying and hearing the truth about you from God?

Pray It!

The Breastplate of Saint Patrick

It is thought that Saint Patrick composed this prayer as he prepared to confront a pagan king. Thus it is called a "breastplate" or body armor of prayer. You may want to pray it at various moments during your day.

Christ with me

Christ before me, Christ behind me

Christ in me

Christ beneath me, Christ above me

Christ on my right, Christ on my left

Christ when I lie down

Christ when I sit down

Christ when I arise

Christ in the heart of everyone who thinks of me

Christ in the mouth of everyone who speaks of me

Christ in every eye that sees me

Christ in every ear that hears me.

Evenings and Weekends

For some of you, the end of the day is a typical time for relaxing. Others may feel exhausted from work or from caring for younger brothers or sisters. All of you hear, "Please set the table, wash the dishes, mow the lawn, take the baby, or wash the car." Life in a household means having shared responsibilities and conflicting needs.

Perhaps you want to snap back at this adult when she or he asks you for help. Let it go and consciously choose to be cooperative for God's sake. Sacrifice your time for God and ask for his help if making this choice is difficult.

Take Responsibility for Your Faith

Being a disciple is up to you. The life of a disciple involves regular participation in the celebration of the Sacraments, the Eucharist on Sundays being the most important. You will want to receive the Sacrament of Penance and Reconciliation for forgiveness and strength. Be aware of the liturgical

Saint Thérèse of Lisieux (1873–1897)

Thérèse Martin of Lisieux, France, entered a Carmelite monastery when she was only fifteen. This was unusual for such a young girl, but she appealed personally to the Pope for this privilege.

Thérèse believed she was called to love in the little ways of everyday life. She called this way of love her "little way to God." She was convinced that anyone could follow it as she did by being considerate of others, by not pouting when disappointed, by volunteering for the job no one else wants. Through her "little way" of love, a teenager showed the rest of the Church just how it's done!

Thérèse died of tuberculosis at the age of twenty-four. Her "little way" had led to spiritual greatness.

seasons and pray with them, as they reflect all aspects of the Christian life.

Take time to pray. Stop by the chapel at school for a few minutes or carve out some regular time at home when you shut out all of the usual distractions. Read the Scriptures, write to God in a journal, pray the Rosary, thank God for the blessings he has given you, or meditate on an important word such as *love* or *Jesus* or *peace*.

A disciple is one who makes conscious choices to follow Christ's example of treating others with care and respect, spending time in prayer, being truthful, and letting God take the lead. And never forget that Christ is with you at all times. ✝

Article 57 Empowered by the Holy Spirit

We conclude our study of the Church by looking at the Nicene Creed. First we profess faith in the Father, then in the Son, and then in the Holy Spirit. In the Creed, the Church comes under the works of the Holy Spirit. The Holy Spirit is central to the life of the Church.

The Holy Spirit in the Church

Throughout this course we have seen the Holy Spirit work in the Church in many ways. On the day of Pentecost, when Jesus poured the Holy Spirit onto the Church, frightened Apostles turned into bold missionaries. Energized by the Holy Spirit, the Apostles then took to the road and spread the Good News of Jesus Christ. The Holy Spirit was at work in the heart and mind of Saint Paul and the early Apostles, guiding them to proclaim Christ's work of salvation among the Jews and Gentiles and to build up the early Church.

The Holy Spirit enabled the early martyrs to willingly accept their impending deaths, led the bishops at the early Church Councils as they articulated the truths of the faith, and set the hearts of the saints on fire with love for God, whether it was through the total renunciation of possessions and power of Saint Francis, the great wisdom of the rule written by Saint Benedict, or the little way to holiness of Saint Thérèse of Lisieux.

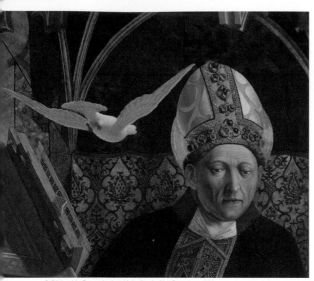

© Bildarchiv Preussischer Kulturbesitz/Art Resource, NY

The Holy Spirit worked through men and women in the Church, such as Pope Gregory the Great, and continues to work today through you.

The Holy Spirit enlivens the mind as well as the heart, and was at work in the endeavors of great theologians such as Saint Augustine and Saint Thomas Aquinas, who helped others grow in their understanding of the faith through their writings.

The gifts of the Holy Spirit help us to honor God through our abilities and talents. Over the centuries, this has resulted in magnificent expressions of praise to God, such as the grand cathedrals of the Middle Ages, the religious art of the Renaissance masters, and the timeless sacred music of Baroque composers.

The Church's history contains countless accounts of the working of the Holy Spirit in the lives of those who, like the Virgin Mary, said "Yes" to God's invitation to work in their lives, to enable them to bring him greater glory. Now, how about you?

The Acts of the Apostles

The Acts of the Apostles is sometimes called the Book of the Holy Spirit. It recounts the early days of the Church, the days after Pentecost, when the Apostles seemed to explode out of the upper room with the joyous message of Jesus' life, death, and Resurrection. The Book of Acts of the Apostles recounts their travels, their troubles, and their triumphs in those first days of the Church.

The Acts of the Apostles was written by the Evangelist Luke. It is considered his "second volume," the first volume being his Gospel. The Acts document the Church's gradual reaching out beyond the Jewish community to people of other places and other cultures. It ends with Saint Paul's imprisonment in Rome. Though this imprisonment almost foretells the unhappy ending of Paul's martyrdom, Luke sees it also as a triumph for the young Church: This little band of disciples, carrying the message of Jesus, has penetrated the very heart of the Roman Empire.

Living with the End in Mind

Maybe you have already started looking at life after high school and the options that await you. You might be investigating colleges and thinking about what you would like to do in your future. Many teens consider the financial implications of choosing one career over another. Some anticipate being parents and would like a career that is flexible to some extent. But most people don't really think beyond their career, maybe a family, and perhaps retirement.

Your destination in life is actually not retirement but life in communion with the Trinity for all eternity. What does career planning look like in light of this destination? These might be some questions you could ask yourself:

- How is the Holy Spirit working in my life now? What talents and gifts have I been given?

- How is the Holy Spirit calling me to serve God and neighbor?

- Does fear keep me from pursuing interests because "philosophy professors do not make any money," for example? (Fear is not from the Holy Spirit, who instead brings faith, hope, and love.)

What are you planning to do after high school? You may choose to go to college, get a job, join the military, or do any number of other things. Whatever you are planning, it is important to remember that our ultimate goal is communion with God in Heaven.

© Richard T. Nowitz/CORBIS

- Are the colleges I like places that will help me grow in faith, or are they places where my faith will constantly be challenged? Will there be a Catholic community on campus that I can belong to?
- Is the career that interests me one that contributes to the well-being of other people, especially the poor?

Throughout your life you will have many significant decisions to make. Keeping in mind your final destination, invite the Holy Spirit to help you in your decision making.

Now

The Holy Spirit is at work within you now, calling you to the Church, to Christ. Instead of drowning out the sound of the Holy Spirit, take time for silence, which can be an opportunity for the Holy Spirit to speak with you. Carve out some silence for him. Exciting possibilities await you! ✝

Live It!

Honor the Holy Spirit

Choose a class project to do in honor of the Holy Spirit. The project should use your gifts and talents in some way and it should also help others. Use a brainstorming session to come up with project ideas. Put all ideas on the board. On folded pieces of paper, write the five or so ideas suggested most often. Put the pieces of paper into a box or hat. Pause for a prayer to the Holy Spirit, asking for grace to choose the best project for your class. Have the youngest person in the class close his or her eyes and draw one of the papers from the box or hat. The selected idea is the project for your class to do in honor of the Holy Spirit!

Part Review

1. What does it mean to be salt for the earth and light for the world?

2. How does Pope Benedict XVI describe you as youth today?

3. What rule does Jesus give us about how to live?

4. What are some of the ways you can take responsibility for your faith?

5. Name two ways we have seen the Holy Spirit at work during this course.

6. What is your final destination in life?

Glossary

A

actual grace: God's interventions and support for us in the everyday moments of our lives. Actual graces are important for conversion and for continuing growth in holiness. *(page 85)*

age of reason: The age at which a person can be morally responsible. This is generally regarded to be the age of seven. *(page 201)*

animate: To give life to. *(page 28)*

apostolate: The Christian person's activity that fulfills the apostolic nature of the whole Church when he or she works to extend the Kingdom of Christ to the entire world. If your school shares the wisdom of its founder, its namesake, or the charism of the religious order that founded it, it is important to learn about this person or order and his or her charism, because as a graduate you will likely want to incorporate this charism into your own apostolate. *(page 120)*

apostolic: To be founded on the Twelve Apostles. *(page 66)*

Apostolic Succession: The uninterrupted passing on of apostolic preaching and authority from the Apostles directly to all bishops. It is accomplished through the laying on of hands when a bishop is ordained in the Sacrament of Holy Orders as instituted by Christ. The office of bishop is permanent, because at Ordination a bishop is marked with an indelible, sacred character. *(page 68)*

aspiration: A short prayer meant to be memorized and repeated throughout the day. The word comes from the Latin *aspirare*, "to breathe upon." In this way we can heed Saint Paul's injunction to pray without ceasing and continually turn our thoughts toward God. *(page 204)*

Assumption of Mary: The dogma that recognizes that the body of the Blessed Virgin Mary was taken directly to Heaven after her life on earth had ended. *(page 95)*

B

bishop: One who has received the fullness of the Sacrament of Holy Orders and is a successor to the Apostles. *(page 114)*

blasphemy: Speaking, acting, or thinking about God, Jesus Christ, the Virgin Mary, or the saints in a way that is irreverent, mocking, or offensive. *(page 45)*

Body of Christ: A term that when capitalized designates Jesus' Body in the Eucharist, or the entire Church, which is also referred to as the Mystical Body of Christ. *(page 53)*

(religious) brother: A lay man in a religious order who has made permanent vows of poverty, chastity, and obedience. *(page 180)*

C

canonized: When a deceased Catholic is publicly and officially proclaimed a saint. *(page 76)*

catholic: Along with one, holy, and apostolic, *catholic* is one of the four marks of the Church. *Catholic* means "universal." The Church is catholic in two senses. She is catholic because Christ is present in her and has given her the fullness of the means of salvation and also because she reaches throughout the world to all people. *(page 98)*

celibacy: The state or condition of those who have chosen or taken vows to remain unmarried in order to devote themselves entirely to the service of the Church and the Kingdom of God. *(page 169)*

chalice: The cup used during the Mass that holds the wine before the Consecration and the Blood of Christ after the Consecration. It represents the cup used at the Last Supper and is a symbol of Jesus' sacrifice and eternal life. *(page 53)*

charism: A special gift or grace of the Holy Spirit given to an individual Christian or community, commonly for the benefit and building up of the entire Church. *(page 32)*

charismatic: The word refers to a person gifted with the charism or graces of the Holy Spirit such as healing, prophecy, and speaking in tongues. Because self-deception is always possible, the charisms claimed by such a person must be verified by the Church. *(page 34)*

chastity: The virtue by which people are able to successfully and healthfully integrate their sexuality into their total person; recognized as one of the fruits of the Holy Spirit. Also one of the vows of religious life. *(page 170)*

Church: The term Church has three inseparable meanings: (1) the entire People of God throughout the world; (2) the diocese, which is also known as the local Church; (3) the assembly of believers gathered for the celebration of the liturgy, especially the Eucharist. In the Nicene Creed, the Church is recognized as one, holy, catholic, and apostolic—traits that together are referred to as "marks of the Church." *(page 10–11)*

college of bishops: The assembly of bishops, headed by the Pope, that holds the teaching authority and responsibility in the Church. *(page 154)*

collegial: Characterized by the equal sharing of responsibility and authority among the members of a group who form a college. The bishops of the Church together with the Pope at their head form a college, which has full authority over the Church. *(page 158)*

Communion: Refers to receiving the Body and Blood of Christ. In general, your companionship and union with Jesus and other baptized Christians in the Church. This union has its origin and high point in the celebration of the Eucharist. In this sense the deepest vocation of the Church is Communion. *(page 23)*

community: A body of individuals that is unified. *(page 50)*

consecrated life: A state of life recognized by the Church in which a person publicly professes vows of poverty, chastity, and obedience. *(page 179)*

conversion: A change of heart, turning away from sin and toward God. *(page 83)*

creed: Based on the Latin credo, meaning, "I believe," a creed is an official presentation of the faith, usually prepared and presented by a council of the Church and used in the Church's liturgy. Two creeds occupy a special place in the Church's life: the Apostles' Creed and the Nicene Creed. *(page 66)*

D

diocese: Also known as a "particular" or "local" Church, the regional community of believers, who commonly gather in parishes, under the leadership of a bishop. At times, a diocese is determined not on the basis of geography but on the basis of language or rite. *(page 11)*

discernment: From a Latin word meaning "to separate or to distinguish between," it is the practice of listening for God's call in our lives and distinguishing between good and bad choices. *(page 162)*

doctrine: An official, authoritative teaching of the Church based on the Revelation of God. *(page 189)*

dogma: Teachings recognized as central to Church teaching, defined by the Magisterium and accorded the fullest weight and authority. *(page 193)*

domestic: Relating to household or family. *(page 176)*

domestic church: Another name for the first and most fundamental community of faith: the family. *(page 153)*

E

ecclesial: Of or relating to a church. *(page 116)*

Ecumenical Council: A gathering of the Church's bishops from around the world convened by the Pope or approved by him to address pressing issues in the Church. *(page 193)*

ecumenism: The movement to restore unity among all Christians. *(page 75)*

episcopal: Of or relating to a bishop. *(page 118)*

eremitic: Having to do with hermits. *(page 183)*

evangelical counsels: The call to go beyond the minimum rules of life required by God (such as the Ten Commandments and the Precepts of the Church) and strive for spiritual perfection through a life marked by a commitment to chastity, poverty, and obedience. *(page 169)*

evangelization: The proclamation of the Good News of Jesus Christ through words and witness. *(page 41)*

excommunication: A severe penalty that results from grave sin against Church law. The penalty is either imposed by a Church official or happens automatically as a result of the offense. An excommunicated person is not permitted to celebrate or receive the Sacraments. *(page 71)*

F

fiat: Latin for "let it be done." *(page 94)*

foreshadow: To represent or prefigure a person before his or her life or an event before it occurs. *(page 13)*

G

Gentile: A non-Jewish person. In the Scriptures, the Gentiles were the uncircumcised, those who did not honor the God of the Torah. In the New Testament, Saint Paul and other evangelists reached out to the Gentiles, baptizing them into the family of God. *(page 42)*

grace: The free and undeserved gift of God's loving and active presence in the universe and in our lives, empowering us to respond to his call and to live as his adopted sons and daughters. Grace restores our loving communion with the Holy Trinity, lost through sin. *(page 84)*

H

Hellenistic: Of or relating to Greek history, culture, or art after Alexander the Great. *(page 42)*

heresy: The conscious and deliberate rejection of a dogma of the Church. *(page 70)*

hermit: A person who lives a solitary life in order to commit himself or herself more fully to prayer and in some cases to be completely free for service to others. *(page 179)*

hierarchy: In general, the line of authority in the Church; more narrowly the Pope and the bishops, as successors of the Apostles, in their authoritative roles as leaders of the Church. *(page 18)*

Holy Orders, Sacrament of: The Sacrament by which members of the Church are ordained for permanent ministry in the Church as bishops, priests, or deacons. *(page 117)*

Holy See: This term is a translation of the Latin *sancta sedes*, which literally means "holy seat." The word see refers to a diocese or seat of a bishop. The Holy See is the seat of the central administration of the whole Church, under the leadership of the Pope, the Bishop of Rome. *(page 152)*

I

icon: Religious painting traditional among many Eastern Christians. Christian iconography expresses in image the same Gospel message that the Scriptures communicate by words. *(page 108)*

iconostasis: A screen or partition with doors and tiers of icons that separates the bema, the raised part of the church with the altar, from the nave, the main part of the church, in Eastern Churches. *(page 108)*

indefectibility of the Church: The Church's remaining uncorrupted and faithful to Christ's teachings, until the end of human history. *(page 191)*

indulgence: The means by which the Church takes away the punishment that a person would receive in Purgatory. *(page 72)*

infallibility: The gift given by the Holy Spirit to the Pope and the bishops in union with him to teach on matters of faith and morals without error. *(page 35)*

institute: An organization devoted to a common cause. Religious orders are a type of religious institute. *(page 179)*

intercession: A prayer on behalf of another person or group. *(page 32)*

K

Kingdom of God: The culmination or goal of God's plan of salvation, the Kingdom of God is announced by the Gospel and present in Jesus Christ. The Kingdom is the reign or rule of God over the hearts of people and, as a consequence of that, the development of a new social order based on unconditional love. The fullness of God's Kingdom will not be realized until the end of time. Also called the Reign of God or the Kingdom of Heaven. *(page 15–16)*

L

Latin Church, Latin Rite: That part of the Catholic Church that follows the disciplines and teachings of the Diocese of Rome, especially the liturgical traditions. It is called the Latin Church or Latin Rite because Latin has been the official language since the fourth century. The majority of the world's Catholics belong to the Latin Rite. *(page 166)*

laypeople (laity): All members of the Church, with the exception of those who are ordained or in consecrted life. The laity shares in Christ's role as priest, prophet, and king, witnessing to God's love and power in the world. *(page 121)*

liturgy: The Church's official, public, communal prayer. It is God's work, in which the People of God participate. The Church's most important liturgy is the Eucharist, or the Mass. *(page 11)*

M
Magisterium: The Church's living teaching office, which consists of all bishops, in communion with the Pope. *(page 34)*

marks of the Church: The four essential features or characteristics of the Church: one, holy, catholic (universal), and apostolic. *(page 63)*

martyr: A person who suffers death because of his or her beliefs. The Church has canonized many martyrs as saints. *(page 45)*

ministry: Based on a word for "service," a way of caring for and serving others and helping the Church fulfill its mission. Ministry especially refers to the work of sanctification performed by those in Holy Orders through the preaching of God's Word and the celebration of the Sacraments. The laity helps the Church fulfill its mission through lay ministries, such as that of lector or catechist. *(page 157)*

monk: Someone who withdraws from ordinary life, and lives alone or in community, in order to devote oneself to prayer and work in total dedication to God. *(page 179)*

mysterium: The hidden reality of God's plan of salvation. *(page 128)*

mystical: Having a spiritual meaning or reality that is neither apparent to the senses nor obvious to the intelligence; the visible sign of the hidden reality of salvation. *(page 57)*

N
Nicene Creed: The formal statement or profession of faith commonly recited during the Eucharist. *(page 66)*

O
Original Sin: From the Latin *origo*, meaning "beginning" or "birth." The term has two meanings: (1) the sin of the first human beings, who disobeyed God's command by choosing to follow their own will and thus lost their original holiness and became subject to death, (2) the fallen state of human nature that affects every person born into the world. *(page 93)*

P
Pentecost: The fiftieth day following Easter, which commemorates the descent of the Holy Spirit on the early Apostles and disciples. *(page 23)*

petition: A prayer form in which one asks God for help and forgiveness. *(page 32)*

presbytery, presbyterate: The name given to priests as a group, especially in a diocese; based on the Greek word *presbyter,* which means "elder." *(page 160)*

province: A grouping of two or more dioceses with an archbishop as its head. *(page 157)*

Purgatory: A state of final purification or cleansing, which one may need to enter following death and before entering Heaven. *(page 88)*

S

sacramental graces: The gifts proper to each of the Seven Sacraments. *(page 85)*

sacramentum: The visible sign of the hidden reality of salvation. *(page 128)*

Sacred Chrism: Perfumed olive oil that has been consecrated. It is used for anointing in the Sacraments of Baptism, Confirmation, and Holy Orders. *(page 201)*

Sacred Tradition: From the Latin *tradere,* meaning "to hand on." Refers to the process of passing on the Gospel message. It began with the oral communication of the Gospel by the Apostles, was written down in the Scriptures, and is interpreted by the Magisterium under the guidance of the Holy Spirit. *(page 114)*

sanctify, sanctification: To make holy; sanctification is the process of becoming closer to God and growing in holiness, taking on the righteousness of Jesus Christ with the gift of sanctifying grace. *(page 28)*

sanctifying grace: The grace that heals our human nature wounded by sin and restores us to friendship with God by giving us a share in the divine life of the Trinity. It is a supernatural gift of God, infused into our souls by the Holy Spirit, that continues the work of making us holy. *(page 85)*

schism: A major break that causes division. A schism in the Church is caused by the refusal to submit to the Pope or to be in communion with the Church's members. *(page 70)*

secular: Relating to worldly concerns; something that is not overtly religious. *(page 184)*

(religious) sister: A lay woman in a religious order who has made permanent vows of poverty, chastity, and obedience. *(page 180)*

supernatural grace: Transcending the power of human intellect and will. *(page 84)*

T

theologian: A person who studies theology. Theology is "the study of God"; the academic discipline and effort to understand, interpret, and order our experience of God and Christian faith; classically defined as "faith seeking understanding." *(page 78)*

Theology of the Body: The name given to Pope John Paul II's teachings on the human body and sexuality delivered via 129 short lectures between September 1979 and November 1984. *(page 57)*

Theotokos: A Greek title for Mary meaning "God bearer." *(page 94)*

Transubstantiation: In the Sacrament of the Eucharist, this is the name given to the action of changing the bread and wine into the Body and Blood of Jesus Christ. *(page 53)*

Trinitarian: Of or relating to the Trinity or the doctrine of the Trinity. *(page 40)*

V

vicar: Someone who serves as a substitute or agent for someone else. As the Vicar of Christ, the Pope acts for Christ, his human representative on earth. *(page 154)*

virtue: A habitual and firm disposition to do good. *(page 58)*

vocation: A call from God to all members of the Church to embrace a life of holiness. Specifically, it refers to a call to live the holy life as an ordained minister, as a vowed religious (sister or brother), in a Christian Marriage, or in single life. *(page 160)*

vow: A free and conscious commitment made to other persons (as in Marriage), to the Church, or to God. *(page 169)*

Index

Page numbers in italics refer to illustrations.

A

actions, 81, 84, 120, 142–143, 212
Acts of the Apostles, 23, 165, 220
advocates, 59, 96
Africa, 41, 44, *121,* 146
African Americans, 22
age of reason, 201
Aloysius Gonzaga, 92
Andrew Dung-Lac, 107
animation, 27–28
Annunciation, *93*
Anthony of Egypt, 107, 183
Anthony of Padua, 91
antichrist, 47
Apostles. *See also* Acts of the Apostles; Apostolic Succession; Tradition (Apostolic/Sacred); *individual Apostles*
    basics, 38
    deacons and, 165
    early Church and, 100
    Holy Spirit and, 219
    Jesus and, 9, 18, 112–114
    mission of, 39–42, 161–162
    Revelation, Book of, and, 135
Apostles' Creed, 66, 67
apostolate, 120–122
"Apostolic Constitution on Penance" (Paul VI), 188
apostolic nature of Church, 111–124
apostolic societies, 184
Apostolic Succession, 68, *72,* 114–115. *See also* bishops
Apostolic Tradition. *See* Tradition
Aquinas, Thomas, 220
archbishops, 156–157
archdioceses, 11
arrow prayer, 204
arts, 83, 220
aspirations, 204

Assumption of the Virgin Mary, 35, 95, 193
Assyrian Church of the East, 70
Athanasius, 90
Athenagoras I, 77
Augustine, 28, 220
authority, 101, 111, 113–114, 118–119, 154, 155, 172. *See also* Magisterium; *specific offices*

B

Bakhita, Josephine, 109
Baptism. *See* Sacrament of Baptism
Bar Mitzvah, *103*
Barnabus, 40
Benedict (saint), 35, 107, 219
Benedictines, 35
Benedict XVI, 28, 63, 69, 75, 152, 158–159, 199, 212
Bible, The, 116. *See* Scriptures
birth, 25, 51
Bishop of Rome, 154, 155
bishops. *See also* college of bishops; United States Conference of Catholic Bishops; *individual bishops*
    authority of, 18, 68, 72, 114–115, 172
    basics, *10,* 111, 117–120
    Body of Christ and, 149, 150, 151
    collegial nature of, 158–159
    Eucharist and, 156, 157, 161
    evangelization and, 144
    hierarchy and, 18, 156–159
    Holy Spirit and, 117, 219
    infallibility and, 35, 192–193
    Magisterium and, 187
    Peter and, 117–120, 153
    responsibilities, 149
    Sacrament of Holy Orders and, 111, 114, 117–118, 156

Black Elk, 146

Black Madonna, 110

blasphemy, 45

bodies, human, 58

Body of Christ. *See also* Eucharist; Sacrament of Baptism; Sacrament of Communion

    basics, 11, 49, 53–57, 209–210

    bishops and, 149, 150, 151

    death and, 88, 95

    friends and, 207

    Holy Spirit and, 28

    laity and, 172

    Paul on, 55

    prayers and, 134

    salvation and, 128

    sinners and, 82, 86

    unity and, 63, 64, 68

bonds of unity, 66

Book of the Holy Spirit, 220

breath, 29

Bride of Christ, 53, 56, 57, 80, 183, 191

British Isles, 41

brothers (religious), 169, 178, 180. *See also individual brothers; individual orders*

building the Church, 28–29

Byzantine Empire, 70

C

callings, 199–202

call of Christ, 81

call of God, 18, 199–200, 202

Calvin, John, 73

Calvinists, 73

canon, official, 116

cardinals, 10, *118*, 157

careers, 221

Carmelites, 178

Cassian, John, 204

Catechism of the Catholic Church, 66, 186, 189–190

cathedra, 150

Catherine of Siena, 88, 184

Catholic Campaign for Human Development (CCHD), 158, 214

Catholic Foreign Mission Society of America (Maryknoll), 184

catholicity, 97–110. *See also* diversity; unity; universality

Catholic Relief Services (CRS), 214

Catholic Worker movement, 214

(CCHD) Catholic Campaign for Human Development, 158, 214

celibacy, 169, 171, 176–177. *See also* virgins, consecrated

cell phones, *139*

chalices, 53

changes, 30

chants, 27, 36

charismatics, 34, 35

charisms, 20, 32–36, 85, 122, 180. *See also* specific charisms

Charitas Christi, 184

charity, 164

chastity, 169, 170–171. *See also* celibacy; virgins, consecrated

Chrism, Sacred, 201

Christ. *See* Jesus Christ

Christian Brothers, 122, 178, 180–181

church, 10–12, 100

The Church in the Modern World (Gaudium et Spes), 138, 139

Church of Christ, 71

Church of England, 73, 76

Church of Rome, 100–101

Cianney, John, 107

circumcision, 114

Clement of Rome, 116

college of bishops, 112, 119, 154, 156

colleges, 221–222

collegial nature of bishops, 158–159

collegial nature of priests, 162–163

"Come, Holy Spirit" ("Veni, Sancte Spiritus"), 26, 27

Commandments, 189

Communion. *See also* Body of Christ; Communion of Saints; Eucharist; Sacrament of Communion; schisms
  Baptism and, 75
  diversity and, 54, 97, 100–101, 108
  God, with, 50–51, 81, 107
  grace and, 84
  Holy Spirit and, 58, 64, 93
  longing for, 68
  martyrs and, 76
  prayer and, 56
Communion of Saints, 87–89
community, 50, 54, 58, 132–135, 206–210. *See also* relationships
Confirmation, 91, 161, 202, 204–205
conformity, 81, 86
Congregation for Bishops, Curia's, 156
consciences, 142
consecrated life, 179–184
Constantine, 41, 70
contemplation, 187
conversion, 83
Corinthians, First Letter to the, 33
Council of Chalcedon, 70
Council of Constantinople, 66
Council of Ephesus, 70
Council of Nicaea, 66
Council of Trent, 74
counterculturalism, 215
Counter-Reformation, 74
covenant, sacrament of the, 57
covenants, 9, 12, 13–14, 49, 51, 56, 104, 135
Creation, 21
creativity, 83
creeds, 66, 189. *See also specific creeds*
CRS (Catholic Relief Services), 214
Crucifixion, 9, 17, 25
crusaders, 71
culture of death, 140–141
Curia, 151, 156
Cyprian, 130
Cyril, 110

Cyril of Jerusalem, 98

D

David, King, 61
Day, Dorothy, 214
Day of Prayer for Peace, 104, 105
deacons, 118, 144, 149, 150, 157, 163–167, 171, 181
death, 88, 89, 95, 113
Declaration on the Relation of the Church to Non-Christian Religions (*Nostra Aetate,* 1965) (Vatican II), 15, 106
Decree on Ecumenism, 77
defects, 191
Dei Verbum (**Word of God**), 117
de La Salle, John Baptist, 122, 181
De La Salle Christian Brothers, 122, 178, 180–181
desert fathers, 182
desires, 30
devil, 182
diaconate, 163–167. *See also* deacons
Diego, Juan, 107
diet, 58, *60*
dignity, 141, 142
dioceses, 11, 152–153, 156
discernment, 162, 163
disciples, 16–17, 23, 28, 32, 42, 172, 211, 212–219
diversity. *See also* catholicity; non-Christians; People of God; unity; universality
  Catholic Church, of, 10, 50, 64–65, 209–210
  communion and, 54, 97, 100–101, 108
  evangelization and, 143, 145
  Paul and, 42
  Pentecost and, 23–24
  sins and, 86
  universality and, 106–110
divine life, 80
divine nature, 193

doctrines, 189, 192
dogmas, 193, 194
Dogmatic Constitution on the Church
(*Lumen Gentium,* 1964) (Paul VI),
64–65
domestic church, 153, 168, 176, 177
Dominic, 91
Dominicans, 143, 178, 180, 181
dove, *21*, 30, 34
Dung-Lac, Andrew, 107

E

early Church, 38–48, 55, 70, 100, 118,
155, 178, 179, 219. *See also* Apostles
earth, 12
Easter, 26
Eastern Catholic Churches, 97, 98,
105, 107–108, 166
Eastern Orthodox Christianity,
70–71, 72, 74, 75, 77, 105
ecclesial, 116
ecclesial communities, 62, 72–75
Ecumenical Councils, 193
ecumenism, 74–78
Egan, Edward, 105
Elijah, 183
Elizabeth of Hungary, 107
episcopacy/episcopate, 156
episcopal, 118
eremitic tradition, 183
error, 35, 192
ethics, 194
Eucharist. *See also* Body of Christ;
Sacrament of Communion
    apostolate and, 120
    basics, 17, 161, 204–205
    bishops and, 156, 157, 161
    Body of Christ and, 17, 23, 87, 202
    Church and, 9, *12,* 25
    holiness and, 84
    laity and, 111
    Paul on, 68
    priests and, 161, 163
    Transubstantiation and, 53

unity and, *54,* 69, 87
    young people and, *200,* 201–202
Eucharistic Adoration, 33
Eucharistic Prayers, 32, 89
Europe, 41, 73
evangelical councils, 169–172, *170*
evangelical counsels, 168
evangelization, 26, 40, 141–148, 175,
178, 184. *See also* missionaries; witnessing; *individual missionaries*
Eve, 95
ex cathedra, 192, 193
excommunication, 71, 77
experience, 84

F

failure, 191
faith. *See also* indefectibility
    Catechism and, 189
    Church and, 115–116
    laity and, 175
    Magisterium and, 188
    understanding and, 78, 128
    unity of, 66
    young people and, 201, 218–219
Fall, the, 93
family, 153, 177–179, 218. *See also*
Marriage
Far East, 143
fasting, 188
fear, 221
Feast of Corpus Christi, 109
Feast of Peter and Paul, 119
Feast of the Assumption, 91
feelings, 84, 217
fiat, 94
fire, *21,* 23
First Vatican Council, 191
flesh, 30, 57. *See also* bodies; sexuality
foreshadowing, 13
forgiveness, 113
*Forming Consciences for Faithful Citi-
zenship* (**U.S. Conference of Catholic
Bishops**), 142

Francis, 35, 219
Franciscans, 143, 178, 180
Francis de Sales, 120, 122
Francis of Assisi, 58
Francis Xavier, 44, 207
free will, 30, 84, 199
Fridays, 188, 194
friends, 81, 207–208
fullness, 126–127

G

Galileo, 195
(Gaudium et Spes) (The Church in the Modern World), 138, 139
generosity, 205
Genesis, Book of, 21
Gentiles, 38, 40, 41, 42, 43, 95, 151, 219
gentleness, 122
gifts, 64, 81, 212–215, 220. *See also* apostolate; Gifts of the Holy Spirit
Gifts of the Holy Spirit, 20, 28, 33, 98–99. *See also* charismatics; charisms; *specific gifts*
God, 17, 50–51, 81, 84–86, 107, 195–196, 199, 206
"God's Grandeur" (Hopkins), 30
Gonzaga, Aloysius, 92
Goretti, Maria, 107
The Gospel of Life **(John Paul II),** 174
grace, 28, 73, 84–86, 128, 130–131, 204. *See also* charisms
grades, 216
Greek Orthodox Church, 71
Greeks, 42, 43
Gregorian chants, 27, 32
Gregory I (the Great), 152, 220
groups, 50

H

happiness, 81
healing, 20, 34, 35, 44, 83, 113, 161
health, 58, *60*
health care, 83, 174, 176

Healy-Murphy, Margaret Mary, 22
Hellenistic culture, 42
Henry VIII, 73
heresy, 70, 90
Hermas, 12
hermits, 168, 179, 182–183, 210. *See also individual hermits*
Herod, 46
hierarchy of the Church, *10*, 18, 150–153, 172, 175
history and the Church, 83
holiness, 79–96, 90, 92–93, 145, 157, 181. *See also* sanctification
Holy Orders, 149. *See also* religious orders
Holy See, 152
Holy Spirit. *See also* disciples; Gifts of the Holy Spirit; Pentecost
    Apostles' mission and, 40–42
    bishops and, 117, 219
    Book of the, 220
    charismatics and, 34
    Church and, 27–29, 32–33, 57–61
    grace and, 84
    human life and, 29, 30–32, 80
    Jesus Christ and, 20–21
    Magisterium and, 187
    mission of, 22–23
    non-Catholics and, 129
    prayer and, 27, *31*, 32
    Sacraments and, 128
    unity and, 64, 202
    young people and, 211–223
Holy Trinity. *See also* God; Holy Spirit; Jesus Christ
    basics, 40, 80, 81, 193–*194*
    Bible and, 117, 135
    evangelization and, 142
    grace and, 84
    Pentecost and, 25–26
    unity and, 63–64
Hopkins, Gerard Manley, 30
human life, 29, 30–32, 80
human nature, 193

I

iconostasis/icons, 108
Ignatius of Antioch, 159, 165
Ignatius of Loyola, 122, 205, 207
images of the Church, 14, 38, 43–44, 49–61
Incarnation, 15, 21
inculturation, 146
indefectibility, 186, 190–193
indulgences, 72
infallibility, 35, 186, 187, 190, 192–193
inquiry, theological, 187
institutes, 179, 184
intellect, 84
intercession, 31, 90–91, 95, 96
invisible dimensions, 66, 80, 128, 129
Irenaeus, 95, 101
Islam, 97, 102, 103, 105
Israel, 9, 10, 12–14, 19, 51, *58*, 86, 183. *See also* Jewish leaders; Jewish People; Judaism
Ivers, Therese, *183*

J

James, 46, 109
Jane de Chantal, 122
Jerome, 95, 203
Jesuits (Society of Jesus), 44, 122, 143, 180, 207
Jesuit Volunteer Corps (JVC), 131
Jesus Christ. *See also* Body of Christ
    Apostles and, 38, 39, 112–113, 118–119, 162
    basics, 15–19
    bridegroom, as, 56
    catholicity, on, 99
    Church and, 22, 25–26, 55
    counterculture and, 215
    eremitic tradition and, 183
    grace and, 85
    hierarchy and, 151
    Holy Spirit and, 20–21
    Judaism and, 14, 104
    keys and, *190*
    Mass and, 100
    missionaries and, 131
    perfection, on, 84
    poverty and, *169*
    prayer and, *205*, 206
    sacrament, as, 127–128
    Sacraments and, 204
    salvation and, 127–128
    Scriptures and, 203
    unity and, 64
    young people and, 202
Jewish leaders, 45–46, 104. *See also* Israel; Judaism
Jewish people, 15, 17, 25–26, 38, 42–43, 49, 103–104. *See also* Israel; Judaism
Joel, 24
John Paul II
    ecumenism, on, 76–77
    evangelization and, *141*, 142
    Galileo and, 195
    inculturation and, 146
    laity and, 174
    martyrs and, 76, 107
    mission, on, 41
    Pope, on, 63, 152
    purifying memories and, 86
    schisms and, 71
    Theology of the Body, 57
    World Day of Prayer for Peace and, 105
John the Apostle, 212
John the Baptist, 183
John XXIII, 193
Joseph, 139
Josephine Bakhita of Sudan, 109
Judaism, 14, 97, 104, 105. *See also* Israel; Jewish leaders; Jewish people
Julius II, 83
JVC (Jesuit Volunteer Corps), 131

K

keys, *190*
Kingdom of God, 9, 15–16, 52, 72
kingly office, 175
Kolbe, Maximilian, 90

L

Lady of the Lamp, 180
laity
    apostolate of, 111, 120–124
    basics, 149, 168, 172–179
    consecrated lives and, 184
    evangelization and, 143
    mission of, 172–175
    prayer and, 181
    religious orders and, 180
    Third Orders and, 178
language, 23–24, 65
Lasallian associates, 178
Last Supper, 14
Latin Church, 107, 166
Latin Rite, 166
Lauds, 182
Law, the, 13–14
Lawrence, 165
laying on of hands, 118
leadership, 20, 35, 149–167, 175
Leo IX, 71, 193
Leo the Great, 107
light, 201, 212–213
liturgy, 11, 58, 65, 133, 146, 164
Liturgy of the Hours, 182, 204
Liturgy of the Word, 164
local churches, 100
loneliness, 206
Lord's Prayer (prayer of the believer), 190
Louis of France, 107
love, 55, 81–82, 87–88, 199, 214, 216
Luke, 220
Luther, Martin, 72, *74*
Lutherans, 72

M

Magisterium, 34, 35, 111, 172, 186–197
Malarias of Metz, 53
maps, *40*
Mark, 112
marks of the Church, 63, 98, 126
Marriage, 56–57, 73, 108, 143, 168, 170, 176–179. *See also* family; Sacrament of Holy Matrimony
Martins, José Saraiva, 89–90
martyrs, 38, 45–48, 76, 219. *See also individual martyrs*
Marxism, 47
Mary, 21, 35, 79, 91, 92–96, 110, 146, 193
Maryknoll (Catholic Foreign Mission Society of America), 178, 184
Mass, 100
materialism, 169–170, 178
Maximilian, *90*
meaning of life, 81, 221
meat, 188, 194
Mediterranean, *40*, 41
Merton, Thomas, *182*
metaphors, 49. *See also* images of the Church
Methodius, 110
Mexico, 109, 143
Michael of Constantinople, 71
Michelangelo, 83
ministry, 156, 157
missionaries, 158, 181, 219. *See also individual missionaries; specific organizations*
Missionaries of Charity, 143
mission of the Church, 29, 38, 39, 41, 111–124, 131–132, 138–148, 149–197
modern world, 89, 138–141, 187, 189
Molla, Gianna Berreta, 177
monasteries, 83
monastic movements, 179
monks, 179. *See also* religious orders
Moran Mar Ignatius Zakka II, 71

Moses, *13*
Mother Teresa, 143–144
musical gifts, *36*, 220
Muslims, 103, 105
mysteries, 26, 49, 57, 80, 83, 106, 130, 183, 193. *See also specific mysteries*
mysterium, 128
Mystical Body of Christ, 57

N

Nagel, Nano, 180
Native Americans, 146
nature, 135
Nazism, 47
Newman, John Henry, *127*, 155
New Testament, 116. *See also specific books*
Nicene Creed, 21, 66, 67, 87, 115, 189, 219
non-Catholic Christians, 69, 73–77, 102, 129–130, 129–131, 142. *See also* diversity; missionaries; universality
non-Christians, 15, 102–106. *See also* missionaries; universality
nuns (sisters), 169, 178, 179, 180. *See also individual nuns; individual orders*

O

obedience, 169, 172
Old Testament, 13, 43, 116. *See also specific books*
openness, 77
opinions, 175
Oratory of Saint Philip Neri, 184
orders, religious, 35, 143, 149, 168, 172, 178, 179–182
ordination, 118, 163
organized religion, 132–135
Oriental Orthodox Churches, 70
origin of the Church, 9–19
Orthodox Christians, 71
others, 29, 30
Our Lady of Lourdes, 110
Out Lady of Czetochowa, 110
Oxford Movement, 127

P

Pachomius, 179
parables, 16, 82–83
parents, 178–179, 200, 202. *See also* family; Marriage
parishes, 10, 152, 153
participation, 202–206
Paschal Mystery, 91
Pastoral Constitution on the Church in the Modern World (Vatican II), 189
pastor of the universal Church, 155
Patrick, 217
Paul
    authority of, 113
    Baptism, on, 28
    bishops and, 117–118
    Body of Christ, on, 55
    charisms, on, 32–33, 35
    diversity, on, 64, 106–107
    Eucharist, on, 68
    Holy Spirit, on, 30–31, 32
    images by, 56–57
    life of, 45, 199–200
    love, on, 87–88
    martyrdom of, 101, 154, 220
    prayer, on, 32, 181, 204
    preaching of, 38, 39, 40, 41, 42–43
    Rome and, 101
    unity and, 54
Paulist Fathers, 184
Paul VI, 34, 64, 77, 163, 166–167, 188
peace, 104
penance, 83, 85
penitence, 188
Pentecost, 20, 21, 23–26, 27, 28, 40
People of God, 49, 50–52, 65, 98, 100, 135. *See also* universality
perfection, 81, 84
persecution, 11, 38, 45–48, 158
Peter
    authority of, 113–114
    basics, 18
    bishops and, 117–120, 153
    Church and, 71, 139

failings of, 120
feast of, 77
indefectibility and, 191
martyrdom of, 46, 101, 154
Pentecost and, 23–24
Pope and, 118–119, 155, 192
petitions, 31, 56
Pius IX, 139
Pius XII, 35, 184, 193
pneuma, 29
Poland, 110
politics, 140–141, 142, 174, 177, 215
Polycarp of Smyrna, 46, 47
poor people, 16, 22, 44, 158. *See also*
poverty
Pope. *See also* infallibility; Magisterium; *individual popes*
    authority of, 101, 111, 118–119,
    155, 172
    basics, 18, 111, 149–155
    Church and, 112
    sins and, 191
    unity and, 63, 68
Portugal, 110
La Posadas, 109
possessions, 169–170
poverty, 169–170
power, 18, 47. *See also* authority
prayer, arrow, 204
prayer in the Communion of Saints,
88
prayer of the believer (Lord's Prayer),
190
prayers. *See also specific prayers*
    basics, 205–206
    Body of Christ and, 134
    Breastplate of Saint Patrick, 217
    Church, for, 192
    deacons, for, 166–167
    Eucharistic, 32, 89
    family and, 173
    generosity, for, 205
    Holy Spirit and, 20, 31, 32, 33
    intentions, 152

intercessory, 119
laity and, 174
martyr's, 46
parents and, 178–179
petition, of, 56
religious orders and, 181–182
unity, for, 73
young people and, 68, 219
preaching, 42–44
presbytery/presbyterate, 159, 160
**Presentation Sisters of the Blessed
Virgin Mary,** 180
priests. *See also* celibacy; religious
orders
    basics, 118, 150, 160–163, 169, 174
    Eucharist and, 157
    evangelization and, 144
    laity and, 173–174
    obedience and, 172
    prayer and, 181
    vows of, 169, 170
prophecy, 35
prophets, 14, 24, 175
Protestant Reformation, 72–73, 74,
75
Proverbs, Book of, 207
provinces, 156, 157
Psalms, 17
public policy, 140–141, 142, 174, 177,
215
Purgatory, 88

R

reading, 82
Redemptoris Missio (**John Paul II**),
142, 145
re-evangelization, 142
reform, 180
Reformation, Protestant, 72–73, 74,
75
Reign of God, 17
relationships, 132–135, 198, 199. *See
also* community
relativism, 186, 194–196

religious orders, 35, 143, 149, 168, 172, 178, 179–182

repentance, 83

Resources for the Week of Prayer for Christian Unity and throughout the year 2009 (Pontifical Council for Christian Unity and Commission on Faith and Order of the World Council of Churches), 73

respect, 61, 145, 170, 171, 176, 196

Revelation, 13, 25, 35, 104, 115, 116, 189, 198

Revelation, Book of, 91, 135

rich people, 169

right conduct, 189

right to life, 140, 215

Rite of Ordination, 163

Roman Catholic Church, 97, 98, 100–101

Roman Empire, 38, 41, 45, 61, 70–71

Rome, 101–102, 154, 220

Romero, Oscar, 76

Russian Orthodox Church, 71

S

Sacrament of Anointing of the Sick, 161, 205

Sacrament of Baptism
  basics, 28–29, 49, 51, 52, 204–205
  conversion and, 83
  grace and, 85
  laity and, 173
  non-Catholic, 75, 130–131
  Peter and, 24
  priesthood and, 160, 161, 162
  salvation and, *127–128*
  young people and, 198, 200–201, 202

Sacrament of Communion, 23, 201–202. *See also* Body of Christ; Eucharist

Sacrament of Confirmation, 91, 161, 202, 204–205

Sacrament of Holy Matrimony, *56,* 161, 205

Sacrament of Holy Orders
  basics, 150, 205
  bishops and, 111, 114, 117–118, 156
  priests and, 160, 162, 163, 169

Sacrament of Penance and Reconciliation, 85, 161, 201, 205

Sacrament of Salvation, 128–129

sacrament of the covenant, 57

Sacraments, 28, 74, 75, 102, 108, 189, 198, 204–205. *See also specific Sacraments*

Sacraments of Christian Initiation, 202

sacramentum, 128

Sacred Tradition. *See* Tradition

Saint Peter Claver Academy, 22

saints, 79, 87, 89–92, 107, 146, 219. *See also* Communion of Saints; *individual saints*

salt, 212–213

salvation
  Church and, 9, 11, 74, 75, 81, 83, 98–99, 125–136
  grace and, 73
  holiness and, 82
  Holy Spirit and, 21–22
  Israel and, 13–14
  Mary and, 94, 95
  non-Catholics and, 129–132

sancta/sancti, 87

sancta sedes, 152

sanctification, 27–28, 80, 81, 82, 84, 88–89, 157

Sara, 183

schisms, 70–71, 77, 107

schools, 122, 180, 201, 208, 215–217

Scriptures. *See also* New Testament; Old Testament
  Apostles and, 115, 116
  basics, 13, 187, 203–204
  holiness and, 82

Reformation and, 73
science *versus*, 195
understanding, 33, 49
young people and, 198
Second Vatican Council, 15, 77, 139, 166, 189, 191, 193
secular, 184
secular institutes, 179, 184
sensus fidei, 175
separation of Church and state, 140–141. *See also* politics
service opportunities, 209, 213–215
Seton, Elizabeth Ann, 107
sexuality, 57. *See also* celibacy; chastity; virgins, consecrated
sharing faith, 128
Shepherd of *Hermas*, 12
Sign of the Cross, 108
signs of the times, 137, 138–139
single people, 177, 184
sinners, 16, 82–84
sins, 65, 80, 86, 95, 191, 195–196, 201, 206
sisters (nuns), 169, 178, 179, 180. *See also individual orders; individual sisters*
Sisters of Charity, 144
Sisters of the Holy Spirit and Mary Immaculate, 22
Sisters of the Visitation, 122
Sistine Chapel, 83
socializing, 208
social needs, 132–133
Societies of Apostolic Life, 184
Society of Jesus (Jesuits), 44, 122, 143, 180, 207
sola gratia/scriptura, 73
Solomon, 61
songs, 32
speaking in tongues, 20, 23–24, 34, 35
spirit, 27

spread of Christianity, 39–41. *See also* Apostles; Paul
Stephen, 45–46, 165
Stewardship and Teenagers: The Challenge of Being a Disciple (U.S. Conference of Catholic Bishops), 152
strength, 122
study groups, 33, 187
suffering, 38, 47, 55. *See also* martyrs; persecution
Sun Dance, 146
Swain, Paul, *183*
Syncletica, 183
synods, 158–159

T

teaching, 32, 43–44. *See also Catechism of the Catholic Church;* Magisterium
technology, *139*, 140, 145, 175
teen centers, 22
Temple of Jerusalem, 58, 59, 61
Temple of the Holy Spirit, 49, 57–59
temptation, 85, 216–217
Ten Commandments, 13–14
terrorism, 105
Tertullian, 46
theology, 78, 187, 220. *See also individual theologians*
Theology of the Body (John Paul II), 57
Theotokos, 94
Thérèse of Lisieux, 82, 91, 218, 219
Third Orders, 178
Thomas Aquinas, 99, 107
thoughts, 217
Timothy, 40, 118
Tower of Babel, *24*
Tradition (Apostolic/Sacred), 32, 38, 111, 114–116, 127, 137–146, 187, 198
traditions of the Church, 47, 108, 132, 166, 183, 188, 194
Transubstantiation, 53

Trinitarian, 40
Trinity. *See* Holy Trinity
trust, 195–196
truth, 44, 126, 187, 188, 190, 193–196. *See also* heresy; infallibility; relativism

U

uniformity, 62, 64, 106
United States Conference of Catholic Bishops, 22, 142, 152, 159, 214
unity, 23, 53–55, 57, 61–78, 114, 119, 128, 156. *See also* catholicity; diversity; universality
universality. *See also* catholicity; diversity; non-Christians; People of God
    Apostles and, 39
    Church and, 126–129
    diversity and, 106–110, 129–132
    eremitic tradition and, 183
    Israel and, 12, 14
    Jesus on, 16
    Pope and, 63, 192
    salvation, of, 129–131
Universal Syrian Orthodox Church, 71
urban audiences, 43

V

Valentine, 91
Vatican Council I, 191
Vatican Council II, 15, 77, 139, 166, 189, 191, 193
Vatican Square, *101*
"Veni, Sancte Spiritus" ("Come, Holy Spirit"), 26, 27
Vespers, 182
Vianney, John, 107
vicars, 154
virgins, consecrated, 168, *183,* 184
virtues, 28, 58–59

visible signs
    Church, 80, 83, 127
    diversity, of, 65
    Mystical Body of Christ, 57
    Pope, 63, *69,* 101, 153, 156
    Sacraments, 128–129
    unity, of, 66, 74, 76
    young people as, 212
vocations, 82, 120–122, 160, 168–185, 176–179
volunteers, 33, 208
vows, 162, 168, 169, 170, 178, 179. *See also specific vows*

W

weak of the world, 18
Week of Prayer for Christian Unity, 73
wind, 29
witnessing. *See also* evangelization
    basics, 41, 42, 45
    diversity and, 103
    hermits and, 183
    institutes and, 184
    laity and, 121, 172, 176, 177
    Marriage and, 57
    religious orders and, 179
women, 86. *See also* Marriage; nuns (sisters); *individual women*
Word, the, 117, 164, 203
World Youth Day, *133,* 141, 209
worship, 68, 133–134

Y

young people, 28, 68, 105, *133,* 143, 145, *174,* 198–210

Z

Zaire, *121*

Acknowledgments

The scriptural quotations in this book are from the New American Bible with Revised New Testament and Revised Psalms. Copyright © 1991, 1986, and 1970 by the Confraternity of Christian Doctrine, Washington, D.C. Used by the permission of the copyright owner. All rights reserved. No part of the New American Bible may be reproduced in any form without permission in writing from the copyright owner.

The excerpts marked *Catechism* and *CCC* are from the English translation of the *Catechism of the Catholic Church* for use in the United States of America, second edition. Copyright © 1994 by the United States Catholic Conference, Inc.—Libreria Editrice Vaticana. English translation of the *Catechism of the Catholic Church: Modifications from the Editio Typica* copyright © 1997 by the United States Catholic Conference, Inc.—Libreria Editrice Vaticana.

Unless otherwise noted, the definitions in this book are taken from *The Catholic Faith Handbook for Youth*, Second Edition, by Brian Singer-Towns et al. (Winona, MN: Saint Mary's Press), copyright © 2008 by Saint Mary's Press; *The Catholic Connections Handbook for Middle Schoolers*, by Janet Claussen et al. (Winona, MN: Saint Mary's Press), copyright © 2009 by Saint Mary's Press; and *Saint Mary's Press® Glossary of Theological Terms*, by John T. Ford (Winona, MN: Saint Mary's Press), copyright © 2006 by Saint Mary's Press. All rights reserved.

The quotation on page 12 is from *The Shepherd of Hermas: Book 1: Visions*, 2.4, at *www.newadvent.org/fathers/02011.htm*.

The definitions on pages 13, 50, and 57 are from the Merriam-Webster Online Dictionary, at *www.merriam-webster.com/dictionary*.

The excerpts on pages 15 and 106 are from *Declaration on the Relation of the Church to Non-Christian Religions* (*Nostra Aetate*, 1965), numbers 4 and 2, at *www.vatican.va/archive/hist_councils/ii_vatican_council/documents/vat-ii_decl_19651028_nostra-aetate_en.html*.

The information about the Sisters of the Holy Spirit and Mary Immaculate on page 22 is from the Healy-Murphy Center Web site, at *www.healymurphy.org/index.cfm?fuseaction=about_History*.

The Pentecostal chant on page 27 was found at the Choral Public Domain Library, at *www1.cpdl.org/wiki/index.php/Veni_Sancte_Spiritus*.

The excerpt on page 28 is from "Homily of His Holiness Benedict XVI," during the 23rd World Youth Day 2008, at *www.vatican.va/holy_father/benedict_xvi/homilies/2008/documents/hf_ben-xvi_hom_20080720_xxiii-wyd_en.html*. Copyright © 2008 Libreria Editrice Vaticana.

The excerpt on page 41 and the quotations on pages 142 and 144 are from *Redemptoris Missio: On the Permanent Validity of the Church's Missionary Mandate*, numbers 92, 33, 33, and 63, respectively, at *www.vatican.va/holy_father/john_paul_ii/encyclicals/documents/hf_jp-ii_enc_07121990_redemptoris-missio_en.html*. Copyright © Libreria Editrice Vaticana.

The quotation on page 51 is from "Message of the Holy Father to the Young People of Israel and Palestine," at *www.vatican.va/holy_father/john_paul_ii/speeches/1999/september/documents/hf_jp-ii_mes_22091999_israel-palest_en.html*.

The quotations on pages 63 and 76 are from *Ut Unum Sint: On Commitment to Ecumenism*, numbers 88 and 84, at *www.vatican.va/holy_father/john_paul_ii/*

encyclicals/documents/hf_jp-ii_enc_25051995_ut-unum-sint_en.html. Copyright ©
Libreria Editrice Vaticana.

The excerpt on pages 65 and the quotations on page 69 and 129 are from *Dogmatic Constitution on the Church* (*Lumen Gentium*, 1964), numbers 13, 23, and 48, respectively, at *www.vatican.va/archive/hist_councils/ii_vatican_council/documents/ vat-ii_const_19641121_lumen-gentium_en.html.*

The excerpt on page 68 is from "Young Adults and Prayer at Taizé," at *www. taize.fr/en_article3148.html.*

The prayer on page 73 is from "Resources for the Week of Prayer for Christian Unity, and Throughout the Year 2009," Day 7, at *www.vatican.va/roman_curia/ pontifical_councils/chrstuni/weeks-prayer-doc/rc_pc_chrstuni_doc_20080630_ week-prayer-2009_en.html.*

The quotations on page 75 from *Decree on Ecumenism* (*Unitatis Redintegratio*, 1964), numbers 3 and 22; the quotation on page 104 from *Declaration on the Relation of the Church to Non-Christian Religions* (*Nostra Aetate*, 1965), number 4; and the quotations on pages 138, 139, and 191 from *Pastoral Constitution on the Church in the Modern World* (*Gaudium et Spes*, 1965), numbers 58, 4, and 43, are from *Vatican Council II: Constitutions, Decrees, Declarations*, Austin Flannery, general editor (Northport, NY: Costello Publishing Company, 1996), pages 502, 520, 573, 165, 234, and 213, respectively. Copyright © 1996 by Reverend Austin Flannery, OP.

The excerpts from Eucharistic Prayer II on page 89 and the excerpt from Eucharistic Prayer I on page 192 are from the English translation of *The Roman Missal* © 2010, International Commission on English in the Liturgy (ICEL). All rights reserved. Used with permission of the ICEL.

The excerpt on pages 89–90 is from "Reflection by Cardinal José Saraiva Martins," number 2, at *www.vatican.va/roman_curia/congregations/csaints/documents/ rc_con_csaints_doc_20030315_martins-saints_en.html.*

The excerpt on page 98 is from "Catechetical Lecture 18," number 23, at *www. newadvent.org/fathers/310118.htm.*

The excerpt on page 99 is from "Exposition of the Apostles' Creed," by Thomas Aquinas, as quoted in *The Catholicity of the Church*, by Avery Dulles (Oxford: Oxford University Press, 1985), page 181.

The quotation on page 101 is from *Against Heresies*, Book III, Chapter 3, number 2, at *www.newadvent.org/fathers/013303.htm.*

The prayer on page 104 is from "Day of Prayer for Peace in the World, January 24, 2002," at *www.vatican.va/news_services/liturgy/documents/ns_lit_doc_20020124_ assisi-impegno_it.html*. Copyright © Libreria Editrice Vaticana.

The words of Saint Josephine Bakhita on page 109 are found on the National Black Catholic Congress Web site, at *congress.org/black-catholics/black-saints-saint-josephine-bakhita.asp.*

The excerpt on page 116 is quoted from *The Apostolic Fathers*, volume one, English translation by Kirsopp Lake (Cambridge, MA: Harvard University Press, 1912), pages 79, 81, and 85, respectively.

The prayer on page 119 is from the English translation of the Intercessions from *The Liturgy of the Hours*, © 1974 ICEL, prepared by the ICEL (New York: Catholic Book Publishing Company, 1976), pages 1180–1181. Copyright © 1976 by the Catholic Book Publishing Company, New York. Used with permission of the ICEL.

The excerpt on page 130 is from "The Unity of the Catholic Church," at *www. ewtn.com/FAITH/TEACHINGS/churc1.htm.*

The "culture of death" phrase on page 140 is from *The Gospel of Life (Evangelium Vitae),* number 19, at *www.vatican.va/holy_father/john_paul_ii/encyclicals/documents/ hf_jp-ii_enc_25031995_evangelium-vitae_en.html.* Copyright © Libreria Editrice Vaticana.

The excerpt on page 141 is from "Message of the Holy Father John Paul II to the Youth of the World on the Occasion of the IV World Youth Day," number 2, at *www.vatican.va/holy_father/john_paul_ii/messages/youth/documents/hf_jp-ii_ mes_27111988_iv-world-youth-day_en.html.* Copyright © 1988 Libreria Editice Vaticana.

The quotation by Mother Teresa on page 144 is from an interview in 1989 for *Time* magazine, found at *www.servelec.net/mothertheresa.htm.*

The quotations from the letters of Ignatius of Antioch on page 159 are from *The Apostolic Fathers,* edited and translated by Bart D. Ehrman (Cambridge, MA: Harvard University Press,2003), pages 247, 225, 247, and 303, respectively. Copyright © 2003 by the President and Fellows of Harvard College.

The prayer for deacons on page 166 and the excerpt on celibacy on page 171 are from the English translation of *Ordination of Deacons, Priests, and Bishops* © 1975, ICEL, numbers 18 and 10, in *Rites of the Catholic Church,* volume 2, prepared by the ICEL, a Joint Commission of Catholic Bishops' Conferences (Collegeville, MN: The Liturgical Press, 1991). Copyright © 1991 by The Order of St. Benedict, Collegeville, MN. Used with permission of the ICEL.

The list of activities on page 167 is adapted from *The Sacred Order of Deacons (Sacrum Diaconatus Ordinem),* number 26, at *www.vatican.va/holy_father/paul_vi/ motu_proprio/documents/hf_p-vi_motu-proprio_19670618_sacrum-diaconatus_en.html.*

The prayer of Saint Gianna Molla on page 177 is from *www.saintgianna.org/ prayersofgianna.htm.* Used with permission of the Society of Saint Gianna Beretta Molla.

The story on page 182 is from *The Desert Fathers: Sayings of the Early Christian Monks,* translated by Benedicta Ward (London: Penguin Books, 2003), page 165. Copyright © 2003 by Benedicta Ward.

The theological inquiry quotation on page 187 and the excerpt on page 189 are from *Pastoral Constitution on the Church in the Modern World (Gaudium et Spes,* 1965), numbers 62 and 1, at *www.vatican.va/archive/hist_councils/ii_vatican_council/ documents/vat-ii_cons_19651207_gaudium-et-spes_en.html.*

The contemplation and study quotation on page 187 is from *Dogmatic Constitution on Divine Revelation (Dei Verbum,* 1965), number 8, at *www.vatican.va/archive/ hist_councils/ii_vatican_council/documents/vat-ii_const_19651118_dei-verbum_en.html.*

The quotation from the First Vatican Council on page 191 is quoted from "The Bishop of Rome Is Peter's Successor," at *www.vatican.va/holy_father/john_paul_ii/ audiences/alpha/data/aud19930127en.html.*

The quotation from the Council of Chalcedon on page 193 is quoted from *Christ, the Eternal King (Sempiternus Rex Christus), Encyclical of Pope Pius XII on the Council of Chalcedon,* number 23, at *www.vatican.va/holy_father/pius_xii/encyclicals/documents/ hf_p-xii_enc_08091951_sempiternus-rex-christus_en.html.*

The Christmas greeting on page 199 is from "Address of His Holiness Benedict XVI to the Members of the Roman Curia for the Traditional Exchange of Christmas Greetings," at *www.vatican.va/holy_father/benedict_xvi/speeches/2008/december/ documents/hf_ben-xvi_spe_20081222_curia-romana_en.html.* Copyright © 2008 Libreria Editrice Vaticana.

The excerpt on page 212 is from "Meeting with Youth: Address of His Holiness Benedict XVI," number 7, during an apostolic journey to Brazil, at *www.vatican.va/ holy_father/benedict_xvi/speeches/2007/may/documents/hf_ben-xvi_spe_20070510_ youth-brazil_en.html*. Copyright © 2007 by Libreria Editrice Vaticana.

The excerpt on page 214 is from "Love Is the Measure," by Dorothy Day, origi-nally published in *The Catholic Worker*, June 1946, and reprinted in *By Little and By Little: The Selected Writings of Dorothy Day*, edited by Robert Ellsberg (New York: Alfred A. Knopf, 1983), page 98. Copyright © 1983 by Robert Ellsberg and Tamar Hennessy.

To view copyright terms and conditions for Internet materials cited here, log on to the home pages for the referenced Web sites.

During this book's preparation, all citations, facts, figures, names, addresses, telephone numbers, Internet URLs, and other pieces of information cited within were verified for accuracy. The authors and Saint Mary's Press staff have made every attempt to reference current and valid sources, but we cannot guarantee the content of any source, and we are not responsible for any changes that may have occurred since our verification. If you find an error in, or have a question or concern about, any of the information or sources listed within, please contact Saint Mary's Press.

Endnotes Cited in Quotations from the *Catechism of the Catholic Church*, Second Edition

Section 1
1. Saint Ignatius of Antioch, *Ad Rom*. 6, 1–2: Sources Chrétiennes (Paris: 1942–) 10, 114.
2. Tertullian, *Apol*. 50, 13: J. P. Migne, ed., Patrologia Latina (Paris: 1841–1855) 1, 603.
3. *Martyrium Polycarpi* 14, 2–3: J. P. Migne, ed., Patrologia Graeca (Paris, 1857–1866) 5, 1040; Sources Chrétiennes (Paris: 1942–) 10, 228.

Section 2
1. Cf. *Matthew* 13:24–30.
2. *Dei Verbum* 8 § 1.
3. *Dei Verbum* 8 § 1.

Section 5
1. *Dei Verbum* 25; cf. *Philippians* 3:8 and Saint Jerome, *Commentariorum in Isaiam libri xviii* prol.: J. P. Migne, ed., Patrologia Latina Supplement (Paris, 1841–1855) 24, 17b.